# ROADSIDE GEOLOGY
## of INDIANA

Mark J. Camp

Graham T. Richardson

Mountain Press Publishing Company
Missoula, Montana
1999

Roadside Geology is a registered trademark
of Mountain Press Publishing Company.

**Library of Congress Cataloging-in-Publication Data**

Camp, Mark J., 1947–
    Roadside geology of Indiana / Mark J. Camp, Graham T. Richardson.
    315 p.    cm. — (Roadside geology series)
    Includes bibliographical references and index.
    ISBN 0-87842-396-6 (alk. paper)
    1. Geology—Indiana Guidebooks.   2. Indiana Guidebooks.
    I. Richardson, Graham T., 1946-    . II. Title.   III. Series.
    QE109.36   1999
    557.72—dc21                                             99-24724
                                                            CIP

PRINTED IN THE UNITED STATES OF AMERICA

Mountain Press Publishing Company
P.O. Box 2399 / Missoula, MT 59806
406-728-1900 / 1-800-234-5308

*We respectfully dedicate*
*this volume to*
*the Hoosier geologists*
*who collected the data*
*that made our work possible,*
*and to the citizens of*
*Indiana.*

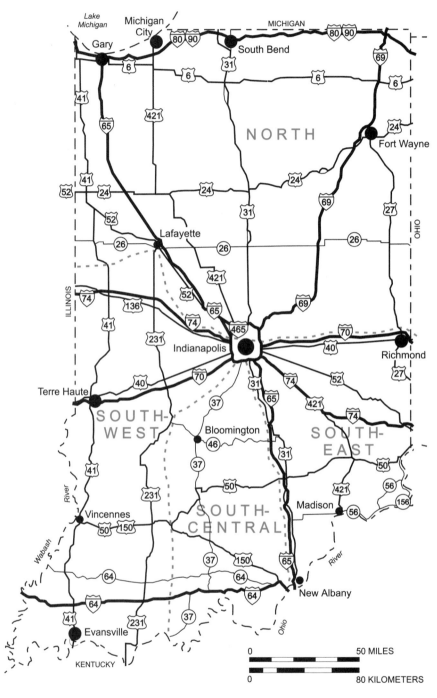

*Roads and sections of* Roadside Geology of Indiana.

# CONTENTS

# PREFACE

Indiana is a great place to see the wonders of geology. The rocks and scenic features of the Hoosier state hold clues that unravel into a history as exciting as any possessed by states with great mountain chains or active volcanoes. True, the clues are sometimes well hidden, but they are there nonetheless. Be a geologic detective and uncover the mysteries of prehistoric Indiana!

Hoosiers can point with pride to many fossil-bearing rocks that attracted pioneer paleontologists: the Ordovician exposures of southeastern Indiana, the Waldron Shale of Bartholomew and Shelby Counties, the Mississippian Salem limestone near Salem, and the Mississippian crinoid beds around Crawfordsville. Collections from these areas greatly enhanced American paleontology. The cultural development of Indiana has close ties with geology. Rivers and landscapes influenced the platting of many towns and led to their growth or, in a few cases, to their demise.

The economic success of Indiana as a new state depended on its development of natural resources. All corners of the state have abundant mineral resources of one type or another. Best known is the building-stone belt stretching from Gosport to Salem across south-central Indiana. Limestone from this region makes up many buildings and other structures throughout North America.

Limestone from other parts of Indiana became well known for its use in the glass industry, as the raw material for lime production, as crushed stone, and as a major component of portland cement. Many important advances in the glass, lime, and cement industry took place in Indiana, including the first plate glass production and the design of more efficient kilns. Clay and coal also played an important role in the economic success of Indiana.

The seeds were sown for this book long ago. After years of data collection, map work, and road checking, we present what we hope is a fair account of the geology of this typical midwestern state. This volume is written for people who are interested in the landscape they see around them—what it is and how it came to be. We begin with an introductory chapter to provide the reader with a foundation of geological knowledge about Indiana. Here are explanations of broad topics that span the wide range of geologic materials and processes that, acting together over geologic time, created today's Indiana.

The introduction precedes chapters on each of the geographic regions of the state—the southeastern hills, south-central hills, southwestern hills and plains, and the northern flatlands. Detailed roadlogs of selected highways in each region show the geology they cross. The road routes run from east to west and north to south, but are written so they serve those traveling in any direction. Just read them in reverse order if you are driving in the opposite direction. The four regional chapters also include selected topics focusing on sites of particular geologic significance along the described routes as well as a number of side trips. These follow the roadlogs and are arranged in the same east-west, north-south order as the roadlogs.

The thirteen geographic provinces used in *Roadside Geology of Indiana* were modified from the long-standing divisions used by Wayne (1956) and Malott (1922). In 1997 the Indiana University Press, in association with the Indiana Department of Natural Resources and the Indiana Academy of Science, published a most beautifully written and illustrated volume entitled *The Natural History of Indiana*. In that work, the authors described the Indiana landscape in terms of twelve different regions (with twenty subordinate sections), each based on features of the terrain and vegetation generally more intricate than what we have attempted in this geology guidebook. We believe this new, largely biologically based system complements, rather than supplants, the older geologically based divisions that we have used in this volume.

Suggested readings and a glossary, explaining the specialized language of geology, close the text. If you want more information or are unfamiliar with a term, be sure to consult these sections.

We try to describe sites and features that are easily seen from the road, but some places are off the road and require permission to visit. Others exist only in history. Quarries, mines, and caves must never be entered without permission and an experienced guide. One careless or thoughtless act by an individual can ruin a site for all responsible visitors.

*Roadside Geology of Indiana* owes its origin to the work of many pioneer and contemporary investigators of Hoosier geology. They unraveled many of the mysteries hidden in the rocks, sorted out the stratigraphic layers, and provided historical records of mineral industries, past and present. Various maps and reports published by the Indiana Geological Survey, the Indiana Academy of Science, and the U.S. Geological Survey provided us a vast data file from which to spin our story. The standard topographic maps of Indiana, published by the U.S. Geological Survey, were particularly valuable in constructing the surface profiles shown throughout this book. Historical photos are from the private collection of Mark J. Camp.

We thank the Indiana Geological Survey for its review of our draft work and the discussions about data mapped by hand and computer. We thank our other reviewers for their comments on our evolving draft manuscript.

The staff of Mountain Press tolerated our schedules and questions; we could not have done this work without them.

We hope that you take every opportunity to drive the roads described and enjoy the great geologic story of Indiana.

| Time Divisions | Began Millions of Years Ago | Typical geological events within Indiana | Millions of years ago | ERA |
|---|---|---|---|---|
| **CENOZOIC ERA**<br>Quaternary Period | 2 | Glacial tills and outwash, river sediments, and soils. Mastodons, giant beavers, other ice-age animals. | 0 —<br>65<br><br>245 | CENOZOIC<br><br>MESOZOIC |
| Tertiary Period | 66 | Scattered gravels and sands. | 570 | PALEOZOIC<br><br>*Spans in red are* |
| **MESOZOIC ERA**<br>Cretaceous Period<br>Jurassic Period<br>Triassic Period | 144<br>208<br>245 | No sediments or fossils found within Indiana. | 1,000 — | *for those periods with rocks and deposits in Indiana.* |
| **PALEOZOIC ERA**<br>Permian Period | 286 | No deposits within Indiana. | | |
| Pennsylvanian Period | 320 | Great swamp forests. Coal, shale, sandstone, and clay laid down in repeated cycles. | | |
| Mississippian Period | 360 | Seas covered Indiana. Limestone, sandstone, shale, and gypsum deposited. Blastoids and crinoids common. | | |
| Devonian Period | 408 | Seas covered Indiana. Limestone, dolomite, and shale deposited. Some Silurian reefs continued to grow. | 2,000 — | |
| Silurian Period | 438 | Shallow seas over Indiana. Dolomite, limestone, and shale deposited. Barrier, patch, and pinnacle reefs began to form. | | P R E C A M B R I A N |
| Ordovician Period | 505 | Shallow seas. Shale and limestone deposited. Bryozoans and brachiopods common. | 3,000 — | *How the geologic time scale appears when the eras are shown in terms of their actual length in years. Precambrian time occupied most of the Earth's history.* |
| Cambrian Period | 570 | Shallow seas. Sandstone and dolomite deposited. No exposures at surface, known only from drilling. | | |
| **PRECAMBRIAN ERA** | 4,600 | Igneous and metamorphic rocks formed in very ancient times. No exposures at surface, known only from drilling. | 4,000 — | |

*Geologic timescale for Indiana.*

# Indiana Rocks and Landscapes

We are about to embark on an excursion back in time to when a vast sea teeming with a myriad of strange creatures covered Indiana, to when tropical vegetation and giant insects flourished, and to when mastodons and giant beavers followed the fluctuating fronts of ice sheets as they scraped and bulldozed across the Indiana countryside. This is the geologic story of Indiana, of how the soils, rocks, and landscapes of the Hoosier state came to be.

## THE STORYBOOK OF LONG TIME

The essence of geology is time, an almost unbelievable amount of time. Geologists can estimate ages based on fossils and relative positions within the Earth's crust, and they can measure the ages of rocks in sophisticated laboratory tests, but they cannot adequately explain the length of geologic time.

The oldest rocks in Indiana date from Precambrian time, billions of years ago. That is when our story begins. The youngest rocks are still forming, so our story has no real end.

No Precambrian rocks are present at the surface anywhere in Indiana, but they underlie the entire state a few thousand feet below the ground surface. Numerous wells drilled through the overlying Paleozoic sedimentary rocks and glacial deposits penetrate them. These ancient rocks are now a complex of igneous and metamorphic rocks, what geologists call the basement.

## PALEOZOIC SEDIMENTARY FORMATIONS

Deposition of Indiana's sedimentary rocks began as a shallow sea flooded across inland North America at the beginning of Cambrian time, about 570 million years ago. That sea persisted, with fluctuations in its level, until the end of Mississippian time, about 320 million years ago. Deposition continued on more or less dry land and along the fluctuating margins of the inland sea during Pennsylvanian time, until about 300 million years ago. From that time to the present, Indiana has been above sea level and eroding. The next sedimentary deposits were laid down by the great ice sheets during the last 2 million years. We have no geologic record of what happened in Indiana during the intervening 300 million years.

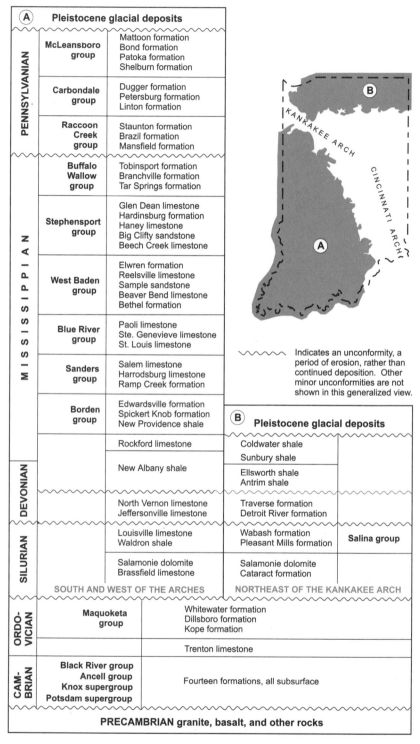

*Generalized geologic column for Indiana.*

Most sedimentary rocks begin as deposits of ordinary sediments such as silt, sand, and gravel, which are common in the modern world, and calcareous mud, which is now extremely rare. Given time, the silt, sand, and gravel solidify into siltstone, sandstone, and conglomerate. The calcareous mud becomes limestone or dolomite, depending on the amount of magnesium the rock contains.

Geologists divide sedimentary rocks into formations, which are simply distinctive rock units that they can recognize from one place to another and can plot on maps. Members are equally distinctive and recognizable parts of formations, but they are usually too thin to plot individually on a map. As the name suggests, groups are sequences of closely related formations that geologists consider a single unit for convenience.

*These limestone layers, or strata, near Ramsey formed from bottom sediments of an ancient sea, beginning some 340 million years ago.*

# MAP SYMBOLS

## Bedrock Geology

Middle Pennsylvanian: Sandstone, shale, limestone, coal

Late Mississippian to Early Pennsylvanian: Sandstone, shale, and limestone

Middle Mississippian: Limestone

Early to Middle Mississippian: Siltstone and shale

Middle Devonian to Early Mississippian: Black shale

Silurian and Devonian: Limestone and dolomite

Late Ordovician: Shale and limestone

*Bedrock geology of Indiana.*

Middle Devonian to Early Mississippian:
Sunbury shale
Ellsworth shale
Antrim shale

Early to Middle Mississippian:
Coldwater shale

Michigan City

South Bend

Gary

Silurian and Devonian:
Traverse formation
Detroit River formation
Salina group
Salamonie dolomite
Cataract formation

Fort Wayne

Kentland disturbed area

Area thickly covered by glacial deposits

Lafayette

Indianapolis

Richmond

Late Ordovician:
Whitewater formation
Dillsboro formation
Kope formation

Southern limit of Wisconsinan ice

Silurian and Devonian:
North Vernon limestone
Jeffersonville limestone
Louisville limestone
Waldron shale
Salamonie dolomite
Brassfield limestone

Terre Haute

Bloomington

Area thinly covered by glacial deposits

Madison

Southern limit of Illinoian ice

Unglaciated bedrock terrain

New Albany

Middle Devonian to Early Mississippian:
New Albany shale

Early to Middle Mississippian:
Borden group
Rockford limestone

Evansville

Middle Pennsylvanian:
McLeansboro group
Carbondale group

Late Mississippian to Early Pennsylvanian:
Raccoon Creek group
Buffalo Wallow group
Stephensport group
West Baden group

Middle Mississippian limestones:
Blue River group
Sanders group

0          50 MILES

0          80 KILOMETERS

## INDIANA'S GEOLOGIC MAP

A geologic map simply shows the distribution of rock formations—where the rocks are. It will tell you what rocks exist where you are, and what to expect where you are going. No enthusiast of geology should be without geologic maps. This book is full of them. You can order at modest expense a colorful geologic map of Indiana from the Geological Survey at Indiana University in Bloomington.

## ARCHES AND SEDIMENTARY BASINS

The sediments in the ancient seas were laid down originally as flat layers, but they did not remain that way. Some areas of the crust sank while others rose, producing what geologists call arches and basins. The Cincinnati Arch stretches along the border of southeastern Indiana. Two smaller arches extend from its northern end, the Kankakee Arch northwestward toward the Chicago area and the Findlay Arch across northwestern Ohio toward Lake Erie. Southwestern Indiana is on the eastern edge of the Illinois Basin. The northern edge of the state is on the southern edge of the Michigan Basin. The sedimentary formations within both basins are much thicker than those around them, and basement rocks lie at great depth. North America contains quite a number of such large sedimentary basins, as do all continents.

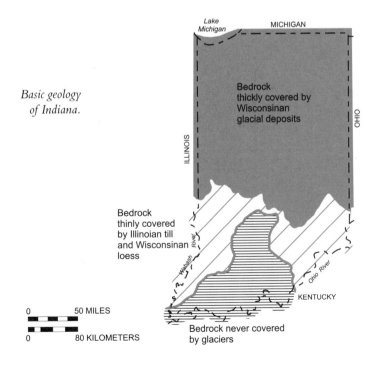

*Basic geology of Indiana.*

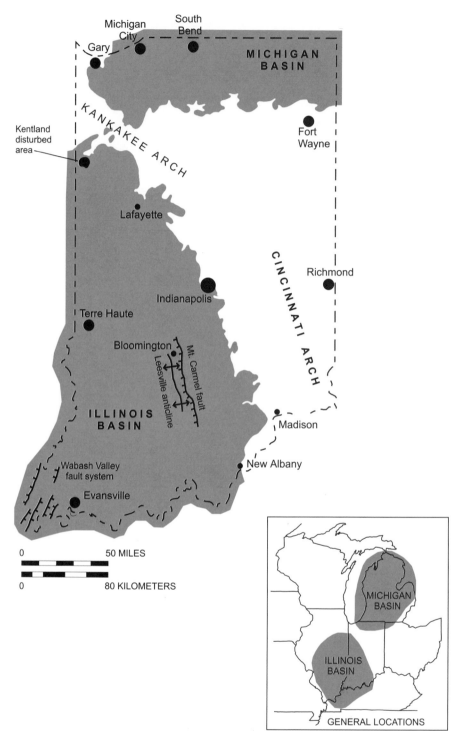

*Major geologic structures of Indiana.*

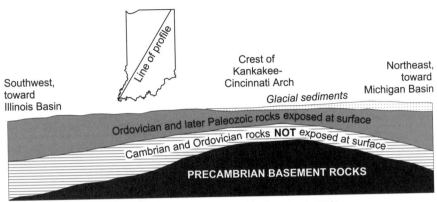

Southwest, toward Illinois Basin

Line of profile

Crest of Kankakee-Cincinnati Arch

Glacial sediments

Northeast, toward Michigan Basin

Ordovician and later Paleozoic rocks exposed at surface

Cambrian and Ordovician rocks **NOT** exposed at surface

PRECAMBRIAN BASEMENT ROCKS

Relative thicknesses and profiles of rock layers are highly exaggerated.

*Generalized northeast-southwest profile across Indiana.*

Sedimentary basins are extremely important because most contain oil and gas and have coal seams around their margins. Oil and gas exist in both east-central and southwestern Indiana, and coal underlies southwestern Indiana, greatly to the benefit of its economy if not the natural beauty of its landscape.

## FOSSILS

The rocks of Indiana are magnificently rich in fossils that provide glimpses of the creatures that lived in the vast shallow seas, swamps, lakes, rivers, and forests that once covered the state. Some fossils form when sediments cover a shell, a piece of wood, or another hard part left after the death of an organism. Groundwater fills openings in these hard parts, turning the organic matter into inorganic mineral matter. Plant fossils often form when leaves and stems compact between sediment layers, leaving only a thin film of black carbon outlining their shapes. Other fossils are molds of the original organism such as the imprint a shell might make when pressed into mud or sand. Fossils range in size from nearly invisible conodonts to pieces of tree trunks 10 feet long or the skeletons of ice-age elephants.

## PLEISTOCENE ICE AGE

The exact time is a matter of some dispute, but sometime around 2 million years ago the earth began to experience periodic ice advances. No one knows why.

Nor do geologists know how many ice sheets came and went, when or why they started and stopped, or exactly what the weather was like. We can say with some confidence that the modern landscape contains clear evidence of the last two ice sheets, and that an unknown number preceded them. And it seems reasonably clear that their weather was both colder and a great deal wetter than what we know today. At least the last ice age ended with an abrupt change in climate and a great melting of ice that sent horrendous summer torrents of water pouring down most of the streams in Indiana.

Geologists call the older of the last two ice sheets that left their signatures on the landscape the Illinoian because its deposits were first identified in Illinois. It happened at an undetermined time, perhaps 100,000 or more years ago. The younger ice sheet, the Wisconsinan, ended approximately 12,000 years ago, very recently as geologic events go.

The standard technique of geologic prediction is to see what happened in the recent past and to predict more of the same for the future. That procedure leads most geologists to presume that the future may bring more ice, but the truth is that no one knows if or when another ice sheet will come.

Most geologists cheerfully assume that anything as geologically significant as an ice age must have a geologic cause. But their efforts to find one have not led to any definitive result. In fact, ice ages are climatic events with widespread geologic consequences. It may be that climatologists, not geologists, will finally figure out what causes ice ages.

## GLACIAL EROSION AND DEPOSITION

Pleistocene snows compacted to become glacial ice. The ice acquired the mass and hardness that allowed it to either push, scrape, or pluck loose material from the ground over which it passed. Most of the loose material probably stayed near the ground, but internal ice movements may have pushed some of the debris higher in the ice sheet.

Sediment deposited directly from glacial ice consists of debris in all sizes and shapes mixed chaotically together. It is called till and typically is gray and plain looking. Glaciers plaster most of their till on the surface to make a flat and rather featureless deposit called ground moraine. End moraine formed where the rate of ice advance matched the rate of melting at the edge of an ice sheet, which dumped till in a hilly ridge around the ice margin in the manner of a conveyor belt.

Glacial meltwater poured down valleys like any other kind of water and deposited sands and gravels as outwash. Outwash in Indiana exists in such outlandish quantities that one can only conclude that torrents of meltwater poured down the valleys in vast floods. It is generally possible to trace outwash deposits upstream into a glacial till, thus leaving no doubt about their origin.

Meltwater streams also deposited outwash in low areas on top of the ice, or as alluvial fans along its margins. When the ice finally melted, it gently lowered these deposits onto the land beneath to make small hills called kames. Most kames stand in flat ground moraine. Outwash also filled the valleys of meltwater streams within the ice; it survived after the ice melted as long winding ridges called eskers. Indiana has many kames but few eskers.

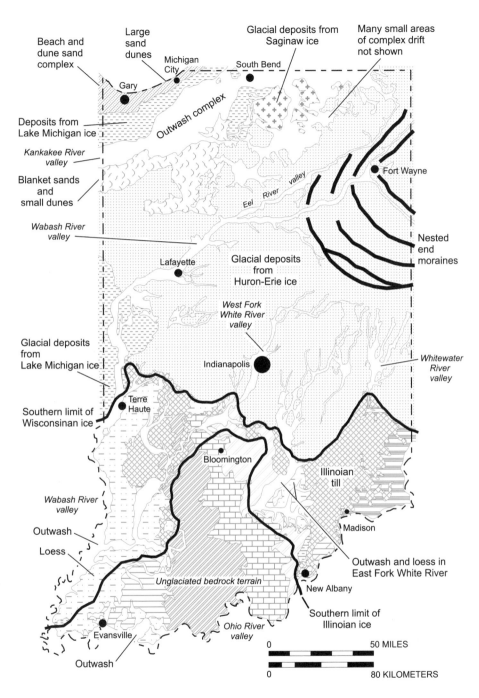

*Generalized glacial geology of Indiana.*

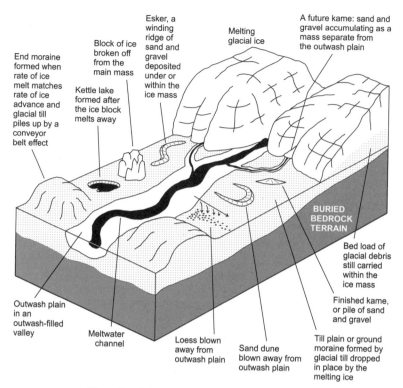

*How glacial deposits and landforms came to be.*

In some places till and outwash are closely mixed because of the particular way the ice moved and melted. To show these materials separately requires large-scale maps covering only a small area. On maps of the scale used in this book, it is more convenient to refer to such areas as mixed till and outwash.

Temporary shallow lakes received thin annual layers of glacial silts and clays to form lake plains that survived after the lakes drained. Some of these lakes formed atop ground moraine as the ice mass blocked the easiest drainage. Most of the lakes formed in side valleys of the major rivers where outwash choked the main valley and ponded the small streams. This type of lake was especially common in the hills of southern Indiana.

## SAND AND GRAVEL

Outwash deposits are, by any reckoning, one of Indiana's most important and valuable natural resources. All industrial economies depend heavily on sand and gravel for construction aggregate and road material. Sand and gravel extraction is the largest mining industry in most of the industrialized world. Any sand and gravel deposit close to a major market is valuable.

Deposits of glacial outwash are so enormous that it seems strange to worry about their reserves. The problem is far more complex than simply estimating the tonnage in the ground. Many formerly good sources may be near their ends either because mineral rights to surrounding areas are not available or because the site is really running out of usable material. Loss to urbanization is an especially difficult problem because sand and gravel must be close to their market, which may then put a gravel pit out of business as urban expansion makes the land more valuable for other uses. Many bedrock quarry operations are producing crushed rock as an alternative to sand and gravel.

## WINDBORNE SEDIMENTS

After the glaciers left their deposits, strong winds began moving numerous areas of sands and silts. Spectacular coastal sand dunes pushed inland from the Lake Michigan shoreline. They are part of a dune complex that stretches into Michigan. Just south of the Kankakee River valley the wind swept a long, wide band of blanket sands and small dunes from the valley. Small areas of river valley sand dunes occur along the east sides of every major river valley across southern Indiana.

A widespread, persistent layer of silt, also called loess, blankets practically the whole state, thinning from as much as 25 feet near the Wabash River to a few inches along the eastern side of Indiana. This dusting originated from silt deposited along with sands and gravels in the major meltwater floodplains. Loess makes fertile soils and may well be Indiana's most valuable natural resource.

*Major areas of windborne sediments across Indiana.* —Modified from Flint, 1971

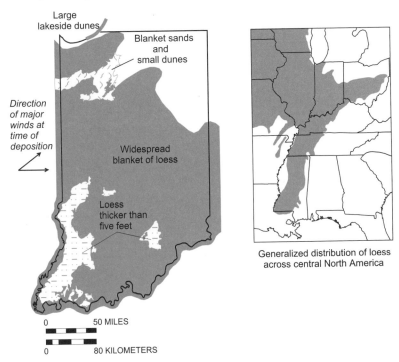

Generalized distribution of loess across central North America

# GROUNDWATER

Groundwater is an absolutely vital natural resource, even in a state blessed with a rich abundance of rain. The deposits of glacial outwash in the floors of most of Indiana's stream valleys contain a bounty of excellent subsurface water in the open spaces between the sand grains and pebbles. The people of Indiana use hundreds of millions of gallons of groundwater from such sources every day.

Areas without much glacial outwash, mostly in the southern half of Indiana, have limited supplies of groundwater, simply because hard rocks contain very little open pore space capable of holding water. And much of that water contains dissolved mineral matter, such as sulfurous compounds, that makes it smell bad and taste worse. People of the nineteenth and early twentieth centuries prized that water because they thought a foul odor and taste indicated medicinal value.

## THE ANCIENT OHIO RIVER

Wells and soundings indicate that a deep buried channel exists below the Ohio River valley southwest of Louisville. This ancient Ohio River probably existed before the Pleistocene ice ages began. The river was much shorter then than now, and it drained a much smaller area.

Glaciers periodically covered the drainage networks of northern Indiana and shed meltwater into the early Ohio River. The increased flow and the tremendous influx of glacial debris greatly changed the early river system. Each major advance of the ice led to more southerly deposits of outwash. Sand and gravel filled the valleys when glaciers melted, creating a higher floodplain. The accumulation of sediments diminished as the ice disappeared. Rivers eroded the valley fill, leaving terraces along the edges of the valley and eventually creating the modern channel.

## OHIO RIVER FLOODS

The power of the Ohio River becomes evident during occasional great floods. Water covers the floodplain and often the lower terraces, leaving a layer of sand, silt, and mud on the bottomlands as it returns to normal river level. The first large flood of record in the Ohio Valley was in 1788. Unfortunately, little information is available about either it or the 1825 flood.

Early towns originated on floodplains to take advantage of the level ground. Their residents lived with floods that raised water as much as 5 feet about the buildings. In 1828 Lawrenceburg residents simply retreated to the upper story and drove the livestock to the hills. Floods were party times. After the water receded, communal cleanup began. Floods were thought to cleanse the earth's surface. The tradition of flood parties ended about 1915, when Lawrenceburg moved to a higher terrace.

Heavy snow in January 1832 and a rapid thaw in February led to the highest flood in the early days on the Ohio River. Four days of rain fell

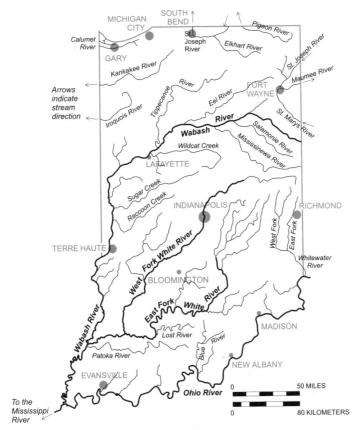

*Rivers of Indiana.*

during the thaw and the river continued to rise. It reached 45 feet above low water level, submerging river towns between Pittsburgh and Louisville. Nearly all frame structures within reach of the flood floated down the river.

An unusual December flood struck the Ohio River valley in 1847. Major winter floods came during three years beginning in 1882. Each year, January or February rains falling on snow raised the river level. A flood in 1884 inspired construction of a number of levees in the valley, including an immense one at Aurora and Lawrenceburg. Parts of the levee slumped during the floods of 1897 and 1898, evidently due to poor construction. An unusually high flood followed the mild and rainy winter of 1906 and 1907.

Most Indiana and Ohio rivers flooded during March 1913 when an intense storm dumped more than 10 inches of rain on a mostly frozen ground. The floods reached record-setting levels and wreaked havoc along many water courses in the Hoosier state. But the greatest flood to date is still the 1937 flood.

In 1937 the Ohio Valley received more than 13 inches of rain between January 14 and 25, including 2 inches on January 15 and almost 3 inches on

*View south across the Ohio River valley. Mauckport bridge in distance.*

January 21. The rain added to water pouring into the river and its tributaries from an unseasonably early snowmelt, especially in the highlands of eastern Ohio and western Pennsylvania. Nearly 13,000 square miles of farmland and riverside communities over twelve states were underwater at its height. The river reached a crest of 80 feet at Cincinnati on January 26, of 57 feet at Tell City on January 28, and of 54 feet at Evansville on January 31. Disaster struck at river communities from Lawrenceburg to Evansville. The river returned to its banks on February 20 in Evansville, more than forty days after the water began rising in early January.

Many small communities, once thriving centers of commerce on the river, essentially washed away during the flood. Bridgeport, on Indiana 111, lost all but one of its buildings; most floated down the river. Landslides, generated by the heavy rains, destroyed several homes at the foot of steep hills south of Bridgeport. Rosewood, now a ghost town and no longer on maps, disappeared during the flood. Buildings at Mauckport, New Amsterdam, and Alton floated down the river or dislodged from foundations. More than sixty homes disappeared or were heavily damaged at Leavenworth.

The flood ravaged Jeffersonville and New Albany. Sightseers lined the Silver Hills above New Albany to watch the swirling waters sweep through

*A submerged Markland during the 1913 Ohio River flood.* —Mark J. Camp Collection

the cities below. Tons of mud and sand accumulated in the downtown buildings. Across the river in Louisville, similar conditions prevailed.

The water was 17 feet above the normal banks at Tell City. Half the town was underwater. Rising waters incapacitated the water and light plant on January 21, leaving the community without electricity or water service. The residents of Tell City learned their lesson the hard way and took immediate steps to prevent future flood disasters. The Army Corps of Engineers completed a reinforced floodwall, supplemented by an earthen levee, around the city in 1940.

At Evansville, conditions were similar. The city waterworks shut down for six days on January 26. Strong currents swept the eastern part of Evansville, knocking buildings off foundations, as waters flowed down the grade of U.S. 41. As floodwaters receded in early February damage estimates came in. Nearly ten thousand homes incurred flood damage. Many riverside buildings either collapsed or were condemned because of weakened foundations. Damage in Evansville amounted to more than $30 million. The Army Corps of Engineers built earthen and concrete levees south of Pollack Avenue on the east side and along Carpenter Creek on the west side between 1939 and 1948. Concrete walls, built in the 1960s, also surround Pigeon Creek, a major tributary to the Ohio River.

Floods continue to plague the Ohio Valley. When will another top the level of 1937?

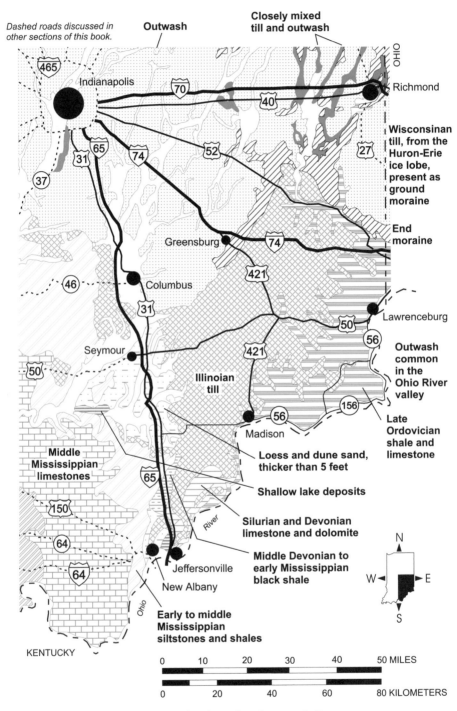

*Highways and geology of southeastern Indiana.*

# Southeastern Indiana
## BRACHIOPODS AND BRYOZOANS

The flat uplands and deep stream valleys of southeastern Indiana display Indiana's earliest and latest geologic history—Paleozoic bedrock and Pleistocene glacial deposits. The rock here dates back to Ordovician time, between 500 and 440 million years ago.

### THE ORDOVICIAN WORLD

Some 480 million years ago, a shallow warm sea covered most of North America. The closest land stretched from what is now Virginia into the Canadian maritime provinces and featured the Taconic Mountains. Streams carried sediments from these eroding mountains and deposited them in deltas where they entered the sea. Gravel and sand settled along the shoreline, and finer particles washed as far west as the seafloor that would become Indiana. Clay that often clouded those ancient waters eventually settled to become shale.

Alternating limestone and shale are typical of Indiana's Ordovician formations. Calcium carbonate precipitated from seawater and seashells accumulated. Limestone layers tend to continue for long distances; the shale

*Ordovician limestone containing brachiopods (concentric-lined shells), bryozoans (branches), crinoid columns (star patterns), and trilobites. Dillsboro formation, near Cedar Grove.*

layers are generally local. The ratio of limestone to shale distinguishes one Ordovician formation from the next.

Sea level and the depth to which waves stirred the water determined the amount of shale deposited between limestone layers. Thick limestone layers dominated in shallow water where wave motion kept the clay in suspension, giving it little chance of settling to the bottom to become shale.

The fossil record here is full. Small brachiopods with thin shells were pioneer colonizers of the muddy bottom. Branching bryozoans then grew up from the shelly foundation in colonies similar to corals. Crinoids—animals related to starfish and that look much like plants because they stand on long stems—followed, and soon a wide range of organisms flourished.

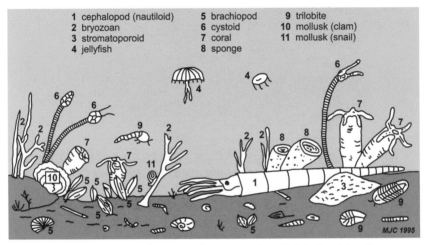

A Late Ordovician seascape showing corals, jellyfish, brachiopods, bryozoans, snails, cephalopods, and cystoids.

**Kope Formation.** A fossiliferous gray shale, the Kope formation appears at the base of several roadcuts and stream banks in Dearborn County. It is the oldest rock formation exposed in southern Indiana. It is as much as 300 to 400 feet thick, but only the upper part is visible. The Kope formation grades upward into the Dillsboro formation through an increase in the proportion of limestone to shale.

**Dillsboro Formation.** The Dillsboro formation, which averages about 400 feet in thickness, crops out from Union County south to the Ohio River. It is the oldest Ordovician formation widely exposed in the state. Near Dillsboro, it contains nearly equal amounts of gray limestone and shale. Limestone layers become more abundant toward the Ohio River; shale dominates near Brookville.

*The Saluda member of the Whitewater formation forms a jutting ledge halfway up the slope along Indiana 101, north of Brookville.*

**Whitewater Formation.** The Whitewater formation, which lies above the Dillsboro formation, was probably deposited in shallow water. Thin seams of mud between the limestone layers explain the rubbly appearance of many exposures.

The Saluda member of the Whitewater formation includes about 50 feet of dolomite, limestone, and mudstone. The scarcity of fossils and presence of dolomite suggest a shallow sea, bounded by reefs, in which rapid evaporation kept the water very salty. Only a few ostracods, tiny arthropods with two hinged shells, and algae could tolerate such conditions. Ripple marks indicate shallow water. Mud cracks formed in the drying dolomite sediments when the Saluda lagoon was exposed to the atmosphere for a long time.

The sea eventually flooded the Saluda lagoon, and more normal sediments again accumulated to become the upper part of the Whitewater formation. It reaches a maximum thickness of 100 feet at Richmond and thins to 60 feet at Madison.

## A LOST INTERVAL

Sea level dropped around 440 million years ago, leaving Indiana high and dry. The old seafloor was exposed and eroded until a rising sea again flooded it in early Silurian time.

The contact between the Whitewater formation and the Silurian rocks above it is the erosion surface, or unconformity, that developed while sea level was low. The best evidence of erosion is truncated stromatoporoids, fossil sponges that normally have a hemispherical shape but whose tops were eroded flat. In other places, fossil burrows filled with Silurian limestone extend down into the Whitewater formation.

## THE SILURIAN WORLD

Erosion during earliest Silurian time reduced the land area to the east, changing its configuration so that less eroded sediment would reach Indiana in periods to come. The inland sea again flooded Indiana in early Silurian time. Limy mud accumulated and hardened into the Brassfield limestone and Salamonie dolomite. After that, clay and mud accumulated to become the Waldron shale. A final layer of more limy mud later became the Louisville limestone.

*Brassfield Limestone.* The Brassfield limestone, the oldest Silurian rock in Indiana, is a tan to gray limestone, 4 to 20 feet thick and full of fossils. Sporadic exposures exist in a belt from Richmond southwest to the Ohio River near Charlestown. After they accumulated, parts of the Brassfield limestone were above sea level and eroded before later Silurian sediments buried them.

*Salamonie Dolomite.* The Osgood member is the lower part of the Salamonie dolomite in southeastern Indiana; the Laurel member is the upper part. The Osgood member, 10 to 30 feet thick, lies mostly on the Brassfield limestone, except in parts of Decatur, Jefferson, Jennings, Ripley, and Scott Counties, where the Brassfield member is missing and the Osgood member rests on the Whitewater formation. In the Madison area, the Osgood member is a calcareous shale; at Rossburg, a muddy limestone; and at Richmond, a dolomite. The variation of the Osgood member causes endless problems for geologists who try to match the Silurian rocks from one place to the next. The shortage of good exposures further complicates matters.

The Laurel member is a tan to gray dolomitic limestone that exists between the Ohio River and the Richmond area. It thickens northward from 27 to 55 feet. Abundant fossil molds indicate the rock began as limestone, then changed to dolomite as magnesium replaced about half the calcium in the original calcite.

*Waldron Shale.* Deposition of the Waldron shale began as more mud entered the Silurian sea. The formation varies from shale in the south, near the apparent source, to muddy limestone in the north. Local concentrations of sea creatures built patch reefs on the muddy bottom. The Waldron shale averages about 5 feet thick in southeastern Indiana. It is famous for its beautifully preserved fossils, which include some extremely rare jellyfish.

*Louisville Limestone.* A rise in sea level probably caused deposition of the fossiliferous Louisville limestone on the Waldron shale. It ranges between 40 and 75 feet thick, becoming thicker in the subsurface of northeastern Indiana. Louisville limestone reaches the surface in Clark County.

**Wabash Formation.** As Silurian time passed, large coral reefs grew in the shallows around the margins of the Illinois Basin, which extended into western Indiana. Debris broken off the reefs accumulated between them to become the Mississinewa member of the Wabash formation. It reaches into southeastern Indiana, where it appears in Clark County as greenish shales and limestones. They are the youngest Silurian rocks in this part of the state.

Parts of southeastern Indiana were above sea level during the transition from Silurian to Devonian time. An erosion surface that developed on the youngest Silurian rocks became an unconformity when Devonian sediments buried it.

## THE DEVONIAN WORLD

A shallow sea once again covered southeastern Indiana by the middle of Devonian time, around 380 million years ago. Fossiliferous Jeffersonville and North Vernon limestones surface periodically in a belt that extends from Hancock and Marion Counties south to Clark County on the Ohio River. The thick New Albany shale accumulated during late Devonian time, when the earth was in the throes of a mass extinction. A large proportion of the earth's animal species vanished while the New Albany shale was being laid down.

**Jeffersonville Limestone.** The oldest readily exposed Devonian rock in the state, the Geneva dolomite member of the Jeffersonville limestone, is at the surface in a narrow band from eastern Illinois across southern Indiana to the Louisville area. As much as 35 feet thick, the Geneva dolomite was

*A middle Devonian seascape showing animals that commonly became fossils.*

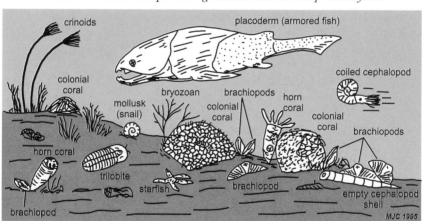

*Devonian Jeffersonville limestone along Indiana 3, south of Vernon.*

originally reef limestone. Percolating water brought magnesium that replaced about half the calcium in the original rock, converting it into dolomite.

The Jeffersonville limestone continues above the Geneva dolomite to a thickness of as much as 200 feet in southwestern Indiana. It is best known as the fossiliferous rock at the Falls of the Ohio. It contains a rich profusion of fossils, especially corals, many of which became extinct by the end of Devonian time.

*North Vernon Limestone.* As sea level continued to rise, limy sediments that became the North Vernon limestone accumulated on top of the Jeffersonville limestone. The North Vernon limestone was deposited in shallow nearshore waters. The sequence thickens to the southwest, averaging about 25 feet thick in southeastern Indiana.

*New Albany Shale.* Brownish fragmentary shale lies on the hillside above U.S. 31W at Sellersburg. It is part of a rock layer that extends over much of the Midwest.

The New Albany shale contains few visible fossils. Many of the fossils are microscopic, most commonly within phosphatic nodules near the top of the formation. The chief exceptions are occasional carbonized twigs and petrified segments of Devonian trees found as individual logs or as the nuclei of large concretions. One log 16 feet long and 2 feet in diameter, unearthed near Henryville, appeared at the Indianapolis Exposition of 1873. The 1874 Exposition featured an even larger log, some 19 feet long and 3 feet in diameter, that came from the New Albany shale northeast of Vienna.

*Devonian New Albany shale overlying the North Vernon limestone in a quarry south of Blocher.*

At least forty species of primitive but nevertheless vascular plants, complete with roots, have been described from the New Albany shale. Many of the fossils occur within phosphatic and pyritic concretions. Fossils of brachiopods occur with the plants, as do the remains of other animals that lived in seawater, including cephalopods and conodonts. The most abundant fossils are spores of ferns and algae, which are often found plastered on bedding surfaces. The association of land plants with marine animals suggests deposition near a coast.

Certain horizons in the New Albany shale contain concretions as large as small boulders. The shale beds warp over the concretions, which suggests that the concretions were solid while the shale was still a soft mud. Some of the concretions are quite dense because they contain a high concentration of siderite, a reddish brown iron carbonate mineral. Siderite, rare in sedimentary rocks deposited in seawater, indicates an extremely peculiar chemical environment.

The origin of the New Albany shale has been much debated. The abundant organic matter shows that life abounded in the depositional environment, but most of the fossils typical of rocks of that age are absent. The New Albany shale probably accumulated in a sea that bloomed with floating algae and whose low oxygen content helped both to preserve organic matter and to permit the rare iron mineral siderite to form. The land plants probably floated into the sea and sank into the fine muds on its bottom. Some of the pieces of petrified wood show signs of transport rounding, like pebbles rounded in a creek. Some have crinoids and other animals attached to them, which suggests that they floated for a while before they sank.

Conodont fossils show that the lower part of the New Albany shale was deposited during late Devonian time and the uppermost part during early Mississippian time. Nothing else in the rock reveals that boundary.

## CINCINNATI ARCH

The geologic map of southeastern Indiana reveals broad north-south bands of rock formations from the older Ordovician rocks between Richmond and Madison westward to the younger Silurian and Devonian rocks between Indianapolis and Jeffersonville.

This is the area of the Cincinnati Arch, a gentle upward warp in the earth's crust east of the Illinois Basin (which may or may not have had anything to do with the warping). The arch appeared during Ordovician time, when it apparently began to shed sediment into the surrounding areas. Many younger formations thin as they approach the Cincinnati Arch, evidently because it has been persistently high. No formations deposited since Devonian time exist on the Cincinnati Arch. It is not completely clear whether none accumulated or some accumulated but later eroded off.

## PLEISTOCENE ICE AGE

The exact number of ice sheets and interglacial episodes during Pleistocene time—the last 2 million years—is unknown. Only the latest two ice sheets, the Illinoian followed by the Wisconsinan, left a clear record in the landscapes of Indiana.

*Illinoian Ice Sheet.* Across most of southeastern Indiana, the landscape has been exposed to erosion ever since the Illinoian ice sheet melted long ago. Streams have cut valleys into the till deposits, which are rather reddish because they have weathered a long time.

Windblown silt or loess 3 to 5 feet thick covers much of the Illinoian till and makes extremely fertile soil. Strong winds blew the silt off the floodplains and into the hills and valleys.

*Wisconsinan Ice Sheet.* North of a line between Liberty and Connersville, four tills, separated by layers of sand or silt, cover the Illinoian glacial deposits. The Wisconsinan ice left them as it advanced and melted at least four times before it finally melted about 12,000 years ago.

Two major late Wisconsinan ice lobes, the Miami lobe coming from Ohio and the East White lobe from central Indiana, met in southeastern Indiana. End moraines record the edges of these two ice lobes and the southern boundary of the Wisconsinan deposits, which do not extend as far south as those of the older Illinoian glacial ice.

Fossil pollen shows that spruce and pine forests persisted for many hundreds of years after the glaciers finally melted, and the climate remained cool and wet. Fossil snails and clams from lake and marsh deposits also show that a cool climate continued after the ice disappeared.

*Early limestone quarry. Note temporary rails laid for stone carts that were pushed by men or pulled by mules.* —Mark J. Camp Collection

## MINERAL INDUSTRIES

Early geological reports tell of many small quarries that peppered southeastern Indiana during its first century of pioneer settlement. Most early quarries were in stream bottoms where rock was most exposed. Such quarries were best worked by prying up stone slabs during low water. Floods tended to fill in such quarries with sediment, making it easier to open a new quarry than to dig out the old one. Most are now hard to find.

Many early quarries also opened along railroads and roads, producing stone for ballast and road gravel. Preferred places were on high ground, well above the water table. Some operators burned limestone to make lime for fertilizer or cement.

The Silurian Brassfield limestone, Salamonie dolomite, and Louisville limestone, and the Devonian Jeffersonville limestone and North Vernon limestone, have been quarried for years for aggregate, agricultural lime, portland cement, and building stone.

Glacial and floodplain clays were mined to make pottery, brick, and tile at numerous locations across southeastern Indiana. In the early days ceramic construction materials were often made at the construction site. As towns grew, tile and brickyards became commonplace in the larger communities. This once flourishing industry has nearly disappeared.

*Belknap's Quarry at Sellersburg, circa 1908. Tunnels permitted exploitation of a formation important in cement production.* —Mark J. Camp Collection

## GEOGRAPHIC REGIONS

*Dearborn Upland.* The Dearborn upland occupies all or part of eleven counties in southeastern Indiana. Most of the region is hills and valleys eroded into late Ordovician shales and limestones overlapping the Cincinnati Arch.

In the southern part of the Dearborn upland, narrow deep valleys with steep sides dominate, and the hilltops are generally long, narrow ridges that end at a nearly common altitude at the Ohio River valley. Northward, the valleys become less prominent and the hilltops wider, eventually looking like gently rolling plains. Elevations are 950 to 1,000 feet in the northern half of this area, between 750 and 850 feet farther south. The elevation along the Ohio River valley is about 450 feet.

Nearly every hilltop south of Franklin County retains an eroded cover of Illinoian glacial deposits, generally less than 50 feet thick. Much of the present landscape is old bedrock hills showing through as erosion strips their glacial cover.

Wisconsinan glacial deposits cover the Illinoian deposits north of Franklin County. These younger glacial deposits are more than 200 feet thick; they have buried valleys and completely masked almost every expression of the underlying bedrock.

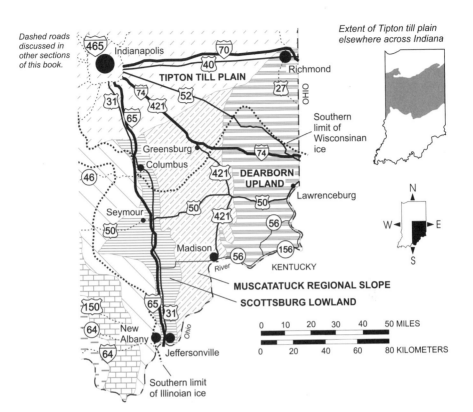

465  Indianapolis  70  40  TIPTON TILL PLAIN  Richmond

Extent of Tipton till plain elsewhere across Indiana

31  74  52  27  OHIO

421  65

Greensburg  Southern limit of Wisconsinan ice

Columbus  74

46  421  DEARBORN UPLAND

Lawrenceburg  50

Seymour  50  421  50

50  421  56

Madison  56  156

River  KENTUCKY

MUSCATATUCK REGIONAL SLOPE

SCOTTSBURG LOWLAND

150  65  31

64  New Albany  0  10  20  30  40  50 MILES

64  Jeffersonville  0  20  40  60  80 KILOMETERS

Ohio

N
W ◄ E
S

Southern limit of Illinoian ice

*Highways and geographic regions of southeastern Indiana.*

*Dearborn upland terrain along Indiana 62, north of Canaan. Late Ordovician bedrock underlies this region.*

A thin dusting of windblown silts and sands caps both the Illinoian and Wisconsinan deposits. These materials are the easternmost extension in Indiana of the sediments blown from the outwash plains in the White and Wabash river valleys. They are hard to see. Only detailed studies of the region's soils and other surficial deposits disclose their extent.

The modern drainage on the Dearborn upland is all south and east to the Ohio River. The major stream is the Whitewater River; it begins just north of Richmond and flows into southwestern Ohio, reaching the Ohio River just at the state line. Laughery Creek and about ten other smaller streams drain from the hilltop areas into the Ohio River.

*Muscatatuck Regional Slope.* The Muscatatuck regional slope descends gently westward from the Dearborn upland. It developed on the generally resistant Silurian and Devonian limestones that dip westward off the Cincinnati Arch. Part of the western side of the Muscatatuck regional slope developed on more easily erodible shales of late Devonian to early Mississippian age. The elevations of the upland areas decrease from 900 or 950 feet along the eastern side of the area to 600 feet near the valley of the East Fork White River. Except near the Ohio River, the Muscatatuck regional slope drains to the west and southwest.

The same range of ages and types of Pleistocene glacial deposits that cover the Dearborn upland also cover the bedrock of the Muscatatuck regional slope. Illinoian glacial deposits cover nearly all the upland areas as a thin remnant less than 50 feet thick. Wisconsinan deposits dominate north of the line between Jennings and Decatur Counties and thicken northward to as much as 100 feet. Windblown sands and silts also cover this province and thicken slightly toward the valley of the East Fork White River, but they are hard to see.

*Scottsburg Lowland.* The Scottsburg lowland stretches north from the Ohio River to southern Johnson and Shelby Counties. It was eroded in soft shales deposited during late Devonian and early Mississippian time. The east side grades into the Muscatatuck regional slope; the west side ends at the base of high hills eroded from more resistant rocks.

The northern three-quarters of this lowland is a broad valley with an elevation of 500 to 700 feet. It is filled with great volumes of outwash to a depth between 50 and 100 feet. The East Fork White River flows south here, and the Muscatatuck River joins it from the east. Their flooding glacial ancestors once joined to erode an extension of the lowland 20 miles westward into the otherwise resistant hills. The hills south and east of Brownstown are an isolated remnant of the hills to the west.

Most glacial deposits in the northern part are Wisconsinan age, but areas of Illinoian till survive in western Bartholomew County. Windblown sands and silts are locally thick along the east side of the lowland, especially in the area of Brownstown, Seymour, and Scottsburg.

The southern quarter of this province is a subtle valley that extends south from the line between Scott and Clark Counties to the Ohio River. Elevations range from 450 to 650 feet. It developed in Silurian and Devonian limestones like those in the Muscatatuck regional slope to the east, and in late Devonian to early Mississippian shales. The valley never carried significant glacial meltwaters. Thin areas of Illinoian till survive on many hilltops. A major lake plain near New Albany formed when Ohio River valley outwash dammed a tributary valley.

## OHIO RIVER

Six terraces of sand and gravel rise like a flight of broad steps from the floodplain of the Ohio River in southeastern Indiana. Judging from a general decrease in sediment grain size from the highest to the lowest terrace, the Ohio River must have been a very different stream when those older terraces were its floodplain.

The Ohio River has also changed during historic time. River channels constantly change their positions as the stream erodes its channel. People who lived in Vevay in the 1850s looked out over a low island just offshore; steamboats cruised between it and the town docks. The island disappeared by 1872 as the channel filled with sediment. In 1872 the Indiana Geological Survey showed that Rising Sun had lost 300 feet of shoreline, and Florence 80 feet, in the preceding twenty-five years. Hardinsburg, now 2 miles west of the Great Miami River, was a port in the middle 1800s. Such changes continue.

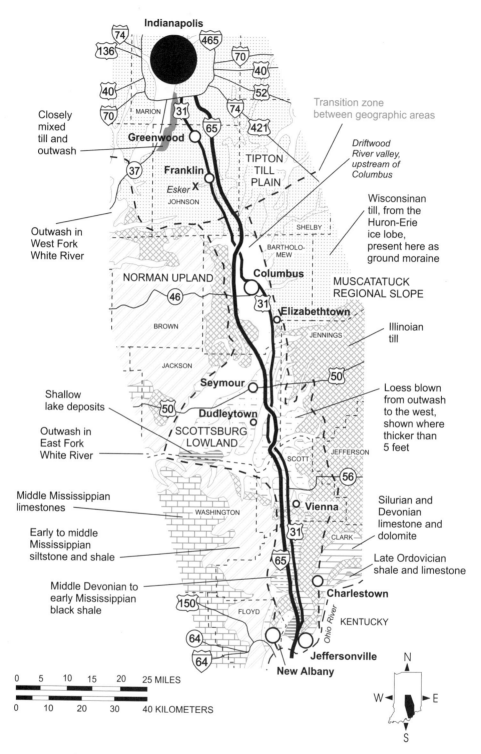

Geology along I-65 and U.S. 31 between Indianapolis and the Kentucky line.

# Interstate 65 and U.S. 31
## Indianapolis—Kentucky Line
### 112 MILES

Interstate 65 and U.S. 31 parallel and cross each other over a variety of glacial deposits and hills eroded in ancient bedrock. They cross the drainage basin of the East Fork White River and its tributaries from the Indianapolis area to northern Clark County. Between northern Clark County and the Ohio River, the highways cross the basin of Silver Creek, a minor tributary of the Ohio River.

Interstate 65 and U.S. 31 cross 20 miles of Wisconsinan ground moraine in the southernmost part of the Tipton till plain between I-465 and the area a few miles south of Franklin. The moraine makes a gently rolling till plain that completely obscures the underlying bedrock, except in quarries.

Interstate 65 and U.S. 31 wander along the western edge of the Scottsburg lowland between the area south of Franklin and the Kentucky line.

Between the area a few miles south of Franklin and the White River, northeast of Seymour, the highways cross or follow 30 miles of stream valleys filled with outwash sands and gravels between 50 and 100 feet deep. This route parallels the boundary between the older Illinoian deposits to the west and the younger Wisconsinan deposits to the east. The valleys in the northern part hold the several tributary streams that join near Columbus to become the East Fork White River. The outwash fill in the valley is between 50 and 100 feet deep.

Southwest of Columbus, I-65 jogs 10 miles across the highlands west of the river valley. They are eroded in siltstone and shale deposited during middle Mississippian time and now have a thin cover of Illinoian till, the Jessup formation, and some windblown silts. Southeast of Columbus, U.S. 31 runs 10 miles across bedrock uplands just east of the outwash valley. Rocks exposed in these eastern uplands are limestones and dolomites that formed during Silurian and Devonian time. Younger siltstones and shales deposited during Mississippian time cap them in places. Wind blew sand out of the White River valley, driving dunes against the base of its eastern valley wall.

The highways cross 23 miles of bedrock highlands capped with thin coverings of Illinoian till and windblown sands and silts between the East Fork White River and the line between Clark and Scott Counties. Three wide valleys of the Muscatatuck River and its tributaries dissect this area. The glacial and windblown sediments are between 50 and 100 feet thick.

Interstate 65 and U.S. 31 parallel each other across 13 to 14 miles of bedrock hills with local caps of windblown silts between the area just north of the line between Scott and Clark Counties and the area just north of Speed and Sellersburg. Bedrock between the Scott and Clark county line and Henryville is Mississippian siltstone and shale of the Borden group. Bedrock south of Henryville is the older New Albany shale, which was deposited during late Devonian and early Mississippian time. A number of weathered outcrops are along the highways near Memphis. State and county roads west of the two highways cross the Norman upland, which includes some hills that rise as much as 450 feet above the shale lowlands to the east. They are eroded in resistant formations deposited during middle Mississippian time.

Interstate 65 and U.S. 31 converge across 11 miles of a mixed terrain between the area just north of Speed and Sellersburg and the Ohio River, where they cross the floodplains of Silver Creek and its tributaries. North of Silver Creek, the roads cut across low bedrock hills capped by Illinoian Jessup till and windblown silts. Between Silver Creek and Jeffersonville, the highways cross 4 miles of gently sloping terrain, sediment deposited in a lake impounded behind outwash dumped in the Ohio River valley. Jeffersonville is on outwash sands and gravels within the Ohio River valley. The hilltops west of the road belong to the Knobstone escarpment, the edge of the Norman upland.

### Johnson County Health Spas and Mineral Water

A well sunk to 1,725 feet at Greenwood in 1894 found mineral water instead of gas in the St. Peter sandstone, a formation deposited during middle Ordovician time. It is the oldest formation that readily yields groundwater in the state. The water was very salty, probably old seawater trapped in the pores of the sand as it was deposited more than 400 million years ago. It supplied the Greenwood Sanitarium, now part of suburban Indianapolis.

Bradley Mineral Spring, 7 miles south of Franklin, was never developed but did provide local people with plenty of water rich in iron carbonate. It flowed from the New Albany shale along Sugar Creek.

### Ridges of Sand and Gravel

An esker, a prominent ridge of sand and gravel, rises above the glacial landscape at the southwestern edge of Franklin. It extends about 3 miles

*Generalized surface and bedrock profiles along I-65 and U.S. 31.*

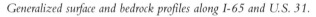
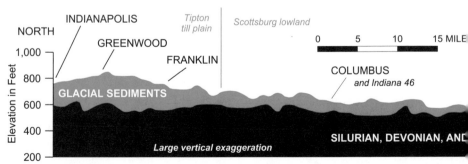

southwest, where it flattens to an apron of sand and gravel. This ridge probably began as a tunnel that ran through the Wisconsinan ice sheet after the ice stopped moving. Meltwater flowing through the tunnel deposited sand and gravel that remained as a winding ridge after the ice melted. Another esker, east of Greenwood, stretches 8 miles. Still others once existed in Indianapolis but were mined for sand and gravel, a common fate of urban eskers.

### Elizabethtown Quarry

Except for a few highway cuts and stream exposures in Clark County and the outcrops at the Falls of the Ohio, quarries provide the only glimpse of the rocks beneath the route of I-65. A deep quarry northeast of Elizabethtown exposes layers of rocks deposited during Devonian and Silurian time. The company produces blocks and crushed stone from the Louisville and Jeffersonville limestones for riprap, concrete aggregate, road metal, agricultural stone, and metallurgical products.

The oldest formations—the Silurian Salamonie dolomite, Waldron shale, and Louisville limestone—appear in the deepest parts of the quarry. A number of nicely preserved crinoids and numerous brachiopods occur in the Waldron shale.

The Mississinewa shale member of the Wabash formation is missing and the Devonian Jeffersonville limestone rests directly on the Louisville limestone. The Jeffersonville limestone is about 75 feet thick at Elizabethtown. The lower part is massive dolomite, brown, and almost without fossils. The uppermost 7 feet are quite fossiliferous. Large brachiopods, bryozoans shaped like fans, and pieces of crinoids are particularly common.

The North Vernon limestone, another fossiliferous unit, lies above the Jeffersonville limestone. The formation is only about 30 inches thick here but thickens considerably to the south and east. The black New Albany shale appears in the upper 3 feet of the quarry face.

The Elizabethtown quarry is well known for its calcite (calcium carbonate), fluorite (calcium fluoride), marcasite (iron sulfide), pyrite (iron sulfide), and sphalerite (zinc sulfide) crystals. The Jeffersonville limestone contains small cavities lined with crystals of calcite and fluorite and filled with asphalt.

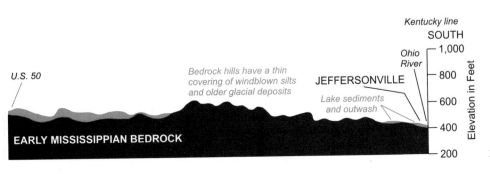

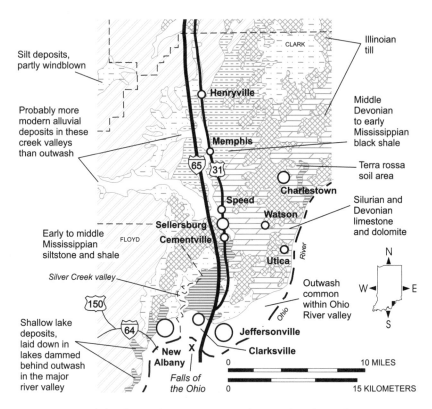

*Detailed geology and important cities and towns along the southern part of I-65 and U.S. 31.*

Small cubes of pyrite mark the boundary between the North Vernon limestone and the New Albany shale.

### Seymour

Sand blown from the glacial outwash in the East Fork White River valley forms dunes along the east side of the valley at Seymour. Look just northeast of Seymour for an oxbow lake that fills an abandoned river meander.

A well drilled for gas at a woolen mill on the southwest side of Seymour in the late 1800s tapped an artesian flow of salty water from Silurian rocks 400 feet below the surface. It provided mineral water for a bathhouse around the turn of the century.

### Kames and Eskers

A side trip to Dudleytown on Indiana 250 leads to the northern end of a chain of kame and esker deposits. Kames are little hills made of glacial outwash. They form as meltwater streams wash sand and gravel into low places on the ice that become high places on the ground after the ice melts. Eskers are

*Clark County Cement Company quarry at Sellersburg, circa 1907.*
—Mark J. Camp Collection

long ridges made of outwash that generally trend in some southerly direction. They form as meltwater streams flowing under the ice fill their channels with sand and gravel that remain as a ridge after the ice melts. Kames and eskers are valuable sources of sand and gravel, partly because they are above the water table and therefore easy to mine.

### Clay and Iron

The Mississippian bedrock of southern Scott and northern Clark Counties provided clay, hematite, and mineral water around the turn of the century. A number of companies, including one at Crothersville and another at Little York, used shale mined from formations in the Borden group to make brick and drain tile. Quarries in the Borden group near Henryville in Clark County supplied nodular hematite or kidney ore. Two to three feet of conglomeratic iron ore once existed in the headwater region of Big Ox Creek.

### Natural Cement Industry

The raw materials for portland cement are limestone and clay. They are fired together in a kiln to drive the carbon dioxide out of the limestone and react the remaining calcium oxide with the clay. This makes a clinker of calcium silicate compounds, which is then ground to a fine powder to make cement. As early as 1826, contractors for the Louisville and Portland Canal used the Silver Creek member of the North Vernon limestone as a source for their cement.

The Beach Mill in Clarksville, the first cement plant in Clark County, was in production in 1866. By the 1890s, more than fifteen cement plants were in operation. Total production peaked in 1890. Cementville, Speed, and Watson boomed. Special trains of cement hoppers served the rapidly expanding industry, carrying the cement to communities throughout the Midwest.

The boom collapsed in 1905, when another source of clay was found in Clark County. That made it possible to mix limestone and clay in consistent proportions instead of taking chances with the varying natural mix in the quarry. The natural cement industry collapsed within a few years. Few traces remain.

## Speed Quarry

The Louisville Cement Company started operating a natural cement quarry and mill at Speed in late 1869. In 1882 the mill expanded to become one of the largest in the state. A new plant built in 1905 allowed production of portland cement from local shales.

The Silurian Wabash formation is at the base of the Speed quarry. This part of the Wabash formation is a grayish green shale and limestone mixture called the Mississinewa shale. The Jeffersonville limestone lies atop it, with an unconformity between them. The Jeffersonville limestone is pure limestone throughout its 35-foot thickness at this quarry; no dolomite is present. Fossils of corals, brachiopods, bryozoans, and crinoids abound throughout. Certain species mark important time horizons within the sequence.

The fossiliferous North Vernon limestone is a layer some 21 feet thick that lies above the Jeffersonville limestone, much thicker than at Elizabethtown. This change in thickness probably reflects a change from open water conditions in Clark County to lagoonal environments in

*Speed Portland Cement Plant in the 1950s.* —Courtesy of Sellersburg Branch of Charlestown-Clark County Public Library

Bartholomew County. Ten feet of black New Albany shale caps the section in the Speed quarry.

## Birth of the Lime Industry

Lime—calcium oxide—was produced at Utica, upriver from Jeffersonville, as early as 1818. The Jeffersonville limestone was broken up with hammers and burned in log fires, then shipped in barrels on Ohio River flatboats. A coal-fired lime kiln built at Utica around 1826 was the first of its kind. Utica lime was shipped to Pennsylvania, Texas, and the Gulf Coast. The plant closed when the company moved its lime division to Milltown in western Harrison County. The Utica quarry turned to producing crushed stone for the construction industry.

## Caves, Sinkholes, and Mineral Springs

Wherever rain falls on limestone bedrock, you are likely to find landscapes full of caves and sinkholes. Rain reacts with carbon dioxide in the atmosphere to make carbonic acid, which dissolves limestone. The acidic water soaks through the limestone along cracks and bedding surfaces, enlarging them into caverns.

Where Silurian and Devonian limestone formations are close to the surface in Clark County and surrounding areas, they are full of caverns, and the landscape is pocked with sinkholes where cavern roofs have caved in or are eroding away to form pits. The reddish brown soils, terra rossa, indicate a limestone origin. You can see terra rossa soils especially well along Indiana 62, northeast of Charlestown.

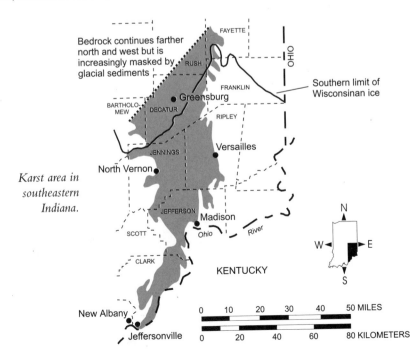

*Karst area in southeastern Indiana.*

Streams commonly disappear into caves or sinkholes, then appear elsewhere as great springs. Fountain Spring, south of Charlestown, and Buffalo Lick Spring, east of Charlestown, are but two of many.

During the late 1800s, many of the major springs were developed or wells were drilled nearby to tap the supposedly curative waters. Bathhouses, sanitariums, and bottling works sprang up like mushrooms. Jeffersonville was famous in the 1840s and 1850s for its Chalybeate Springs; railroad construction later destroyed them.

The earliest health resort was about 4 miles west of Memphis, where a well drilled around 1870 yielded sulfate water on the farm of Samson King. He knew a bonanza when he saw one and built a hotel and bathhouse, which he ran until his death. The well caved in by 1898 and a nearby spring replaced it during the early 1900s. Stores sold water from nearby Indiana Blue Lick Spring, Payne's Mineral Springs at Henryville, and King's Mineral Spring near Dallas.

### Falls of the Ohio State Park

Falls of the Ohio State Park is just west of downtown Jeffersonville, where the Ohio River flows over resistant Devonian limestone in a series of rapids. The rapids owe their origin to changes in the drainage of southeastern Indiana.

Before the ice ages, the Salt River flowed north into Indiana from the Jeffersonville area and the Kentucky River flowed north into western Ohio. Early Pleistocene ice deflected the Salt River from its northern channel into Indiana. Ice of middle Pleistocene time dammed the Kentucky River. Meltwater streams flowing south from the ice eroded deep valleys into the bedrock. As water ponded along the edge of the ice rose, it poured across one divide after another, establishing streams that flowed west along the

*Ledges of Devonian Jeffersonville limestone along the Ohio River at Falls of the Ohio State Park, Clarksville.*

southern margin of the ice. Those combined to become the modern Ohio River, which eroded down through a ridge of resistant Jeffersonville limestone. The Falls of the Ohio River tumbles across the remains of that ridge.

The Falls of the Ohio River was well known to explorers and the military by the late 1700s because no boats could pass at low water. Towns sprang up where boatmen were forced to portage the rapids or wait for high water. The Louisville and Portland Canal was built in the 1820s to provide a safe passage around the rapids. The canal separated portions of Kentucky to create Shippingsport Island.

A description of the fossils preserved in the Jeffersonville limestone at the Falls of the Ohio was published in 1882. The site has been much studied since and is famous among paleontologists and fossil collectors. Corals and brachiopods dominate the hundreds of fossil species collected over the years. The lower beds of the Jeffersonville limestone, near river level, contain numerous corals, especially branching ones, apparently preserved in living position. This indicates a calm environment of deposition, most likely in water deep enough to escape the effects of wave motion. Corals are preserved as fragments associated with mats of stromatoporoids in the upper parts of the Jeffersonville limestone. These probably indicate that the water was shallower and more subject to wave action during later Devonian time.

The Falls of the Ohio Interpretive Center, on the river bluff overlooking the fossil beds, is on West Riverside Drive in Clarksville. Steps lead from the parking area down to the famous fossil beds.

Geophysical evidence and drilling show that the Falls of the Ohio lies above the northern edge of a mass of gabbro buried more than 1 mile below the surface. The gabbro rises above the general level of the old Precambrian erosion surface over which Paleozoic rocks were draped in a gentle arch, an anticline, at the falls. The sedimentary layers tilt down to the southeast near the Pennsylvania Railroad bridge, upstream from the visitor center.

*A slab of Devonian Jeffersonville limestone showing abundant coral fossils. Falls of the Ohio State Park, Clarksville.*

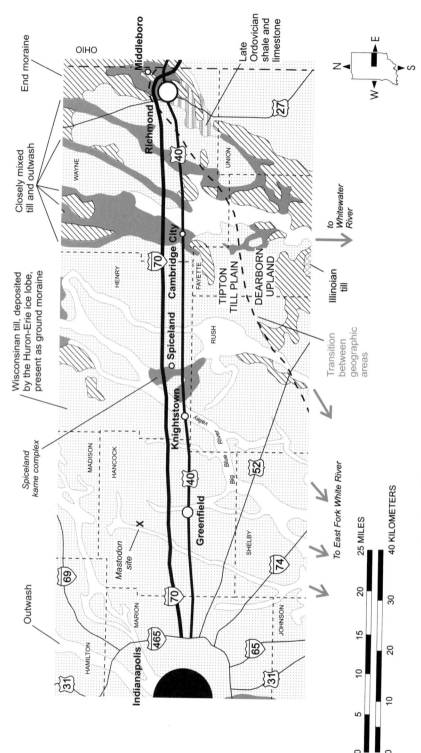

*Geology along I-70 and U.S. 40 between the Ohio line and Indianapolis.*

# Interstate 70 and U.S. 40
## Ohio Line—Indianapolis
### 66 MILES

Interstate 70 and U.S. 40 cross a wide expanse of ground moraine deposited during the Wisconsinan ice age, interrupted only by minor occurrences of end moraine, mixed till and outwash, and stream valleys filled with outwash. Although glacial deposits extend much farther south, the two roads are sometimes considered the dividing line between northern Indiana, with its thick cover of glacial sediments, and the southern part of the state, with its thinning glacial cover and widely exposed bedrock.

East and north of Richmond, U.S. 40 and I-70 cross 4 to 5 miles of deep stream valleys filled with closely mixed till and outwash. End moraine caps the hilltops. These valleys were drastically enlarged when glacial meltwater poured through them. Comparing the size of each valley with its diminutive present stream will give you some idea of the decrease in stream flow after the last ice sheet melted.

Richmond is on the Dearborn upland, between the Tipton till plain to the north and the bedrock hills to the south. Between the west side of Richmond and I-465 at Indianapolis, U.S. 40 and I-70 cross 61 miles of ground moraine near the southern edge of the Tipton till plain. Between Richmond and Indiana 1, the routes cross four small stream valleys filled with glacial outwash and moraines. Two other valleys filled with similar deposits exist west of Indiana 103 and Indiana 3 in central and southern Henry County.

The thickness of the glacial sediments below U.S. 40 and I-70 generally ranges between 100 and 200 feet. A buried bedrock valley beneath the Flatrock River just west of Indiana 103 contains more than 400 feet of glacial fill.

Between the Ohio line and eastern Henry County, U.S. 40 and I-70 cross seven streams that flow south to feed the Whitewater River, a tributary of the Ohio River. Between eastern Henry County and the Indianapolis area, the highways cross six small streams that are tributaries to the East Fork White River. These small valleys are subtle, largely because they contain enormous quantities of outwash sands and gravels.

### Rocks near Richmond

In the late 1800s, several wells penetrated Ordovician formations at Glen Miller Park and produced artesian flows of both fresh and sulfurous water. Water from Reid's and Hawkins Springs on the north side of town was sold as a cure for all ailments.

*Ordovician Whitewater formation at Thistlethwaite Falls, Richmond.*

The fossiliferous Whitewater formation is exposed along the gorge carved by the East Fork Whitewater River, which bisects the city. The Whitewater Gorge trail, starting at Thistlethwaite Falls, offers a close view.

An abandoned quarry near the intersection of Wernle and Garwood roads on the southeast edge of Richmond exposes the Silurian Salamonie dolomite. It lies on a buried erosion surface developed on the Brassfield limestone. If you exit to Indiana 227 North at Richmond, you will come to another quarry near Middleboro that exposes this same unconformity.

### The Crawfordsville Moraine

A rise in elevation in the Cambridge City area marks the crest of the Crawfordsville end moraine, a deposit of glacial till laid down at the margin of the last great ice sheet. Some glacial geologists include it on their maps; others do not.

*Generalized surface and bedrock profiles along I-70 and U.S. 40.*

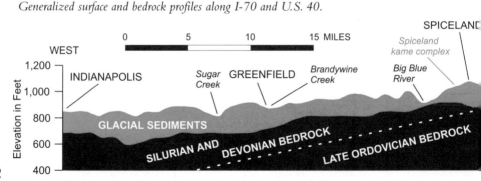

## Spiceland Kame Complex and Its Mineral Springs

Regular drivers on I-70 know the sandy hills of the Spiceland kame field just west of the New Castle exit simply because they provide some relief from the flat monotony of the till plain. These hills are one of the largest kame fields in the state. The Big Blue River flows in a former meltwater valley on the west side of the Spiceland kame field.

Kames are mounds of glacial outwash sands and gravels originally deposited as alluvial fans along the edge of the ice, in depressions on its surface, or in cracks in the ice. When the ice melted, the deposits of sediment settled gently onto the ground beneath to become low hills. Outwash sands and gravels from this valley were used as early as 1853 to pave the old mud and corduroy roads around Knightstown, including the old National Road, America's first interstate highway completed between Maryland and Illinois in 1832.

Settlers believed in the medicinal properties of three springs on the property that became the Spiceland Sanitarium Company in 1893. Patrons drank the water and took mud baths. A company formed to rebuild the sanitarium after it burned in 1913, but three small spring houses were the only structures built. Meanwhile, the water was bottled as Bezor Spa Spring Water. One spring still flows.

## Mastodons in Hancock County

In 1977, geologists excavated mastodon bones and remains of giant beaver, caribou (first Indiana record), deer, raccoon, muskrat, mink, turkey, ducks, turtles, and frogs from a pond site 6 miles northwest of Greenfield, in Hancock County. The Children's Museum in Indianapolis displays the mastodon remains.

The site was a kettle lake that filled in with vegetation and became a bog from about 14,500 to 12,000 years ago. The oldest vegetation was a spruce forest with some fir and birch trees, like Canada's Hudson Bay area today; modern trees came later. Most plant and animals dug up here cannot be found today anywhere across North America. The region's ecology shifted after the ice melted.

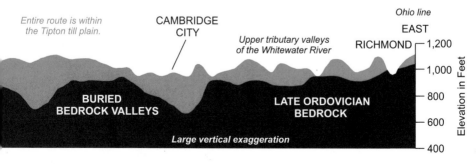

Entire route is within the Tipton till plain.

CAMBRIDGE CITY

Upper tributary valleys of the Whitewater River

Ohio line

EAST RICHMOND

Elevation in Feet

— 1,200
— 1,000
— 800
— 600
— 400

BURIED BEDROCK VALLEYS

LATE ORDOVICIAN BEDROCK

*Large vertical exaggeration*

43

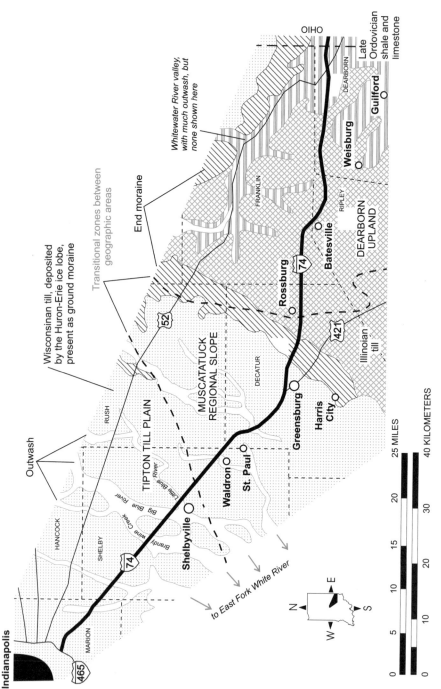

Geology along I-74 between the Ohio line and Indianapolis.

# Interstate 74
## Ohio Line—Indianapolis
### 79 MILES

Near the Ohio line, I-74 crosses old and thin glacial deposits that cover ancient bedrock hills. Farther west, the glacial deposits become younger and thicker until they completely bury the old bedrock landscape. The route crosses the Whitewater River basin near the Ohio border, the collective basins of several small streams across northern Dearborn and Ripley Counties that flow to the Ohio River, and the East Fork White River basin between Greensburg and Indianapolis.

Interstate 74 crosses 33 miles of the Dearborn upland between the Ohio line and the area just east of Greensburg. It is a hilly landscape eroded in fossiliferous bedrock formations that were deposited during Ordovician time. Thin deposits of glacial till cover many of the hilltops, along with some windblown silt.

The till is part of the Jessup formation, which was deposited during the Illinoian ice age. Most of the original deposit is now lost to erosion, but remnants still cover the upland surfaces west of the interchange with Indiana 1. The landscape east of Indiana 1 is almost entirely bedrock, except for some glacial outwash in the floor of the Whitewater River valley. Thin deposits of silt were blown from the wide outwash plains of the major river valleys to the west, from even as far as the Wabash River valley. The plant cover effectively hides both the glacial till and the windblown silt. The thickness of the glacial deposits in this area is generally much less than 50 feet, although one completely buried valley east of Greensburg contains more than 100 feet of glacial sediments.

Interstate 74 traces a nearly straight path across 46 miles of ground moraine left by the Huron-Erie ice lobe between the area east of Greensburg and I-465 near Indianapolis. This part of the route crosses the southern edge of the Tipton till plain. The glacial cover is about 50 feet thick between Greensburg and Shelbyville but thickens to more than 250 feet near Indianapolis.

A few shallow stream valleys that once carried torrents of meltwater interrupt the monotony of the ground moraine. They are now full of glacial outwash, a source of sand, gravel, and huge volumes of groundwater. The largest valleys are those of the Little Blue River, Big Blue River, and Brandywine Creek, all near Shelbyville.

### Buckets of Fossils

Fossils abound in most outcrops of Ordovician rocks in southeastern Indiana but are best known from several remarkable sites. One of these is a series of railroad cuts between Guilford and Weisburg, along Tanners Creek.

Paleontologic studies commenced here when the railroad was built in the early 1900s. The sites, now overgrown and slumped, still yield specimens of brachiopods, bryozoans, corals, and mollusks from the Dillsboro formation.

### Ordovician-Silurian Boundary

Boundaries between rocks of different ages are important because they help unravel the events that created the many rock layers. A quarry just west of Rossburg, off I-74, exposes the boundary between the Ordovician Whitewater formation and the Silurian Brassfield limestone. The contact is easy to see because the Ordovician rocks are gray and the Silurian rocks on top of them are a yellowish to reddish brown. Close examination reveals that the Whitewater formation was eroded before the Brassfield limestone was deposited.

The Rossburg quarry contains a second unconformity that separates the Brassfield limestone from the overlying Salamonie dolomite. This unconformity is harder to distinguish because the rocks above and below the contact are essentially the same color. The Rossburg quarry is known for its specimens of barite (barium sulfate), calcite, and pyrite. Barite generally occurs as white crystals that look waxy and are denser than calcite. Pyrite generally crystallizes into cubes with a brassy metallic luster.

### Decatur County Dimension Stone

Tan beds of the Laurel limestone member of the Salamonie dolomite crop out along Clifty, Muddy Fork, and Sand Creeks and along the Flatrock River of Decatur County. Settlers of the early 1800s discovered that chunks and slabs of Laurel limestone were durable and made good foundation stone for buildings, fence posts, curbing, and flagstone. Quarrying it soon became a major industry. The layers come in varying thickness, so quarry workers could usually find stone of the needed thickness somewhere in the quarry walls, pry it out, and have it ready for shipment with little or no trimming. Its pale color made it a desirable facing stone.

When the Lawrenceburg and Indianapolis Railroad was laid through the county in the 1850s, its surveyors noted that the limestones around

*Generalized surface and bedrock profiles along I-74.*

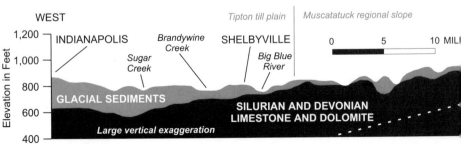

*Silurian Salamonie dolomite in Rossburg quarry near New Point.*

Greensburg were hard and massive. Quarrying began near Rossburg to provide heavy stone for bridge piers and abutments. The stone was also in demand for curbing, facing, sidewalks, steps, and porches. Inferior stone was crushed for railroad ballast.

Abandoned quarries exist in Sand Creek valley, between Letts and Westport. Farther south, Indiana 3 passes the old Westport quarries, east and south of Westport along Sand Creek. Although as much as 15 feet of limestone were exposed here, the quarries were unable to compete and were abandoned by the early 1900s.

A large quarry operates in Harris City, east of Horace. In the 1870s, more than three hundred people lived here in houses built by the Greensburg Limestone Company. Large derricks surrounded the quarry to hoist slabs and blocks onto railroad cars. The operation shipped stone throughout In-

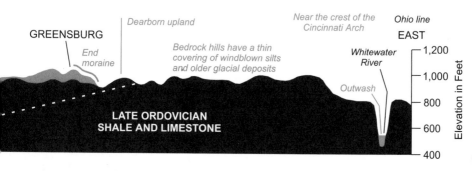

*Dimension stone quarrying, circa 1907, of Silurian Salamonie dolomite, near Westport.* —Mark J. Camp Collection

diana and the surrounding states. The quarry now produces crushed stone for the construction industry.

### St. Paul–Hartsville Boulder Belt

A trail of boulders, some several feet in diameter, extends from St. Paul 15 miles southwest to the vicinity of Hartsville in a belt 2 to 3 miles wide. Some of the boulders are red gneiss, which must have come from Canada. The belt is probably a remnant of an eroded moraine.

### Waldron Shale

A professor from Cincinnati discovered the fossiliferous Waldron shale in 1860 along the west bank of Conn's Creek, across from the Avery Quarry, a little more than 1 mile south of Waldron. James Hall, state geologist of New York, examined the fossils that same year. His reporting aroused wide interest. The original site is now buried, but others nearby still yield abundant fossils. Exposures of thick limestone with interbeds of calcareous shale yield more than 160 species of crinoids, brachiopods, corals, snails, trilobites, and other marine creatures, all remarkably preserved.

Numerous quarries in the St. Paul and Waldron area produced limestone above and below the Waldron shale starting in the 1850s. Two quarries at St. Paul produced dimension stone for foundations, piers, and building construction, including many jails in Indiana and Ohio. Other products included flags and curb stones for sidewalk construction as well as lime. Sains Creek was at one time dotted with small quarries, as was Clifty Creek in the Hartsville area.

## Shelbyville—Mineral and Thermal Wells

A well drilled in 1870 near the Little Blue River on the east side of Shelbyville encountered groundwater 25 feet below the surface, at a temperature of 76 degrees Fahrenheit. Four miles west of town at the former site of Barlow's Mill, the temperature of the water from an earlier well rose from 52 to 86 degrees within one year. This warm water was of little use, so the wells were abandoned. Shallow wells normally produce water at the mean annual temperature of the area. No one knows why these produced such warm water.

*A fossiliferous slab of Silurian Waldron shale from a quarry near Waldron. Note the trilobite, crinoid stems, and brachiopods.*

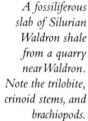

*Silurian Salamonie dolomite overlain by Waldron shale in the Waldron quarry. This quarry is now part of a recreation area.*

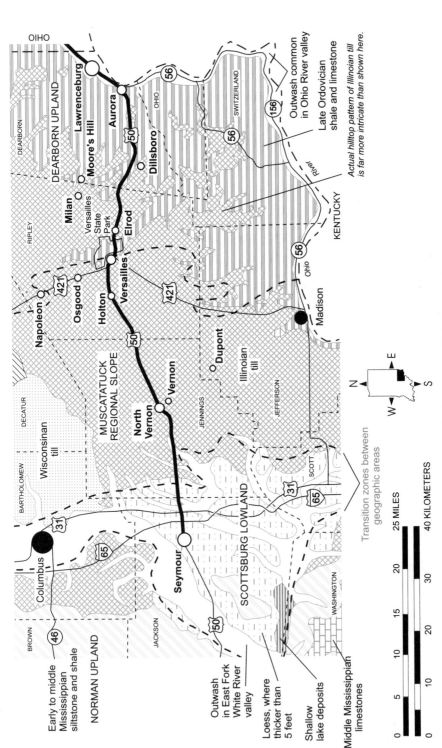

Geology along U.S. 50 between the Ohio line and Seymour.

The Shelbyville Mineral Well was drilled more than 400 feet into Or-dovician formations in 1901. It yielded no oil or gas but did produce flows of water rich in calcium carbonate, lithium chloride, magnesium carbonate, sodium chloride, and sodium sulfate. The water supplied a sanitarium and was sold as Shelbyville Lithia Water. It came from the St. Peter sandstone, which was deposited across much of the Midwest during middle Ordovi-cian time.

# U.S. 50
## Ohio Line—Seymour
### 65 MILES

The eastern end of the route is on floodplains east of the bedrock hills of the Dearborn upland with their caps of old Illinoian till and windblown silts. Farther west, U.S. 50 crosses the Muscatatuck regional slope to the Scottsburg lowland. East of Versailles, the highway crosses small drainage basins that empty directly into the Ohio River; west of Versailles, the road crosses the eastern part of the East Fork White River basin.

Between the Ohio line and Aurora, U.S. 50 crosses 8 miles of floodplain deposits within the Miami and Ohio River valleys. Glacial outwash sands and gravels underlie much of these floodplains to a depth of 100 or more feet.

The highway crosses the bedrock hills of the Dearborn upland in the 20 miles between Aurora and Versailles. The bedrock is late Ordovician shales and limestones with widely scattered thin caps of Illinoian till, the Jessup formation.

A side trip into Versailles State Park provides a closer look at the bedrock in the hillsides of the Laughery Creek valley, the western border of the Dearborn upland. The lookout tower offers a view of the creek valley, the nearby ridgetops, and the sinkholes eroded in the limestone bedrock. The heavy plant cover hides the thin cap of the Jessup till and windblown silts that blanket the ridgetops.

Between Versailles and the line between Jennings and Jackson Counties, the highway crosses 33 miles of the Muscatatuck regional slope with its hilly bedrock terrain capped with till of the Jessup formation and wind-blown silts. The bedrock in this area is Silurian and Devonian limestone and dolomite, overlain by late Devonian to early Mississippian shales. The up-land cover of windblown silt increases in thickness westward, toward its source in the outwash plains from which the winds blew the silts.

The highway crosses 4 miles of the Scottsburg lowland between the boundary of Jackson and Jennings Counties and Seymour. Neither the bedrock nor the elevation differ from those in the Muscatatuck regional slope to the east, but the windblown cover changes to a blanket of sand thicker than any to the east. Its source area is the floodplain of the East Fork White River, only a few miles to the west.

### Aurora, Dillsboro, and Milan

Roadcuts just west of Aurora on U.S. 50 expose some 150 feet of limestones and shales deposited during late Ordovician time. The lower 20 feet contain gray shales of the Kope formation. Broken fossils occur in the thin limestone beds but much less abundantly than in the layers above. The rest of the section, the Dillsboro formation, contains more limestone than shale and also yields abundant and nicely preserved fossils of brachiopods, bryozoans, snails, clams, and assorted tracks and trails.

An exploratory gas well drilled in 1890 near the old railroad depot in Aurora found flowing artesian water. The well became a source of medicinal water, as did nearby Cheek's Spring.

Dillsboro was the site of the Dillsboro Sanitarium, which was organized in 1911 after the Dillsboro Oil and Gas Company struck artesian water instead of oil at a depth of 1,387 feet in 1900. Starting in 1915, mineral water was pumped into a building with fifty-six rooms. Business dwindled in the late 1920s and the facility quietly closed.

The Miwogco Mineral Springs Hotel flourished in Milan on Indiana 101, north of U.S. 50, from 1920 until it burned in 1928. It was established after exploratory drilling by the Milan Indiana Water, Oil, and Gas Company yielded mineral water instead of petroleum.

### Ripley County Karst and Versailles State Park

Indiana has two regions, both mostly south of the limit of Wisconsinan ice, where water has dissolved limestone to create cave and sinkhole landscapes—karst topography. The larger of these areas is in the Mississippian limestone belt of south-central Indiana; the other is in the area of Silurian

*Generalized surface and bedrock profiles along U.S. 50.*

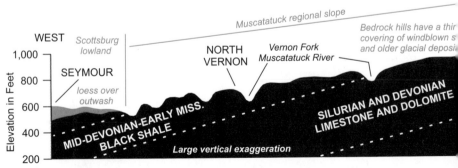

*Ordovician Dillsboro strata along U.S. 50 west of Aurora. Limestone beds jut out from the cliff face; less-resistant shale forms the slope.*

and Devonian limestones from Clark County on the Ohio River north to the southern part of Rush County. One of the better places to see this kind of landscape is in Versailles State Park, just east of Versailles on U.S. 50.

Many small sinkholes pock the hilltops within and outside the park boundaries. Some formed as collapsing caves broke through to the surface. Others may have formed where water dissolved the limestone bedrock more effectively than elsewhere. Watch for them along Trail 1, especially when the trees are bare. A number of deep valleys in the park lack permanent streams because the drainage is underground, through caverns in the limestone bedrock.

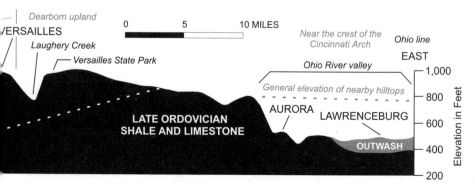

53

### Ordovician and Silurian Bedrock

U.S. 50 crosses meandering Laughery Creek just west of the entrance to Versailles State Park, where the creek cuts into gray Ordovician shales and limestones filled with fossils. A large roadside quarry south of Versailles exposes the Laurel limestone member of the Salamonie dolomite. Similar rocks exist to the north, off U.S. 421, at Osgood and Napoleon.

The Ohio and Mississippi Railroad, later the Baltimore & Ohio Railroad, quarried stone in the early 1850s at Elrod and Moores Hill for bridge abutments. Watch for the abutments along the tracks on the north side of U.S. 50 between Versailles and North Vernon. Abandoned quarries south of Versailles, west of Holton, and at Brewersville on Sand Creek expose the Laurel limestone.

### Devonian Bedrock

A quarry on the north side of North Vernon works the Devonian North Vernon and Jeffersonville limestones beneath the New Albany shale. Concretions in the shale sometimes contain the zinc sulfide mineral sphalerite or pink dolomite crystals. At Hayden, another quarry displays zones of broken rock in the North Vernon and Jeffersonville limestones, probably ancient caves that filled with rubble as their roofs collapsed. The time of their formation is unknown.

*The valley of Vernon Fork Muscatatuck River, carved into Devonian Jeffersonville limestone. Bank to left is undercut due to strong current. Note toppled trees. Muscatatuck County Park, Vernon.*

*The stone viaduct of the Madison & Indianapolis Railroad at Vernon. Blocks of Devonian Jeffersonville limestone were quarried more than 150 years ago.*

### Vernon Area

A short drive south on Indiana 3 from North Vernon leads to nice exposures of Silurian and Devonian rocks around the historic town of Vernon. Muscatatuck County Park was the site of Vinegar Mill, a water power operation that sawed limestone from the nearby quarries into sills, lintels and other building trimmings from the late 1840s through 1875. You can see stone dressed in this mill in many of the old buildings in Vernon. The mill was abandoned when ice destroyed the dam in Vernon Fork. Only the foundation and a few quarries remain. The fossiliferous Jeffersonville limestone is exposed in them and in the nearby streamcuts. A trail leads into the valley of Vernon Fork along undercut rocky cliffs.

A roadcut just south of where Indiana 3 branches from Indiana 7 exposes the New Albany shale and Jeffersonville limestone, which continue into the valley west of the road. Some 53 feet of Jeffersonville limestone are exposed in an abandoned quarry and on the hillside. Below this are the Silurian Louisville limestone and Waldron shale. Four to five feet of highly fossiliferous Waldron shale are exposed in an old tunnel that once served a grist mill, some 300 yards down the hill.

The meandering Vernon Fork carved a channel in the Salamonie dolomite, which is now part of the Crosley Fish and Wildlife Area. Follow county road 25 W west from Indiana 3/7 just south of Vernon to the parking area. Two small caves are along Vernon Fork and Biehle Branch.

The viaduct of the Madison & Indianapolis Railroad in Vernon was made of local limestone in 1837. The railroad line, the first in Indiana, passes through Vernon on an elevated embankment to avoid flooding by Vernon Fork. Vernon is on a narrow ridge within a meander loop of Vernon Fork. This restricted site prevented growth and helps explain why Vernon is the smallest county seat in the state.

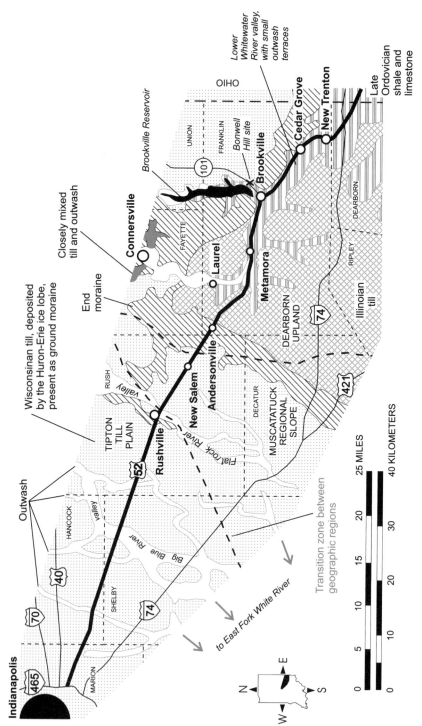

*Geology along U.S. 52 between the Ohio line and Indianapolis.*

A quarry that opened in 1874 at Dupont on Indiana 7 produced North Vernon limestone used in the old Southern Railway bridge on the west side of downtown Cincinnati, some 50 miles to the southeast. Stone for this bridge also came from the Paris Crossing area, and from the old Kerchner Quarry at North Vernon.

# U.S. 52
## Ohio Line—Indianapolis
**78 MILES**

U.S. 52 crosses some of Indiana's oldest and youngest geologic materials, from the hills near the Ohio border eroded in Ordovician bedrock to the nearly flat glacial plains near Indianapolis.

U.S. 52 follows the Whitewater River valley between the Ohio line and the area 2 miles west of Metamora. The valley existed before the great Pleistocene ice age began. Then the great torrents of meltwater that poured out of the melting glaciers as the various ice sheets ended enlarged it and left deposits of outwash sands and gravels.

Since the end of the Wisconsinan ice, the Whitewater River has eroded much of the outwash out of its valley floor, leaving a number of terraces along the valley walls. Trenton, Cedar Grove, and Brookville stand on these terraces and take advantage of an elevation 50 to 80 feet above the floodplain. Some of the terraces also provided clay that was used to make bricks and tile. Four partial skeletons of mastodons—hairy elephants that inhabited Indiana until about 10,000 years ago—were found in the clay deposits.

The hills along the Whitewater Valley are part of the Dearborn upland. Before the Pleistocene ice came along, the hills were eroded from shales and limestones of the Dillsboro formation and the overlying Whitewater formation, both of which were deposited during Ordovician time, perhaps some 500 million years ago. The hilltops are between 450 and 500 feet above the highway near the Ohio line but are only about 250 feet above the highway west of Metamora. This change is due in part to the outwash fill in the upstream portions of the valley.

The hilltops on both sides of the valley between the Ohio line and Cedar Grove carry a thin cap of till, the Jessup formation. The Illinoian ice sheets plastered it onto the surface as ground and end moraines long before the latest, Wisconsinan, ice sheet began. In the hundreds of thousands of years since, erosion has reduced the Jessup till to a thin frosting on the ridge crests. The plant cover makes it hard to see.

*View of Cedar Grove nestled on an outwash terrace in the Whitewater River valley. The valley is also partly filled with outwash. The bluffs in foreground and background are Ordovician bedrock.* —Mark J. Camp Collection

Wisconsinan till, the Trafalgar formation, covers the hills northeast of the valley from the Cedar Grove area north. It records the most southern advance of the Wisconsinan ice sheets in this part of Indiana.

Between the hillside 2 miles west of Metamora and the area just east of Andersonville, U.S. 52 climbs onto an upland surface eroded in Ordovician bedrock and thinly capped with glacial till of the Jessup formation.

Between the east side of Andersonville and I–465 at Indianapolis, U.S. 52 crosses a nearly level to gently rolling plain of Wisconsinan till, the Trafalgar formation. Valleys filled with glacial outwash punctuate it in several places. Geologists have mapped the land surface between Andersonville and the area a few miles west of the town as end moraine. They interpret the rest of this surface near Indianapolis as ground moraine.

*Generalized surface and bedrock profiles along U.S. 52.*

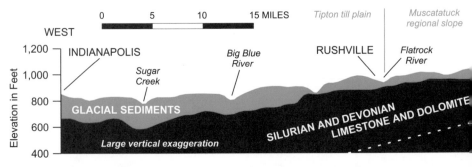

*The Ordovician Whitewater and Dillsboro formations form the walls of this roadcut along Indiana 1 near Cedar Grove.*

Between Andersonville and New Salem, U.S. 52 crosses the drainage divide between streams that flow south into the Whitewater River basin and others that flow southeast into the East Fork White River.

### Ordovician Fossils and Pleistocene Till

A 30-foot cutbank exposes Wisconsinan valley fill along the Whitewater River where Indiana 1 leaves U.S. 52, just north of Cedar Grove. The highway ascends the bluff of the Whitewater Valley and offers some scenic views of the valley and the Dearborn upland. Illinoian till, the Jessup formation, thinly covers the Ordovician bedrock. Ordovician fossils abound in the high, terraced roadcut west of Cedar Grove on Indiana 1, which exposes the Dillsboro and Whitewater formations.

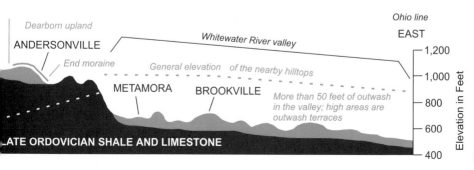

59

## Indiana 101—A Side Trip

Follow Indiana 101 north from Brookville to impressive roadcuts in Ordovician limestones and shales that yield a treasure trove of fossils. Watch for a large outcrop of the Dillsboro formation about 1 mile north of Brookville at the intersection with the road to Brookville Dam, along Bonwell Hill. Blocks of rock in the talus contain typical Dillsboro fossils. Drive across the dam to see the thick section of beds in the lower part of the Dillsboro formation exposed in the spillway.

Just south of the entrance to Mounds State Recreation Area, watch for nearly 90 feet of Ordovician rocks exposed on both sides of Indiana 101. Dillsboro rocks, on the south side of the valley, contain alternating beds of limestone and shale that yield abundant brachiopods, clams, bryozoans, and fragments of a large species of trilobite.

Across the valley to the north, the section continues with more Dillsboro formation and includes more limestone. Prominent fossils include brachiopods and bryozoans. The formation grades upward into the Whitewater formation.

The lower layers of the Whitewater formation contain fewer fossils than the Dillsboro formation. Large coral heads and sponges that jut from the cliff face in the Whitewater formation mark the Saluda member. Look for the cavities lined with lovely crystals of dogtooth calcite.

Sulfurous water flowed from several springs along Brier's (Logan) Creek just north of the line between Franklin and Union Counties. During the 1800s this was a busy health spa known as Bath Sulphur Springs. A small cave eroded in the Ordovician bedrock is near the old site of Quakertown, now on the west bank of Brookville Reservoir.

## Birthplace of the Indiana Academy of Science

The decline of New Harmony in the 1830s caused a corresponding decline in scientific research in Indiana. The Joseph Moore Museum at Earlham College, Hanover Museum, and other colleges only partially filled the gap. In 1881 at Brookville, the Brookville Society of Natural History was organized to collect, record, and preserve elements of the natural environment of Brookville and Franklin County. The society established a museum and sponsored a series of lectures by prominent naturalists and scientists. In 1885 the members established a statewide association of scientists, which continues to this day as the Indiana Academy of Science.

## The Whitewater Canal

Metamora is a good place to see part of the restored section of the Whitewater Canal, first planned and excavated in the 1830s. The restored section runs between Laurel and Brookville, about 14 miles. The original canal was meant to be a watery highway 40 feet wide and 4 feet deep, connecting the rich farmlands of southeastern Indiana with the growing urban markets of the Ohio River valley. Early plans called for a northward extension to Richmond and other connections with the Wabash and Erie Canal across northern Indiana, but these never materialized.

The Whitewater Canal had fifty-six locks for raising and lowering barges. Their doors were wood, but their walls and abutments were made of blocks quarried from nearby hillsides. Seven dams provided water from feeder streams. Ten aqueducts crossed small creeks, one of them at Metamora, and two crossed the Whitewater River. Few of these structures survive outside the Metamora area.

Like all the ambitious Indiana canal projects of its time, the Whitewater Canal never fulfilled its promise. It worked part-time at best. Poor construction and maintenance, floods, water management problems, and the varying values of the crops it was meant to transport all impeded its operation. In 1865 the Indiana legislature authorized a railroad over part of the canal tow path. Some of the northernmost portions were retained for some years to drive water mills and generate electricity.

### Indiana 121—A Side Trip

A side trip north on Indiana 121 brings you to Laurel. Quarries along the tributaries of the West Fork Whitewater River supplied dimension stone for local use until about 1900, when stone from the Bloomington-Bedford belt of south-central Indiana began to dominate the market. The local limestone was used in many of the early buildings, especially in their foundations.

Cave Hollow, Derbyshire, and Rieboldt's Falls tumble across ledges of the resistant Laurel limestone. These falls were sites of early quarries in the Laurel area, including a large one near Derbyshire Falls. The Laurel Steam Stone

*The Silurian Laurel limestone member was used in a number of early buildings in Laurel, along Indiana 121.*

Company operated this quarry around the turn of the century. Lime was another product of the Laurel hillsides, beginning around 1870. Paper mills at Laurel and elsewhere in the Whitewater Valley used it.

Clay was once used to make brick and tile in the West Fork Whitewater River valley at Connersville. Large amounts of Silurian limestone were also quarried along Big Williams Creek for the locks along the Whitewater Canal.

### Ice Block Lakes

A number of small depressions that contain marl and peat exist on either side of the Flatrock River north and east of Rushville. The Flatrock River follows the channel that carried glacial meltwater along the edge of the moraine as the last ice age was ending. The stranded ice blocks finally melted, leaving low spots in the till and outwash that filled with water to become ponds. Vegetation and sediment encroached on the open water, gradually reducing the ponds to marshes and finally to meadows. These sediments contain snail shells and other remnants of the old ponds now filled with peat and marl.

An end moraine near Rushville records an advance of the Wisconsinan ice sheet some 20,000 years ago. The glacier had reached its farthest south a thousand years earlier, then melted back, only to advance again. This end moraine is patchy and hard to recognize in this region between ice lobes.

# U.S. 421
## Indianapolis—Madison
**91 MILES**

U.S. 421 angles across the Wisconsinan till plain and the hills capped with Illinoian till in southeastern Indiana on its way to the bedrock hills along the Ohio River. Between Indianapolis and the area south of Versailles, the highway crosses and then follows the edge of the drainage basin of the East Fork White River. Between Greensburg and Versailles, and farther south, the route crosses minor streams that flow to the Ohio River.

Between I-465 near Indianapolis and the area just east of Greensburg, U.S. 421 crosses 44 miles of Wisconsinan ground moraine. The glacial cover is more than 250 feet thick near Indianapolis but thins to slightly more than 50 feet near Greensburg. Brandywine Creek, Big Blue River, and the Little Blue River near Shelbyville flow through subtle, shallow valleys with 10 to 40 feet of outwash that supply groundwater, sand, and gravel. Just southeast of Greensburg, U.S. 421 crosses 3 miles of end moraine.

Between the area 3 miles southeast of Greensburg and that just north of Madison, U.S. 421 angles across 44 miles of gently rolling uplands and hilly

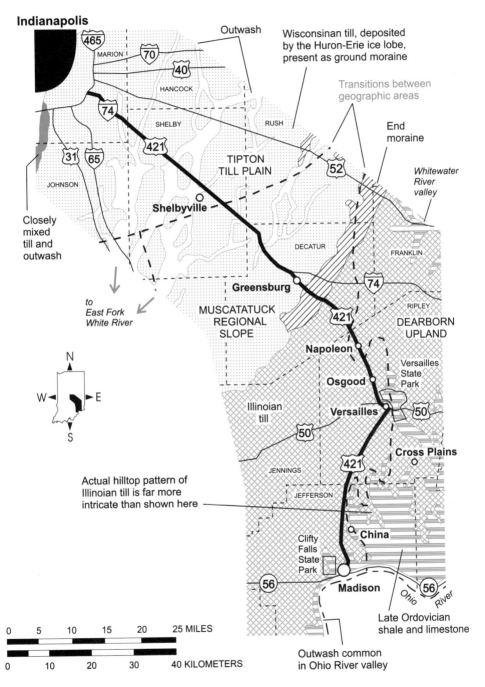

*Geology along U.S. 421 between Indianapolis and Madison.*

terrain, a bedrock landscape with less than 50 feet of Illinoian till on the hilltops. The bedrock formations are limestones deposited during Silurian time, lying on older shales and limestones deposited during Ordovician time. More than 100,000 years of erosion have shaped the rolling landscape since the Illinoian ice sheets melted. Windblown silts cap this area and are some of the easternmost in the state.

Immediately north of Madison, U.S. 421 descends from the upland surface to the floodplain of the Ohio River through a roadcut that continues for 3 miles. It provides wonderful exposures of approximately 300 feet of the sedimentary formations that lie beneath southeastern Indiana. At the top of the sequence you see the Silurian Salamonie dolomite and Brassfield limestone overlying the Ordovician Saluda member of the Whitewater formation. Look closely below a massive ledge in the Saluda member for a layer of large fossil sponge and coral heads, the remains of one of the ancient shallow reefs. The Dillsboro formation is the lowest, and oldest, bedrock unit exposed in this roadcut.

## Decatur and Ripley Counties

The Silurian Laurel limestone is exposed in a quarry on the east edge of Napoleon. You can watch the quarry operations from an adjacent road. Follow the road west from the center of town to near Millhousen for a view of Pompey's Pillar. This erosional remnant of the Laurel limestone stands high above Honey Creek near its juncture with the Muscatatuck River.

The glacial till at Napoleon provided raw material for a small tile and brick plant that operated a few miles east of town, along Indiana 229. Glacial clays were dug and fired in a single beehive kiln. This operation was typical of many such small plants that served a local area. They went out of business when all the fields were tiled, streets were paved, and buildings were completed.

The Salamonie dolomite was worked by hand for curbing and architectural stone just south of Osgood as early as the 1870s. After other building stones eclipsed the Salamonie dolomite, the quarries produced crushed stone

*Generalized surface and bedrock profiles along U.S. 421.*

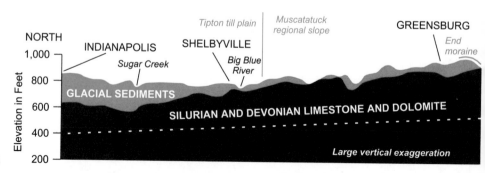

**64**

*The upper part of this quarry at Napoleon exposes the Silurian Laurel limestone member. Deeper parts of the quarry show the Osgood member and Brassfield limestone.*

and agricultural lime. One of these pits now serves the waterworks on the southwest edge of town, off Tanglewood Road.

Quarrying also began in the Versailles area in the 1870s. The Salamonie dolomite is quarried along the east side of the road 2 miles south of town. You can see it from U.S. 421. An abandoned quarry in the Silurian Brassfield limestone is south of Cross Plains on Indiana 129.

### Stone Architecture

Stone houses of early-nineteenth-century vintage dot the countryside of Jefferson County, especially around China, along Indiana 62, and at Hanover. Many of the early settlers came from Scotland and Ireland, where stone

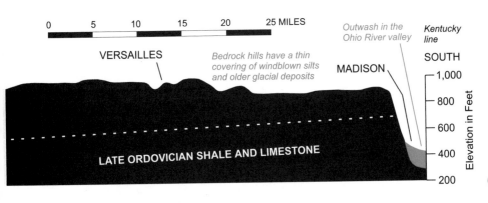

homes were standard because wood was scarce. In southern Indiana they built with gray limestone. The early railroad that connected Madison with Indianapolis used outcrops of Silurian rocks in North Madison, particularly those along Big and Middlefork Creeks, for bridgework. In the late 1800s, Ordovician rocks quarried around Madison were shipped by river steamer to various towns along the Ohio River.

*A house made of slabs of Salamonie dolomite of Silurian age along Indiana 62 in China.*

# Indiana 56 and Indiana 156
## Lawrenceburg—Scottsburg
### 89 MILES

The southeastern part of Indiana 56, with Indiana 156, follows a scenic route in the Ohio valley. The highways parallel the Ohio River along its floodplain for about 60 miles, generally following close to the base of the valley walls eroded in Ordovician shale and limestone. Erosion over a very long time has deeply cut the side valleys, doubtless with the help of glacial meltwaters. Small waterfalls tumble over resistant ledges in the tributary valleys.

Glacial outwash sands and gravels underlie the Ohio River floodplain, to a depth of more than 100 feet in places. Watch for the many sand and gravel pits, especially the large one near Patriot. This river route is remarkably flat, declining from about 470 feet near Lawrenceburg to about 460 feet at Madison. The elevation of the riverside hilltops, the Dearborn upland, is about 800 to 850 feet.

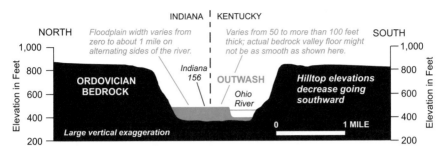

*Generalized surface and bedrock profiles across Indiana 156 near Florence.*

Hillsides facing the Ohio River near Madison expose Ordovician to Silurian rock—along old U.S. 421 in its sloping hillside route just north of downtown Madison, along Indiana 56 west of town, and as fascinating cliffs and overhangs along Indiana 7, where it curls between the upland and the river valley west of Madison.

Indiana 56 crosses 20 miles of bedrock uplands capped with till of the Illinoian Jessup formation and windblown silts between a hillside about 3

*Geology along Indiana 56 and Indiana 156 between Lawrenceburg and Scottsburg.*

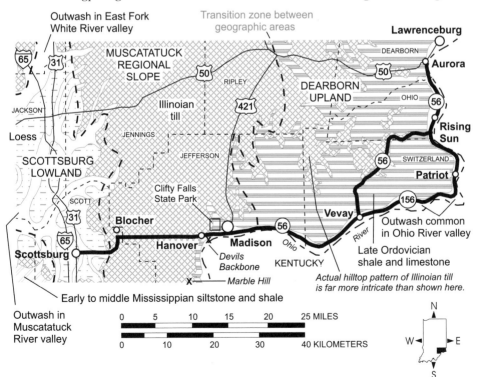

miles west of Madison and Scottsburg. The bedrock is Silurian to Devonian limestone and dolomite overlain by upper Devonian and lower Mississippian shale. The plant cover effectively obscures the break between the bedrock surfaces and the hilltop tills and silts. Glacial outwash sands and gravels underlie the flat stream valley east of Scottsburg.

### Ohio River Sediments

The modern floodplain deposits of the Ohio River valley contain sediments that vary from clay to gravel. In the early 1900s, many tile, brick, and pottery manufacturers operated plants in the valley. Most of the kilns were at the clay pits to eliminate transportation costs.

Bricks were made of clays dug from the bottomlands. The clay was mixed with sand, molded, then baked in a kiln. Aurora, Jeffersonville, Lawrenceburg, Madison, Rising Sun, and Vevay had brick factories.

An alluvial blue clay was used at Port Fulton to make stoneware before 1900. In the early to middle 1800s, red pottery ware came from Vevay and yellow ware from Rising Sun. Drain tile factories were also a common industry, but most lasted only until the wetlands were drained. Then, as now, it was possible to work yourself out of a market for your goods.

Huge sand and gravel pits that gape on both sides of Indiana 156 between Patriot and Rising Sun give a good view of what lies beneath the valley floor. They show intricately sandwiched layers of clay, sand, and gravel, the record of a continually changing channel. Sand and gravel are big business in Indiana, as they are anywhere with a busy industrial economy. The tremendous volumes mined here are used mainly for construction aggregate.

### Clifty Falls State Park

The old river town of Madison adds historic charm to the scenic beauty of the Ohio River valley. Clifty Falls State Park is just west of Madison on

*Generalized surface and bedrock profiles along Indiana 56 and 156.*

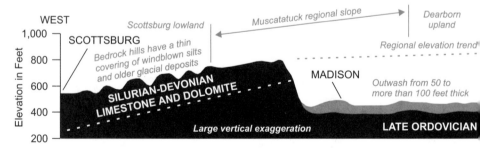

the Ohio River bluff, where Big Clifty Creek and its tributaries cut narrow gorges complete with four waterfalls before emptying into the Ohio River.

Ordovician and Silurian strata form outcrops along Big Clifty Creek. The Silurian limestones cap the bluff, while the older Ordovician units are in the walls of the gorge. If you start at the south end of the gorge, you first encounter gray shales and limestones of the Dillsboro formation. It accumulated for millions of years in a series of layers about 270 feet thick.

The Saluda member of the Whitewater formation overlies the Dillsboro rocks. It so strongly resists erosion that it forms the overhanging lip of the four waterfalls. Younger Silurian rocks, eroded from this area when it was above sea level during early Silurian time, appear just to the east along the U.S. 421 roadcut, north of Madison. The Brassfield limestone occurs only in the southern part of the park. It is not present at Clifty Falls, where the Salamonie dolomite rests directly on the Saluda member. Try to spot the buried erosion surface between them in the rock cliff below the falls.

Any rocks laid down in the Madison area after Silurian time are long since lost to erosion. A thin glacial deposit of Illinoian age, representing the next to last stage in the development of Big Clifty Creek gorge, is above the Salamonie dolomite.

The glaciers scraped the bedrock as they spread a short distance into northern Kentucky. The new Ohio River channel more or less followed the ice front. As the ice sheet melted back to the north, tremendous torrents of meltwater washed through the new channel, widening and deepening it. At the same time, smaller stream valleys developed as meltwater flowed to the Ohio valley through tributary channels. The valley of Big Clifty Creek contained such a stream. As the Ohio River rapidly deepened its valley, this little stream also eroded its valley, cascading over the Silurian rocks. The rushing waters eroded the soft shales of Ordovician age, undercutting the more resistant Silurian rocks, which toppled in great blocks into the channel. Big Clifty Creek cut upstream until today the waterfalls are some 2 miles from the Ohio River.

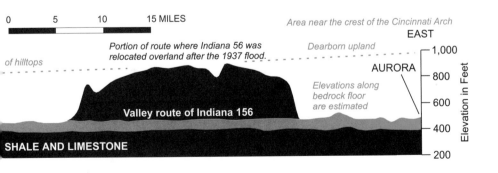

*Big Clifty Creek cascades over a jutting ledge of Ordovician Saluda member at Clifty Falls in Clifty Falls State Park, Madison.*

### Devils Backbone

An observation tower just west of Clifty Inn along Trail 1 in Clifty Falls State Park offers a panoramic view to the south across the valley of the Ohio River. To the southeast is a long bedrock ridge, Devils Backbone, which rises 200 feet from the river bed. The Ohio River flowed around its northern side until a change in the river's course long ago left the ridge standing between the old and present valleys. Indiana 56 follows this short abandoned valley west out of Madison. More Ordovician rocks with abundant fossils lie where the highway ascends the bluff toward Hanover.

### Marble Hill

The old quarries south of Hanover led people of the middle 1800s to call the area Marble Hill. Although the Ordovician limestone took a nice polish and Silurian Laurel limestone sold as dimension stone, rocks from this area were poor quality because they weathered rapidly. A number of the original buildings at Hanover College were built of Laurel limestone. The Marble Hill quarries closed by the late 1850s; this area is now on the grounds of the abandoned Marble Hill Nuclear Power Station.

*Cliffs of Devonian North Vernon and Jeffersonville limestones in a quarry along Indiana 3, south of Blocher.*

### Devonian Fossils and Rocks

An abandoned quarry west of Hanover, visible south of Indiana 56, exposes the New Albany shale and underlying North Vernon limestone. In the late 1800s fossiliferous Devonian rocks along nearby Big Spring Creek yielded well-preserved cystoids (primitive echinoderms related to crinoids) and parts of bony armored fish.

A quarry at the intersection of Indiana 56 and Indiana 203 south of Blocher exposes a section of Devonian rocks that extends from the Geneva dolomite member of the Jeffersonville limestone up through the North Vernon limestone to the cap of New Albany shale. Quarries farther south, in the Jeffersonville area, do not contain the Geneva dolomite, which occurs only along the trend of an ancient reef. Nice specimens of sphalerite, a zinc sulfide mineral, occur in this quarry.

### Salt Works at Lexington

A salt works operated in the early 1800s about 1 mile east of Lexington, on Indiana 356. Brine originally came from a seep and was boiled in large kettles to make salt. A deep well drilled in 1815 produced brine that was sold across southeastern Indiana.

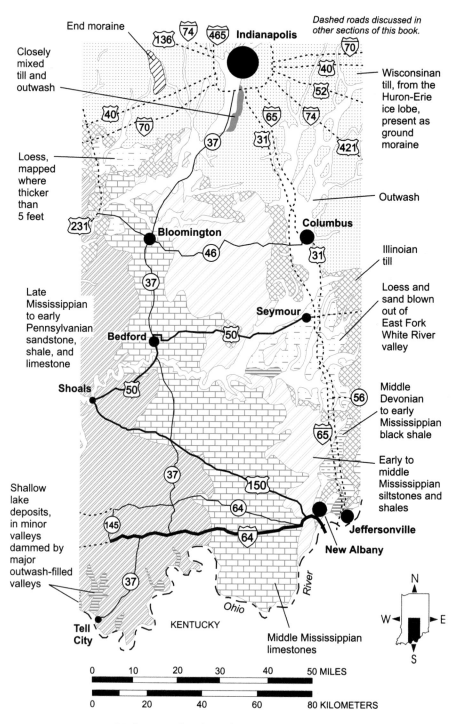

*Highways and geology of south-central Indiana.*

# South-Central Indiana
## BUILDING STONES AND CRINOIDS

### THE MISSISSIPPIAN WORLD

Shallow seas flooded all of Indiana during Mississippian time, 345 to 325 million years ago. Mississippian rocks are conspicuous through the unglaciated part of the state southwest of the East Fork White River valley. They are missing farther east on the flank of the Cincinnati Arch, where erosion stripped them off the older Paleozoic formations. Farther west, these rocks disappear beneath younger Pennsylvanian formations on the eastern flank of the Illinois Basin. Glacial deposits cover the Mississippian rocks in the north.

*New Albany Shale.* Devonian time ended and Mississippian time began with the continued deposition in shallow seawater of the New Albany shale, dark with organic matter. The upper 2 to 6 feet contain Mississippian fossils, mostly conodonts, which look like jaws or teeth no larger than the head of

*Mississippian seascape. Crinoids, blastoids, bryozoans, and brachiopods were major inhabitants of Mississippian seas and are now common fossils in many Mississippian rocks.*

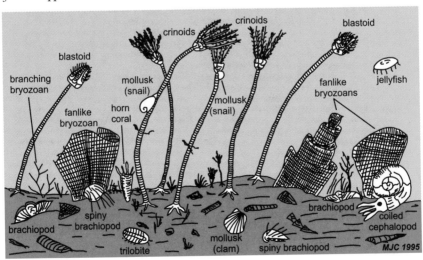

73

a pin. The thickness of the New Albany shale ranges from more than 300 feet near the edge of the Illinois Basin in southwestern Indiana to 85 feet in the Scottsburg lowland, north of New Albany. You can see outcrops of the shale only along the boundary between the Scottsburg lowland and Norman upland.

*Rockford Limestone.* The Rockford limestone, a bed of gray limestone between 2 and 4 feet thick, lies on the New Albany shale in the Norman upland as far north as Rockford in Jackson County.

Although most parts of the Rockford limestone contain few fossils, one exposure in the East Fork White River at Rockford contains an exceptional fauna of fossil cephalopods, some eighteen species of shelled animals closely related to modern squids. This limestone records the return of normal environmental conditions in the shallow sea that then flooded Indiana. After the Rockford limestone accumulated, part of the Mississippian seabed rose briefly above sea level and underwent erosion before the Borden group accumulated.

*Borden Group.* The Borden group is a sequence of shales, siltstones, and sandstones that ranges from 485 to 800 feet thick. It is the submarine part of a large delta that spread across Indiana and surrounding states during early Mississippian time. Rivers and streams flowing southwest from the rising Appalachian Mountains spread sediments that survive from Benton County on the Illinois border to Harrison County on the Ohio River.

*Mississippian Borden group strata along U.S. 50 where it ascends the Norman upland west of Seymour.*

*Ramp Creek formation with numerous geodes near Bloomington along Indiana 37.*

Its lowest formation is the New Providence shale, which erodes easily and is present at the surface in only a few places along the boundary of the Scottsburg lowland and Norman upland. The Spickert Knob formation accumulated on top of the New Providence shale. It was deposited in a continually shifting complex of delta lobes, which include sediments laid down in the open sea, in swamps, on floodplains, and in river channels. It contains a good many fossils, including crinoid stems, and ironstone nodules. It also contains geodes.

The Edwardsville formation is at the top of the Borden group. It consists of 40 to 200 feet of sediments deposited on top of the delta, mostly siltstone, shale, and sandstone, along with small amounts of limestone. Geodes abound in its lower part. The Edwardsville formation is well known for its remarkably preserved crinoids, especially from around Crawfordsville.

**Sanders Group.** The next youngest series of formations belong to the Sanders group. The Ramp Creek formation was the first to accumulate above the Edwardsville formation of the Borden delta. It consists of 20 to 25 feet of evenly bedded limestones and dolomites, full of geodes.

The Harrodsburg limestone, above the Ramp Creek formation, was laid down in a shallow sea after Mississippian seawater covered the Borden delta. It averages about 70 feet thick and contains fossils of crinoids, bryozoans, and brachiopods. This formation is at the base of a thick sequence of Mississippian limestones that makes south-central Indiana world-famous among fanciers of building stones.

The Salem limestone is the youngest formation of the Sanders group. It ranges from 60 to 100 feet thick in south-central Indiana. It consists mostly of tiny fossils and fragments of fossils cemented into solid rock. The Mississippian sea had numerous shoals where waves washed and sorted broken pieces of shells, bryozoans, crinoid stems, and other small fossils. Finer sediments filled troughs on the seafloor. The homogeneous nature of this bedrock made it an excellent stone for buildings and carvings.

***Blue River Group.*** Overlying the Salem limestone are formations of the Blue River group, also laid down in a shallow sea. The oldest is the St. Louis limestone, which consists of much finer sediment than the Salem limestone. Its lower part contains gypsum that probably accumulated in quiet and uncommonly salty water. The St. Louis limestone ranges in thickness from 70 feet in Putnam County to 300 feet in southern Crawford County

The Ste. Genevieve limestone, from 45 to 220 feet thick, is above the St. Louis limestone, but the boundary between them is hard to find. A bed of chert as much as 6 feet thick in the lower part of this formation may help distinguish it. The Ste. Genevieve limestone contains some oolites, spherical carbonate grains about the size of bird shot. Oolites normally form where waves agitate shallow water, in places such as the Bahama Islands.

The Paoli limestone, the uppermost formation of the Blue River group, also contains some oolitic beds. It contains more shale than the rocks beneath, and grades upward into the shales of the overlying West Baden group. The Paoli limestone varies in thickness from 20 to 35 feet.

***West Baden Group.*** The West Baden group thickens from 100 feet in Putnam County to 140 feet at the Ohio River. It consists of five formations that contain shale, sandstone, and limestone. The rivers of late Mississippian time continued to bring sediments from the Appalachian Mountains to the in-

*A railroad cut in the Mississippian Ste. Genevieve limestone near Milltown.*

land sea, where they deposited another delta on the limestones of middle Mississippian time. As with the earlier Borden delta, sandstones were deposited in stream channels or nearshore areas, shales on floodplains and in quiet basins, and limestones in open water, offshore.

The Bethel formation, a mix of gray sandstone, shale, and coal seams as much as 42 feet thick, is the oldest of the West Baden group and includes the oldest coal seams in the state.

The Beaver Bend limestone, where present, is generally 10 to 14 feet thick and locally contains masses of blastoids, crinoids, bryozoans, and brachiopods that resemble modern patch reefs. After it accumulated, sea level dropped and parts of the Beaver Bend sediments eroded.

The Sample sandstone buried reefs as it accumulated. It consists of 15 to 50 feet of brightly colored shale and sandstone. Where the Beaver Bend limestone is missing, the Sample sandstone lies directly on the Bethel formation, making a single thick layer of sandstone.

The Reelsville limestone locally caps the Sample sandstone. It is 2 to 7 feet thick and loaded with fossils of brachiopods, corals, bryozoans, blastoids, and crinoids. It is missing in many places, no doubt because limestones are rarely deposited on the top of a delta.

The top of the West Baden group is the Elwren formation, a sequence of shale, siltstone, and sandstone between 20 and 60 feet thick. This formation correlates with the Cypress sandstone in the Illinois basin, where it is a prolific oil producer.

The West Baden group contains a belt from 2 to 8 miles wide in which a branching network of sandstone, siltstone, and shale deposits extends 20 miles south from Owen and Greene Counties into Kentucky. It is on the crest of the delta, where only coarse sediments settled out of the water. The sandstone formations within it are thicker than usual and limestone and dolomite are entirely absent. It includes more than 200 vertical feet of rock in which the sandstone formations are nearly impossible to distinguish.

***Stephensport Group.*** Marine sedimentation continued with deposition of formations of the Stephensport group. Sandstone was deposited in deltas, nearshore bars, and tidal channels. Shale was laid down in lagoons, and limestone accumulated offshore.

The gray Beech Creek limestone, 8 to 33 feet thick, is the lowest formation of the Stephensport group. It contains fossils of brachiopods, blastoids, and crinoid stems, some as much as 1 inch in diameter.

The Beech Creek limestone grades upward into 30 to 70 feet of Big Clifty sandstone. The lower part of the Big Clifty sandstone is a black shale overlain by a tan sandstone. Siltstone in various colors lies on the sandstone, and gray fossiliferous shale and limestone, called the Indiana Springs shale, cap this formation. Small animals that lived on the sandy seafloor left numerous tracks on bedding surfaces, what geologists call trace fossils. The Big

Clifty sandstone probably accumulated on a delta along the eastern margin of the shallow inland sea.

The Haney limestone is above the Big Clifty sandstone and is 20 to 40 feet thick. It contains abundant blastoids, crinoids, and bryozoans. Paleontologists interpret them as evidence that the Haney limestone was deposited after a rise in sea level flooded the delta on which the Big Clifty sandstone was deposited. Sea level again fell as the Hardinsburg formation was deposited on the Haney limestone. The Hardinsburg formation is about 20 to 60 feet of interbedded gray shale and sandstone.

The gray Glen Dean limestone is 10 to 30 feet thick and contains blastoids, brachiopods, and bryozoans. It is the top formation of the Stephensport group.

*Buffalo Wallow Group.* Alternating rise and fall of sea level continued during latest Mississippian time, when the formations of the Buffalo Wallow group accumulated. The thickness of the Buffalo Wallow group varies from zero to more than 300 feet. It seems that a landscape was eroded on the older rocks; then the rocks of the Buffalo Wallow group filled the valleys and finally covered it all. At a few places in west-central Indiana, the entire Mississippian sequence was eroded, and the Pennsylvanian rocks rest directly on the New Albany shale.

The Tar Springs formation is the oldest and lowest formation in the Buffalo Wallow group. It consists mostly of shale with a few thin beds of limestone and commonly reaches thicknesses of 65 feet. At places, a prominent cliff of sandstone makes up most of the formation; all that sand suggests that a shoreline was somewhere near. The lowest part of the Tar Springs formation contains quite an abundance of nicely preserved fossils, including blastoids and crinoids.

Above the Tar Springs formation, the Branchville formation, 85 to 105 feet thick, consists of thin beds of shale, siltstone, and sandstone. In most places, it is hard to tell where the Tar Springs formation ends and the Branchville formation begins; they form a single rock unit. In some areas of Perry and Crawford Counties, a prominent bed of limestone called the Vienna limestone is at the base of the Branchville formation, neatly marking the boundary.

The Tobinsport formation lies on the Branchville formation and looks just like it. The two form a single rock unit, except in a belt from southwestern Orange County southward to the Ohio River, where the Leopold limestone is at the top of the Branchville formation. The Tobinsport formation is the top of the Buffalo Wallow group.

## PENNSYLVANIAN RACCOON CREEK GROUP

Sea level rose and fell across western Indiana during Pennsylvanian time, leaving repetitions of different sedimentary rocks. The rocks of the Raccoon Creek group, the oldest Pennsylvanian rocks in Indiana, record rapidly changing environments of sediment deposition, from shallow sea to shore-line swamp, to river channel, to floodplain, and back again.

The typical sequence begins with sandstone, shale, and siltstone deposited in streambeds and on floodplains, when the shore of the inland sea lay somewhere to the west. Then, as sea level rose, the shallow coastal waters accumulated sediments full of marine fossils that buried previous deposits of plant material laid down in coastal swamps. The weight of the rocks compacted the organic materials into thin coal seams that are not economically important. Some time later, sea level fell and the shoreline migrated westward once again, and the deposition of sandstone, shale, and siltstone began anew. Geologists call these repetitions cyclothems.

## PLEISTOCENE TIME IN SOUTH-CENTRAL INDIANA

The bedrock uplands of south-central Indiana contain no till. They were beyond the reach of both the Illinoian and Wisconsinan glaciers.

The Illinoian ice advanced down the Wabash Valley on the west side of Indiana and across the Ohio River valley in southeastern Indiana. This ice overlapped the eastern and western sides of the bedrock highlands. Most of the Illinoian till has eroded in the 100,000 or so years since it accumulated, leaving only a thin cover of till that tops so many of the hills. Dense plant cover generally hides the Illinoian till.

Although it did not reach as far south, the Wisconsinan ice also left souvenirs. Outwash sands and gravels were sluiced into the stream valleys in the bedrock uplands. The enormous volumes of the torrents of meltwater helped erode some of the bedrock valleys.

The windblown silt that caps nearly all the landscape becomes locally thicker along the western edge of south-central Indiana. The wind probably blew the silt off the glacial outwash plain in the Wabash Valley. This silt cap makes fertile soil.

## MT. CARMEL FAULT

Early geologists observed that the Sanders group occurs at a much lower elevation in a stretch from Monroe to Lawrence Counties than elsewhere in south-central Indiana. In 1903 geologists recognized that this is due to movement along the Mt. Carmel fault, named from an exposure near Mt. Carmel Church in northwestern Washington County. There the Spickert Knob formation of the Borden group on the east butts against the Harrodsburg and Salem limestones of the Sanders group on the west. The block on the west side dropped as much as 175 feet in some areas. Judging from the youngest rock layers it broke, the fault moved in late Mississippian or early Pennsylvanian time.

The fault dips steeply down to the west and trends slightly northwest, paralleling the edge of the Illinois Basin for 50 miles from southern Morgan

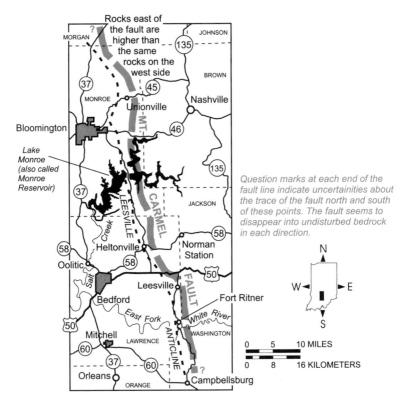

Question marks at each end of the fault line indicate uncertainies about the trace of the fault north and south of these points. The fault seems to disappear into undisturbed bedrock in each direction.

*The Mt. Carmel fault stretches for 50 miles in south-central Indiana.*

County, just east of Indiana 37, southeast to just west of Campbellsburg in northwestern Washington County. It disappears under glacial deposits to the north and under weathered sedimentary rocks to the south.

## CAVES AND SINKHOLES

Aside from its status as a primary source of building stone, south-central Indiana is perhaps best known for its caves and sinkholes.

During the War of 1812, caves with large bat populations were sources of saltpeter—potassium nitrate—the major ingredient of black powder. Early settlers used flowing springs and waterfalls at cave entrances to turn waterwheels that drove sawmills and gristmills. Some caves became fruit cellars and others became commercial tourist attractions.

Marengo Cave and Big Wyandotte Cave in Harrison County are the most famous of the more than four hundred caves known in south-central Indiana. The Lost River cave system in Orange County is one of the better-known underground drainage systems in America. Binkley's Cave, just south of Corydon, and Blue Springs Caverns, west of Bedford, each have more

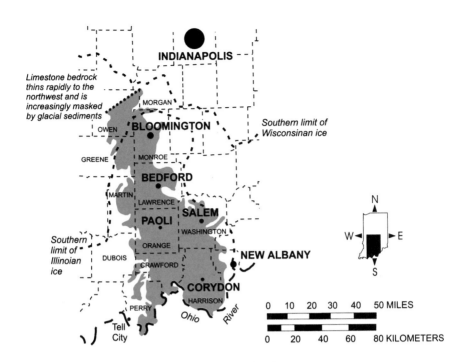

*Karst area in south-central Indiana.*

than 20 miles of passages and now rank as the longest two caves in Indiana, both among the ten longest in the world.

These caves and others are in the Mitchell plain—actually a plateau—where limestones of the Sanders and Blue River groups are exposed in a belt that stretches from northern Putnam County to the Ohio River in Harrison County and then into Kentucky. Thousands of sinkholes pock the landscape. The Crawford upland, to the west, has much less limestone bedrock, hence fewer caves, and stands higher in elevation.

Streams first eroded the Mitchell plain during Tertiary time and removed sandstones, siltstones, and shales, carving deep valleys into the underlying limestones. Rainwater and groundwater, naturally slightly acidic, dissolved the increasingly exposed limestone along fractures in the rock and then along bedding surfaces. Solution widening of fractures near the surface created small crevices, which you can easily see at the tops of roadcuts and quarry walls around Bloomington and Bedford.

The elevation of surface streams largely controls subsurface cave development. The larger streams eroded their valleys before the caverns formed, and the levels of these main valleys controlled the level of cavern development. The multiple levels of caverns record changes in the depths of the valleys.

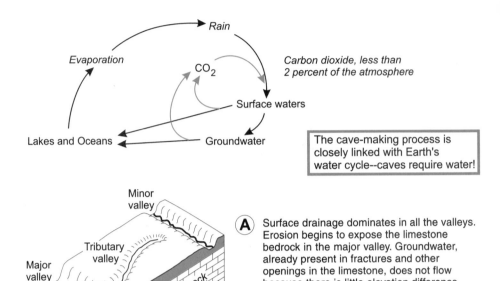

Carbon dioxide, less than
2 percent of the atmosphere

The cave-making process is
closely linked with Earth's
water cycle--caves require water!

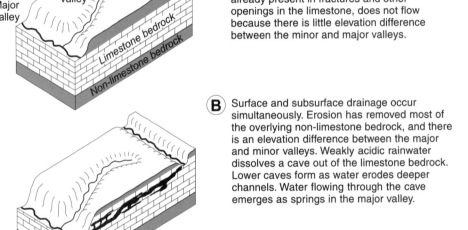

**A** Surface drainage dominates in all the valleys.
Erosion begins to expose the limestone
bedrock in the major valley. Groundwater,
already present in fractures and other
openings in the limestone, does not flow
because there is little elevation difference
between the minor and major valleys.

**B** Surface and subsurface drainage occur
simultaneously. Erosion has removed most of
the overlying non-limestone bedrock, and there
is an elevation difference between the major
and minor valleys. Weakly acidic rainwater
dissolves a cave out of the limestone bedrock.
Lower caves form as water erodes deeper
channels. Water flowing through the cave
emerges as springs in the major valley.

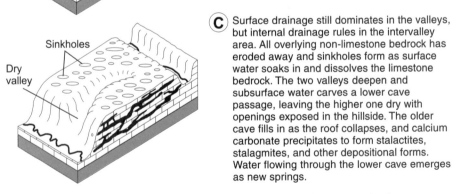

**C** Surface drainage still dominates in the valleys,
but internal drainage rules in the intervalley
area. All overlying non-limestone bedrock has
eroded away and sinkholes form as surface
water soaks in and dissolves the limestone
bedrock. The two valleys deepen and
subsurface water carves a lower cave
passage, leaving the higher one dry with
openings exposed in the hillside. The older
cave fills in as the roof collapses, and calcium
carbonate precipitates to form stalactites,
stalagmites, and other depositional forms.
Water flowing through the lower cave emerges
as new springs.

*The process of cave formation: carbon dioxide and rainwater form a karst landscape.*

*Fractures widened by groundwater solution in the Mississippian Paoli limestone along I-64 at Corydon exit. Terra rossa partially fills the cracks.*

Most of the drainage in cave country is underground. Many streams in south-central Indiana flow on the surface, then suddenly disappear either under a rocky ledge or into a small sinkhole or swallow hole. That is why so many caves contain underground streams. Most sinkholes are open and dry, but some are clogged and hold water as circular ponds. At other places, streams rise to the surface in great springs. In some areas, such as along the Lost River, water flows in the surface channel only during torrential rains that completely fill the underground channels with water. Dry valleys, originally carved by surface streams, are common, especially along the western edge of the Mitchell plain, where it meets the Crawford upland. The streams that once flowed in these valleys now flow through caverns.

Caves are voids in solid rock; therefore they are unstable and tend to collapse. Rubble on a cave floor occupies more volume than it did as intact rock in the ceiling. Successive collapses backfill caves with broken rubble.

Some caves are too large or too shallow to fill themselves with rubble. They eventually break through to the surface to become collapse sinkholes, which commonly appear quite suddenly. Many people in Indiana cave country call them "gulfs," such as the Wesley Chapel Gulf in the Lost River area of Orange County. Occasionally collapses open lateral passages, exposing the cave in two places. That happened at Twin Caves in Spring Mill State Park near Mitchell.

Mention a cave and most people immediately picture stalactites, the pendants of calcium carbonate that hang from the ceiling, and stalagmites, the pedestals that rise from the floor. Both form when drops of water lose dissolved carbon dioxide to the cave atmosphere. That causes immediate precipitation of calcium carbonate as a thin skin around the drop. Continued evaporation from more drops adds to the mineral skin, which lengthens, drop by drop, to become a stalactite that is initially hollow like a soda straw. As the drops fall, they splatter on the floor of the cave, where they lose more calcium carbonate to build a stalagmite. Water also seeps from cracks and flows in sheets down the walls, precipitating calcium carbonate in the form of flowstone. In the drier parts of some caves, gypsum—hydrous calcium sulfate—dissolves out of rock layers above the cave and precipitates to form clumps of gypsum crystals that cling to cave walls like ghostly white flowers.

Further evidence that enormous amounts of limestone have dissolved exists in the orange and brown soils, called terra rossa, that cover the Mitchell plain and the eastern part of the Crawford upland. Terra rossa soils consist mostly of the insoluble sand, chert, and iron oxide–stained clay left as the limestone that once contained it dissolved.

## GEODES

Geodes, masses of quartz crystals that fill rounded cavities in rock, abound in the upper part of the Borden group and the lower part of the Harrodsburg limestone. It is easy to see them in roadcuts, harder to spot them after they weather free to become brownish rocks. Geodes may be as large as basketballs but typically come in the size range and irregular forms of potatoes.

Geodes obviously form in cavities. Some were the interiors of fossils, but in most cases their origin is unclear. Once the cavity is open, circulating groundwater fills it with crystals from the outside edge inward. The commonest filling is quartz. Other possibilities include such rarities as barite, dolomite, or sphalerite.

## BUILDING STONE CAPITAL

South-central Indiana is widely known for its building stone. A number of other areas, in Indiana and elsewhere, produced locally important building stones, particularly in the middle to late 1800s. After the coming of the railroads, the better-quality Mississippian limestones of the Bloomington and Bedford area became the building material of choice.

The first quarry in this part of the state opened in 1827 near Stinesville to supply stone for bridge piers and chimneys. David Dale Owen, the Indiana state geologist, advertised the quality of the Mississippian limestones in the late 1830s. Improving railroads led to the development of many new quarries in the 1850s and 1860s, both to serve the construction needs of the railroads and to carry the building stone to such places as Chicago, Cincinnati, and Louisville.

*Typical Hoosier geodes. Quartz crystals line the interior of the opened specimen.*

Work in the early stone-belt quarries was tiring and hazardous. Men shoveled the overburden into wheelbarrows and horse-drawn wagons. Then they drilled holes with hammer and steel rod, filled them with black powder, and broke blocks of stone free, trying not to shatter them. Large wooden derricks hoisted the blocks onto wagons for the trip to the railroad. Accidents were frequent; many were fatal.

Many early quarries lacked mills. The operators either shipped blocks to be cut elsewhere or cut them with two-man saws as much as 10 feet long. The Watts and Biddle Quarry at Stinesville installed the first steam gang saw in 1855. Three other companies installed them by 1866, two at Ellettsville and the other in Bedford.

The rock that brought fame to south-central Indiana is the Salem limestone, which is 60 to 100 feet thick in the Bloomington and Bedford area. It is at the surface from the White River valley at Gosport and Romona southeast in a belt about 3 miles wide through the quarry districts of Stinesville, Ellettsville, and Hunter Valley to Bloomington. The belt nearly doubles in width near Clear Creek, then narrows toward Salem. South of Salem, the formation appears in quarries at Georgetown and Corydon.

The qualities that make the Salem limestone such good building stone are its massiveness, homogeneity, and softness. Massive rocks lack directional grain; they look the same from any direction. Freshly quarried stone can be sawed, planed, and shaped. Then it hardens as it dries. Some parts of the Salem limestone make better building stone than others. Too many fractures or layers of clay led to the abandonment of many quarries.

Later quarries used mechanized methods to get at the stone. Channelers traveled on railroad tracks across the bedding surface, noisily hammering a furrow 5 to 13 feet deep into the limestone. Wire saws began to replace

*Discarded blocks of Salem limestone at a quarry along Buff Ridge near Oolitic.*

channelers in the 1930s. After sets of parallel channels were cut across the quarry floor in a checkerboard pattern, the first block was wedged loose and hoisted from its place. Then the others were freed by drilling holes across their bases. The blocks were hauled to the mill for cutting, shaping, and finishing. Today, large carbide and diamond saws are commonly used.

Cutting Salem limestone into architectural shapes and designs became important in the early 1900s. Numerous stone mills worked in Bloomington and Bedford. Some were part of quarrying firms, others simply purchased blocks. By 1910 the mills shipped tremendous volumes of waste rock to Gary and Chicago for use as flux in steel mills. Crushed mill scrap later found use in the glass industry. In 1967 the town of Burns Harbor dumped more than a half million tons of waste blocks along the south shore of Lake Michigan to form a breakwater.

Salem limestone was used in the foundation and trim of the original Monroe County courthouse built in 1819. The contractors hauled the stone by wagon from a creekbed 8 miles away, apparently not realizing that the same stone lay beneath the construction site in Bloomington.

The first major use of Salem limestone was in the United States Customs House and Court House in Louisville, where construction began in 1853. Further use awaited an increase in the population of the midwestern states, changes in construction methods and architectural designs, and an increase in the numbers of people affluent enough to build mansions. Demand increased sharply as Chicago and Boston rebuilt after their great fires of 1871 and 1872. Another increase followed the use of Salem limestone in the Indiana capitol in 1878. Salem limestone became increasingly popular on the east coast as an alternative to the darker stones locally available. By 1917 more than two hundred midwestern county courthouses were made of Salem limestone. In 1980 Indiana limestone was used in Indiana's tallest skyscraper of the time, the American Life Insurance Company building in Indianapolis.

A stone supermarket started at Oolitic in 1959, where a 15-acre display offered different varieties. Customers drove in and bought stone on the spot.

Once you learn to recognize Salem limestone, you see it in buildings all over the country, including the Pentagon and the Empire State Building. Bloomington and Bedford contain many examples that celebrate the fine craftsmanship of the stoneworkers. To celebrate the U.S. Bicentennial, Indiana stonecutters made a full-scale reproduction of the famous painting of George Washington crossing the Delaware. It is now on exhibit at Washington Crossing Park in Pennsylvania—all 40 tons of it. A visit to the Limestone Heritage Museum in Bedford is also well worth the time.

*Blackford County Courthouse at Hartford City, one of many county courthouses built of Salem limestone.*

# GEOGRAPHIC REGIONS

*Norman Upland.* The Norman upland is a high area eroded into middle Mississippian sandstones, siltstones, and shales of the Borden group, which tilt gently to the west, toward the Illinois Basin. This upland extends from the Ohio River north to Johnson and Morgan Counties. The area is less than 1 mile wide near the Ohio River, but widens northward to as much as 30 miles across.

The eastern edge of the Norman upland is a steep rise, the Knobstone escarpment, especially obvious from the New Albany area northward. Its western edge grades into hills eroded in middle Mississippian limestones. The southern edges of the great till sheets define its northern boundary. Elevations range from about 900 feet along its eastern edge to about 700 feet along the western edge.

Most of the Norman upland was never glaciated, and few of its streams ever carried much meltwater. The main exception is the East Fork White

*Geographic regions of south-central Indiana.*

River, which is entrenched in an oversized valley partly filled with glacial outwash. Torrents of meltwater enlarged the valley, then left the outwash as they ceased to flow.

The Illinoian ice sheet covered most of Indiana. Scattered remnants of Illinoian till survive on hilltops north of the East Fork White River, from Jackson to Morgan Counties.

*Mitchell Plain.* The Mitchell plain is eroded into middle Mississippian limestones of the Sanders and Blue River groups. It is between the Norman upland on the east and the Crawford upland on the west. Its southern portion is pitted with thousands of sinkholes that capture much of the surface drainage and send it underground. South of the East Fork White River, the Mitchell plain is generally 10 to 15 miles wide and 650 to 850 feet high. Farther north, it is far less distinct, from 3 to 10 miles wide, with elevations that range from as high as 900 feet to as low as 450 feet in the major valleys.

The wide sinkhole plains south of the East Fork White River are best known for their caves, including the Wyandotte, Marengo, and Blue Springs caves. In northern Orange County, the plain features the Lost River, part of which flows underground.

*Crawford Upland.* At the west edge of the Mitchell plain, especially south of the East Fork White River, the Chester escarpment is the eastern edge of the Crawford upland. It is less obvious than the Knobstone escarpment but does stand several hundred feet above the plains to the east. It becomes less obvious north of the East Fork White River.

*Mitchell plain landscape at Depauw. Low-lying areas are sinkholes.*

*A view across the Crawford upland at Wyandotte Cave along Indiana 62.*

The west side of the Crawford upland is the transition between rugged topography eroded in late Mississippian formations and rounded topography eroded in Pennsylvanian rocks. This transition extends north from the line between Perry and Spencer Counties near the Ohio River to the southern edge of the Tipton till plain. The Crawford upland ranges between 30 and 7 miles wide, narrowing from south to north.

The Crawford upland includes some of southern Indiana's most rugged topography. Elevations range from 450 feet along its west side to 900 feet along the east side, especially north of the East Fork White River. The highest elevations south of the East Fork White River are 850 feet.

Numerous small rivers and creeks drain the Crawford upland, but only the major valleys of the West and East Forks of the White River cross it. These existed before the glaciers came south; later floods of meltwater enlarged them.

# Interstate 64 and Indiana 64
## Kentucky Line—Indiana 145
**50 MILES**

These roads cross the bedrock hills of south-central Indiana, some of the most picturesque scenery in the state. Between New Albany and Indiana 37, both routes cross the drainage basins of the small streams that flow south directly into the Ohio River. West of Indiana 37, Indiana 64 crosses the southern edge of the Patoka River drainage basin, while I-64 crosses the northern edges of small basins that drain into the Ohio River.

At New Albany, I-64 traverses 1.5 miles of the Ohio River floodplain on a terrace of outwash dumped from great floods of glacial meltwater. It dammed a side valley on the west side of New Albany to make a lake in which sediments accumulated.

Just west of New Albany, the roadway ascends the Knobstone escarpment to emerge atop the bedrock hills of the Norman upland. Roadcuts on the west side of New Albany expose rocks deposited on the Borden delta during Mississippian time.

Three miles west of where it enters the Norman upland, Indiana 64 diverges northwest from the interstate to follow a more or less parallel path 6 to 10 miles north. Limestones of the Edwardsville formation are exposed near the Edwardsville exit.

The western edge of the Norman upland is transitional near the junction of I-64 and Indiana 64. Between there and eastern Crawford County, the two routes cross bedrock hills in the Mitchell plain. The hills are eroded in limestones of the middle Mississippian Sanders group. Sinkholes are locally common, mainly along a line that trends north across central Harrison County, in a sinkhole plain 3 to 6 miles wide.

Some of the larger creeks that flow south across the Mitchell plain have entrenched meanders. You can see them along side roads. They must have developed when the stream was flowing on some easily eroded material above the level of the present landscape. Then the stream eroded through that vanished cover and into the hard limestone beneath as erosion reduced the general level of the landscape. The Blue River west of Corydon flows through an entrenched valley in an angular course that probably follows the fracture pattern in the underlying bedrock.

Between eastern Crawford County and the intersections with Indiana 145, the two highways cross 20 to 25 miles of bedrock hills in the Crawford upland. The bedrock is sandstones, shales, and limestones deposited during Mississippian and Pennsylvanian time. The countryside does not have flat ridgetops like those in the Norman upland to the east, nor does it contain many sinkholes. During low water levels, the Little Blue River flows into caverns dissolved along fractures in the Paoli limestone near English.

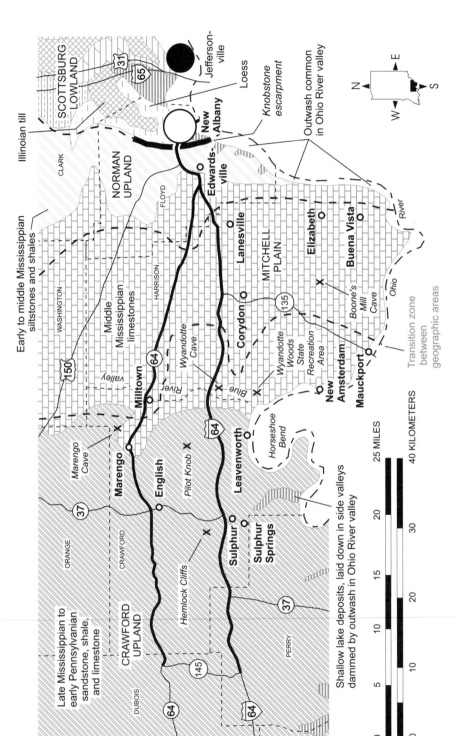

Geology along I-64 and Indiana 64 between the Kentucky line and Indiana 145.

## *A Glacial Lake*

Some 30 feet of finely stratified silt and clay lie beneath Falling Run Park on the west side of New Albany. They are souvenirs of a vanished lake. The Wisconsinan ice sheet never reached farther south than some 55 miles north of New Albany, but it did shed torrents of meltwater choked with sediments. These followed the northern tributaries of the glacial Ohio River through southeastern Indiana. Tremendous deposits of sand and gravel in the Ohio River valley dammed the mouths of smaller streams, such as the one that flowed through the New Albany area. Two sequences of lake sediments indicate this damming occurred twice, with enough time in between to form soil atop the lower layer.

## *Knobstone Escarpment*

As I-64 winds west from New Albany, it climbs the Knobstone escarpment, 500 feet of impressive cuts in the Mississippian Borden group. These lie just above the Devonian rocks so well exposed at the nearby Falls of the Ohio. The rocks tilt gently to the west because they are on the western flank of the Cincinnati Arch and the eastern side of the Illinois Basin.

Fossils abound in parts of the Edwardsville formation and the overlying Sanders group. In the late 1800s, a thick limestone layer near Lanesville yielded a bonanza of Paleozoic fish teeth, more than three thousand specimens representing a number of different species.

One of the best rock exposures in the Knobstone escarpment is 10 miles south of Edwardsville, near Elizabeth. Leave I-64 at Edwardsville and follow

*View east from atop the Knobstone escarpment into the Ohio River valley. Mississippian strata form the bluff along Indiana 211, east of Elizabeth.*

Indiana 11 south 10 miles, then turn east on Indiana 211 and descend past a long roadcut into the Ohio Valley. This is the base of the Knobstone escarpment. The New Providence shale is just below the surface.

*Sinkhole in Mississippian Salem limestone on edge of old quarry along Indiana 211, east of Elizabeth.*

*Generalized surface and bedrock profiles along I-64 and Indiana 64.*

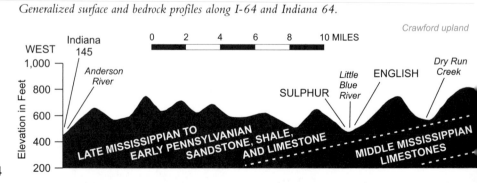

94

The lowest exposed rocks are about 125 feet of massive gray siltstone, the Spickert Knob formation. Many of the limestone nodules that stick out of these rocks contain fossil crinoid fragments. Thirteen feet of Edwardsville formation overlie the Spickert Knob formation farther up the roadcut. The Edwardsville formation looks much like the Spickert Knob formation, but a layer about 1 foot thick at its base contains some small geodes, tracks and trails of crawling animals, and a concentration of fossils. Overlying this are 65 feet of the Ramp Creek formation of the Sanders group, which include gray siltstone and limestone complete with crinoids, chert nodules, and geodes. Farther up the road are 35 feet of the overlying Harrodsburg limestone and 55 feet of Salem limestone. Some 30 feet of tan St. Louis limestone cap the Knobstone escarpment. An abandoned quarry along the road produced lesser-quality Salem limestone.

## Plate Glass

New Albany was the home of John B. Ford, one of the founders of the Libbey-Owens-Ford Company. He built a glass plant on the banks of the Ohio River shortly after the Civil War. At that time, the tendency of glass to bulge in places during cooling limited the size of the sheets that early manufacturers could make. But Ford improved the process, and during the 1880s the New Albany Glass Works produced the first large sheets of glass that did not bulge. The company ceremoniously installed the first large store window in a shop along Pearl Street.

In 1870 Ford's cousin, Washington DePauw, built the adjacent Starr Glass Company. In 1872 Ford sold his factory to DePauw and started over in Pennsylvania. DePauw's Starr Glass Company quarried sandstones of the Mississippian Bethel formation that capped ridgetops of Mississippian limestones at Martinsburg and Elizabeth. Coal came by way of the Ohio River. In the 1890s the glassworks moved to Alexandria to use natural gas. The Ohio Falls Cooperative Window Glass Company failed to keep the local industry alive. It closed in 1905 because refinements in the glass industry established more exacting specifications for glass sands. In 1964 a plant opened

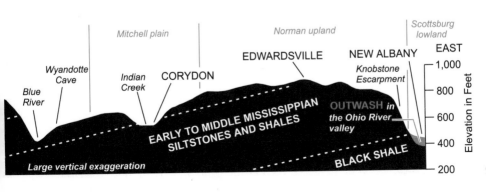

east of Elizabeth to produce glass sand from a particularly thick section of the Bethel formation.

### Kilns in the Hills

Shales of the Borden group yielded raw material for pressed bricks around 1900. The Hoosier Brick Company built a plant just west of New Albany in 1894, along the Southern Railway. Pits dug into the banks south of the tracks exposed a bluish shale in a cut that was 60 feet high by 1904. Workers mixed shale with river sand and baked the mixture in kilns. The bricks were first used to pave alleys and walks and later to pave streets, some of which are still in use. The Goetz Pressed Brick Company produced similar products from a nearby plant. Kentucky Vitrified Brick mined Borden shale in the Silver Hills and shipped it to Louisville. There they mixed it with underclay from beneath a coal seam to make paving blocks.

### Harrison County Meteorite

A meteorite fell on Buena Vista on the afternoon of March 28, 1859. The place is south of I-64, off Indiana 11. A few people noticed a slight glare, then everyone heard a series of loud noises like thunder. Some people reported that the fragments sounded like a heavy rain shower as they fell into the woods. Two of the pieces that were found are now in the British Museum and one is at Harvard. Little remains of Buena Vista, but pieces of its meteorite still lie buried in the countryside, waiting to be found.

### Corydon—The First Capital

Corydon, the first capital of Indiana, snuggles among the hills of the Norman upland. Blocks of St. Louis and Ste. Genevieve limestone dug from the bed of Indian Creek form the walls of the historic courthouse on the town square. Window sills and lintels are St. Louis limestone quarried at New Salisbury, north of Corydon.

Quarries produced small amounts of lithographic limestone in the hills southwest of town during the 1870s. The quality was good but the quantity was not, so the operation closed within a few years. The same quarry produced limestones that took a nice polish and found use as table tops, mantels, counters, and so forth.

Someone found a mineral spring east of town, along the north side of Little Indian Creek, in 1871. A well dug some 40 feet into the Mississippian bedrock produced water that the local people used to treat their ailments. The area became a popular picnic grounds, complete with dance pavilion and bathhouse. A raging flood ruined the picnic grounds in 1903, and they were never rebuilt.

Watch for caves and springs between Corydon and St. Croix. Blind fish and crayfish that show up in springs and wells show that the water is part of cave systems. Water flows in just a few deeply incised streams and rivers. Most of the drainage is through caverns. The Blue Springs Bottling Works of Corydon used water from Blue Springs, east of town, to make soft drinks during the early 1900s.

Areas between the incised valleys are known as barrens because the first settlers found them treeless and covered with prairie grasses and low shrubs. Sinkholes are common on the barrens, and their soil is the reddish terra rossa that develops on weathering limestone. Compacted terra rossa makes a natural cement that was used in the sidewalks of early Corydon.

The Corydon Stone Company began quarrying Ste. Genevieve limestone in 1885 to supply contractors in many East Coast cities. The limestone was paler than the Salem limestone and in great demand for buildings, monuments, and bridge piers. The stone company bought the railroad that served the quarry after a terrible train wreck forced the railroad into bankruptcy in 1886. That railroad, the Louisville, New Albany & Corydon, still operates.

A few quarries near Corydon still work the Paoli and Ste. Genevieve limestones. Cavities in the Ste. Genevieve limestone commonly contain a lining of dolomite crystals, beautiful pink blades, much admired among mineral collectors. Fluorite, the mineral form of calcium fluoride, and various sulfide minerals also occur.

Corydon is vulnerable to serious floods along Big and Little Indian Creeks. Torrents of water periodically rush through the bottomlands, carrying away tremendous volumes of topsoil and causing washouts and landslides. Floodwaters covered Courthouse Square most recently in March 1943 and in January 1959.

*Pink dolomite crystals in Ste. Genevieve limestone from a quarry at Corydon.*

### Boone's Mill Cave and Mauckport

A side trip south on Indiana 135 leads to a historic cave and the historic river town of Mauckport. Boone's Mill Cave is 3 miles east from the sign on Indiana 135. A stream flowing from the cave provided the power to drive a gristmill. The owner was Squire Boone, brother of Daniel Boone. According to legend, Squire and Daniel discovered this cave in 1790 while hunting, and Squire later returned to establish a homestead. Squire was buried in a small nearby cave that reportedly once saved him from marauding Indians. Boone's Mill Cave is now a tourist attraction called Squire Boone Caverns, and it features high waterfalls along the main passageway and rare cave pearls as well as the usual stalactites and stalagmites. A metal walkway crosses a gushing underground stream.

At Mauckport, Indiana 135 drops off the bedrock highlands into the valley of the Ohio River. Watch 1 mile north of Mauckport for an overlook east of the highway that provides a spectacular view of the present and former river valleys. Look a half-mile south of the overlook for a small hill that rises about 150 feet above the valley that encircles it. Sometime before

*A large column towers over visitors in Squire Boone Caverns.*
—Courtesy of Squire Boone Caverns

*The Ohio River once flowed in the valley at the bottom of this slope near Mauckport. Later the river abandoned this course and assumed its present route, in the background of this view.*

the ice ages began about 2 million years ago, the Ohio River made a meander loop around the area that later became this hill. The river has since entrenched its valley south of the hill, leaving the hill standing above the modern floodplain.

No rocks are now cut for building stone in this part of Indiana, but many were in the middle and late 1800s. The Jacob Stockslager Quarry in the Ste. Genevieve limestone 2 miles north of Mauckport produced dimension limestone for many years and shipped it down the Ohio River on barges. It finally closed after railroads opened up the stone belt, bringing competition from the quarries in the Bloomington and Bedford area.

The Jacob Stockslager Quarry sold stone cut from a layer of white oolitic limestone that would take a high polish. The oolites appear as spherical bodies the size of fine bird shot. Chert nodules added a certain beauty to the stone, which was used for tombstones, monuments, and decorative facing. Burning of broken pieces and cuttings produced very pure chemical lime used for plaster and purifying sugar. The quarry closed in 1878.

### Horseshoe Bend and Vicinity

A short jaunt south at the Indiana 66 exit of I-64 leads to Leavenworth, built on Horseshoe Bend, a meander of the Ohio River. High bluffs of Ste. Genevieve limestone flank both sides of the Ohio River at this point, so it was a natural site for a town. The narrow channel constricted floods to great depths in 1884, 1913, 1925, 1933, and 1936. Some were as much as 70 feet above low water. After the flood of 1937 exceeded all previous levels, some 84 feet above low water at the nearby dam, much of Leavenworth was moved onto the bluff.

*Along Indiana 62 at Leavenworth, the Ohio River flows in a loop-shaped meander—Horseshoe Bend—far below the bluff.*

The new site of Leavenworth is on the edge of the Crawford upland. The overlook along Indiana 62 provides a great view of Horseshoe Bend. Follow the winding road on the east side of town down to the remains of old Leavenworth, past an old quarry in the Ste. Genevieve limestone. Springs are common along the escarpment, where the Mississippian rocks lie on Mississippian limestones of the Norman upland. Years ago, Cave Spring on the west side of Leavenworth occasionally shot water several feet into the air.

Limestone was quarried at many places north of Leavenworth, and sandstone grindstones were shipped down the river for many years. The limestone was used for purifying sugar. Two quarries east of Cape Sandy, south and southwest of Leavenworth, produce crushed stone from the West Baden and Blue River groups.

### Wyandotte Caves State Recreation Area

Wyandotte Caves State Recreation Area is just south of I-64, in the Ste. Genevieve limestone along the Blue River valley and includes Big Wyandotte and Little Wyandotte Caves. Big Wyandotte Cave was known as Indiana Saltpeter Cave in 1812 for the potassium nitrate that covered the floors of some passageways. Early settlers mined it.

Some early visitors to the cave vandalized easily accessible passageways and defaced many beautiful rock formations. The state finally intervened, requiring the owner to fence the entrance to "prevent cattle from licking

*Entrance to Big Wyandotte Cave in the Mississippian Ste. Genevieve limestone.*

the epsom salts." An explorer found a new entrance in 1850. Other discoveries quickly followed, opening long passageways. The owners finally recognized the bonanza below their property and opened the cave for tours. A lodge was built in 1856 to accommodate visitors who came in hacks and carriages from Leavenworth, New Albany, and Corydon. A few minor discoveries in the late 1800s and early 1900s further increased the known size of the cave. In 1941 a number of important passages displaying branching formations called helictites were opened in the eastern part of the cave.

The state bought the cave area in 1966 and now operates it as part of the Harrison-Crawford-Wyandotte Complex. Passageways are large, some rooms as much as 70 feet high and 80 feet long. More than 5 miles of passageways are known.

Indian hammer stones were found in one large cave room, along with a deep gouge in the side of a large stalagmite and rock chips on the floor. Evidently they were mining aragonite, a mineral similar to calcite, that makes up many cave formations. Ornate Indian pipes made of aragonite from Big Wyandotte Cave have been found in several nearby states.

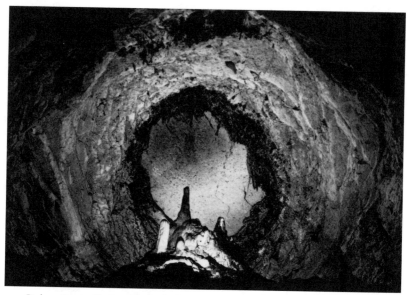

*Stalagmites in Rothrock's Cathedral, Big Wyandotte Cave.* —Courtesy of Indiana Department of Natural Resources, Forestry

## Wyandotte Woods State Recreation Area

Wyandotte Woods State Recreation Area is just south of I-64, off Indiana 62. Watch for Devil's Elbow, a narrow meander of the Blue River south of Indiana 62 east of Wyandotte Cave.

The park is between the Blue and Ohio Rivers along the eastern border of the Crawford upland. Sinkholes in the valley floors swallow most of the stream flow, leaving the valleys dry. The road follows a deep valley, dry except in very wet weather, to the Ohio River. Ledges of limestone in the Blue River group make steps in the streams. Potato Creek winds through a tight meander loop near the Ohio River. The creek will someday cut across the narrow neck, leaving the meander bend abandoned on the floodplain as an oxbow lake.

## The Underground World of Marengo

Marengo Cave, northeast of Marengo, contains some of the nicest cave formations in the state. It was discovered in 1883, when children crawled into a hole that had opened within a sinkhole and found themselves in a large room decorated with cave formations. Further exploration showed that the cave was nearly 1 mile long. Today the cave is known to contain more than 4 miles of passages.

Marengo Cave is in Ste. Genevieve limestone. The upper passageways lack cave formations, have muddy floors, and are oval in cross section. Beautiful cave formations decorate the lower passageways. A stream flows through

*Dry streambed in Wyandotte Woods State Recreation Area.*

*Stalactites and stalagmites in Crystal Palace section of Marengo Cave.* —Courtesy of Marengo Cave

the lowest level, which is not open to the public. Town Spring, west of Marengo Cave, is one of the largest in the state.

Marengo started at Town Spring and was the site of an early underground limestone mine that produced from the Ste. Genevieve limestone until 1983. Look for the old mine on the southeast edge of town, along the bluff east of the railroad tracks. Other quarries tap the Paoli and Ste. Genevieve limestones near Ramsey and Depauw, north of Indiana 64.

### Other Notable Caves and Springs

More than eighty caves are less than 10 miles north or south of I-64, all within the Norman upland, Mitchell plain, and eastern Crawford upland. Saltpeter, Everton, and Tinsel Miller caves are but a few.

Numerous rises—streams coming out of cave openings—include Wilson's and Harrison Springs northwest of Corydon, Blue Spring near New Amsterdam, the Stygean River near the mouth of the Blue River, Blue Spouter in Walnut Valley near the Blue River, and many others in the general area.

### Blue River Valley

Late Mississippian sandstones of the West Baden group cap the rocky ridges that rise nearly 300 feet above the Blue River at Milltown, south of Indiana 64. The river carved its channel into older Mississippian limestones of the Blue River group, which includes in ascending order the Paoli, Ste. Genevieve, and St. Louis limestones.

Look for the crumbling remains of an old lime kiln, vintage 1886, along Main Street. Behind it is the original quarry of the Louisville Cement Company, later the J. B. Speed Company, opened in 1885. In its early years, the

*Abandoned lime kiln of the Louisville Cement Company, Milltown.*

104

*Speed Quarry along Indiana 64 at Milltown. Tunnels were excavated into the Ste. Genevieve limestone.*

operation produced about 300 bushels of lime per day from the lower part of the Ste. Genevieve limestone. The rest of the stone was crushed. In the early 1900s, another company opened a quarry across the Blue River. The J. B. Speed Company followed suit around 1910, and in 1913 bought out the other operation and closed its old quarry in Milltown. During the First World War, the operators began tunneling for more high-grade limestone after crushed stone was declared not essential for the war effort. Lime manufacture was phased out in the late 1940s, and crushed stone became the main product until the operation was abandoned in 1953. You can see the tunnels blasted into the lower walls of the abandoned quarry along Indiana 64.

### Sulphur Springs and Mississippian Fossils

High, terraced cuts in the late Mississippian formations, from the Sample sandstone at the base to the Hardinsburg sandstone at the top, dominate the English exit at Indiana 37. Fossil crinoids, bryozoans, and brachiopods are common, especially in the interbedded limestones and shales of the Indian Springs shale within the Big Clifty sandstone. More roadcuts in these rocks exist farther north along Indiana 37.

The small towns of Sulphur and Sulphur Springs are just south of I-64. A well drilled in search of oil in 1862 found mineral water along the West

*Mississippian strata from the Sample to the Hardinsburg formations form the terraced cuts at the Indiana 37 exchange.*

Fork of the Little Blue River. The water terminated the drilling but launched a health spa boom that lasted well into the twentieth century. Visitors to the White Sulphur Hotel and bathhouse were soon wallowing in the water, enjoying its purported medicinal benefits. The water was bottled and distributed throughout the southern hills as "16 to 1 White Sulphur Water." Tar Springs, actually an oil seep, was 3.5 miles northwest of Sulphur Springs. Mineral springs also existed there, but their remoteness inhibited development.

# U.S. 50
## Seymour—Shoals
**60 MILES**

In south-central Indiana, U.S. 50 crosses lowlands filled with outwash in its eastern part and unglaciated bedrock hills in its western part. The highway is completely within the drainage basin of the East Fork White River, which it parallels and repeatedly crosses.

Between Seymour and the area 5 miles west of Brownstown, U.S. 50 crosses 15 miles of outwash deposited during Wisconsinan time, now a part of the Scottsburg lowland. In the area 4 miles southwest of Seymour, the highway crosses a blanket of sand and silt about 50 feet thick, blown off the bare surface of the outwash plain to the west, as the last ice sheet was melting.

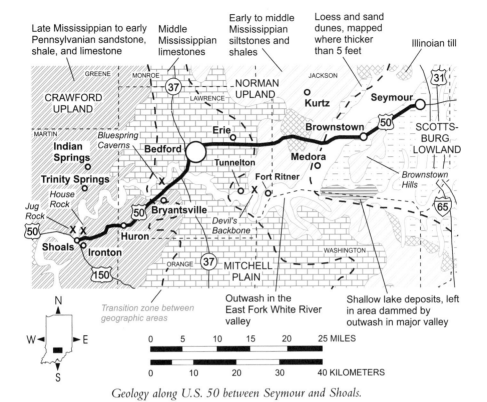

*Geology along U.S. 50 between Seymour and Shoals.*

U.S. 50 crosses almost 6 miles of dune sand, about 50 feet thick, blown against the east side of the East Fork White River valley between the area 4 miles southwest of Seymour and the west side of Brownstown. This sand is essentially continuous with the blanket sands near Seymour but is piled higher against and on top of the bedrock hills near Brownstown.

In the area 5 miles west of Brownstown, U.S. 50 cuts across the valley of the East Fork White River with its fill of glacial outwash. Torrents of water that poured through this valley when the last glaciers were melting dumped this tremendous expanse of sand and gravel. The modern White River is an underfit stream, a ghost of the mighty river that eroded this valley.

Between the area 5 miles west of Brownstown and that around Erie, U.S. 50 ascends the hillsides of the Knobstone escarpment and crosses 12 miles of bedrock hills, part of the Norman upland. The hills are eroded mostly in siltstones and shales of the middle Mississippian Borden group of formations. Some of the hills have caps of middle Mississippian limestone. The hilltops in the eastern half of this short stretch of road have thin coverings of Illinoian till. Limestones exposed in roadcuts and hillsides near Bedford belong to the Sanders group.

Side trips along other highways and along almost any of the back roads in these hills bring you to the scenic valley that the East Fork White River

*A view west to the Knobstone escarpment on the horizon and the town of Medora.*

carved into the bedrock. The original valley existed long before the glaciers came. Then the torrents of meltwater from the glaciers entrenched the old valley about 100 to 200 feet.

The back road between Fort Ritner and Tunnelton crosses Devil's Backbone, a thin fin of bedrock a quarter-mile wide that stands about 220 feet above the valleys of Guthrie Creek to the north and the East Fork White River to the south. The flat valley floors of the main river and several of the nearby creeks testify to the quantity of glacial outwash in them.

U.S. 50 crosses 15 miles of bedrock hills, part of the Mitchell plain, between the area around Erie and that around Bryantsville, both just off the highway. Bedrock formations are cave-riddled limestones that belong to the middle Mississippian Sanders group. The highway crosses a conspicuous sinkhole plain between the East Fork White River and Bryantsville.

Between Bryantsville and Shoals, U.S. 50 crosses 12 miles of bedrock hills, part of the Crawford upland. The East Fork White River flows through these hills in more of its entrenched valley. At Shoals, U.S. 50 again enters the East Fork White River valley and its outwash fill. The small sand dunes on the valley wall east of Shoals are difficult to see.

*Generalized surface and bedrock profiles along U.S. 50.*

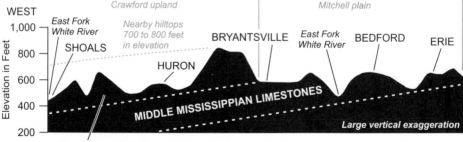

## Brownstown Hills and Glacial Outwash

Watch southeast of Brownstown for the Brownstown Hills, an erosional outlier of the Norman upland. They are eroded in formations of the Borden group, the same rocks that make the knobs of the Norman upland on the horizon to the north and south. The East Fork White River and its tributary, the Muscatatuck River, isolated these hills as they eroded their valleys. Any of the back roads provide good views of the splendid scenery.

U.S. 50 follows the southern edge of the wide valley of the East Fork White River between Seymour and Brownstown. It was the pathway for many torrents of glacial meltwater. No one can say when the valley received its first slug of meltwater, because any sediments it left were probably swept away during later floods. Some 60 feet of outwash now fills the valley and makes terraces that look like giant steps on the valley walls.

The dunes at the base of the Brownstown Hills tell of strong southeasterly winds that blew sand off the great outwash plain. This probably happened mainly in winter, when meltwater flow stopped and cold winds whipped sand and silt across the valley floor. Here, as elsewhere in Indiana, silt blew onto the hills, accumulating to depths as great as 12 feet in the low areas. It is the basis for much of the excellent soil in the Brownstown area.

## Bricks and Tile in the Seymour-Brownstown Area

Around the turn of the century, buff glacial clays and Borden shales were stripped from a farm west of Seymour to make paving bricks and tile. Production stopped by 1904, but you can still see the bricks in the older streets and alleys of Seymour.

Another plant made housing brick. The Brownstown Brick and Tile Company used Borden shales from pits in the Brownstown area. The New Providence shale, near Brownstown, supplied clay to a cement plant at Mitchell. Still another plant stripped shale and clay for brick and tile manufacture at the village of Kurtz. The abandoned Medora Brick Company stands near Medora. It made common brick into the late 1980s. Abandoned shale pits form scars along Indiana 235 north of Medora.

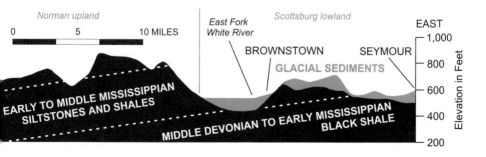

### Blue Springs Caverns

Blue Springs Caverns, in western Lawrence County, contain more than 20 miles of passageways eroded in the Salem and St. Louis limestones. The damming of the East Fork White River at Williams in 1911 drowned the springs that issued from the cave and flooded most of its lower passages.

The present main entrance appeared in 1941, when a sinkhole pond suddenly drained during a heavy rainstorm. The cave contains four levels, the deepest far below the East Fork White River. The right angle arrangement of the passageways follows the pattern of fractures in the bedrock. Some fifty-five streams flow within the cave and join the main stream, which surfaces at Blue Spring. The tour, a boat trip, follows the main passageway to near the junction of a long but low tributary passage. Cave formations are scarce.

*A shale pit in the Mississippian Borden group, just north of Medora.*

*Kilns of the Medora Brick Company just southwest of Medora. Knobstone escarpment in background.*

*Entrance to Blue Springs Caverns is at the bottom of a sink.*

### Dimension Stone Quarrying in the Huron Area

An old mill west of Huron is a relic of a dimension stone industry that cut slabs of the Big Clifty sandstone into ornamental facing. The fresh rock splits readily into thick slabs that harden as they dry. They vary greatly in color, depending on the amount of iron oxide stain. At least four companies worked the sandstone between the 1940s and 1980s.

### Mississippian-Pennsylvanian Unconformity

The contact between Mississippian and Pennsylvanian rocks is exposed in the area around Huron and Shoals. It is an unconformity—an old land surface eroded on the Mississippian rocks and then buried beneath the Pennsylvanian rocks. The Pennsylvanian Mansfield formation lies on Mississippian formations as old as the Elwren formation and as young as the Tar Springs formation. Evidently, the buried erosion surface cuts across the older rocks at a slight angle.

### Clay Deposits near Huron

Clay, once called indianaite, exists along the Mississippian-Pennsylvanian unconformity. It is a mixture of several clay minerals that become white porcelain when fired. Mining continued from the 1870s until 1891, revived briefly in the 1920s, and then died out.

Indianaite clay occurs from Owen and Monroe Counties south to Crawford County. It is probably buried soil that weathered when the Mississippian terrain was above sea level and eroding, before the Pennsylvanian rocks were laid down on them. The North and South Gardner mines, northeast of Huron, were the largest producers.

### Indiana Gypsum

The first official note of gypsum deposits in southern Indiana came in the 1920s, after a discovery near Huron. Considering all the mineral springs and wells that produce water rich in sulfates in this part of Indiana, the discovery should not have surprised anyone. In fact, thick beds of gypsum and anhydrite were known in the lower part of the Mississippian St. Louis limestone by the 1850s.

Gypsum and anhydrite are mineral forms of calcium sulfate; they differ in that gypsum also contains water. The gypsum is entirely subsurface, from Perry, Crawford, and Harrison Counties on the Ohio River northwest to Vigo and Clay Counties. The beds reach a maximum thickness of 16 feet near Shoals.

Two mines opened near Shoals about 1955: one is 2 miles east of town, south of U.S. 50; the other is 5 miles east of town, near Willow Valley. One is about 400 feet deep, the other about 500 feet, one of the deepest gypsum mines in the country. Front-end loaders and side-dump tractors mine rooms in the layer of gypsum, leaving pillars to support the roof. Large conveyor belts help bring the rock to the surface, where mills process it into plasterboard and many other products. The reserves are enough to keep the mine alive at least another hundred years.

### Martin County Iron Ores

Ironton, just southeast of Shoals, grew up around the blast furnace of the Nelson Furnace Company in the 1870s. Several hundred people worked here around 1873, the high point of the operation. This was the last blast furnace in southern Indiana and was part of a revival of iron smelting after the early companies, which used local iron ores, closed after the Civil War. The new activity followed the discovery that the blocky coal seams in the lower Pennsylvanian rocks made good fuel for blast furnaces.

Ironton seemed an excellent site for a blast furnace because the Mansfield formation contained iron ore, coal could be mined from outcrops at Sampson Hill, and flux came from local Mississippian limestones. When the operators found they could make better pig iron by mixing local ore with richer ore from Missouri, they began using less local ore. Astronomic rises in freight rates during the Civil War, mechanical and financial problems with the blast furnace, and a disastrous explosion in the late 1870s all helped end the operation.

Renewed mining of the Martin County iron deposits began around 1900 and provided ore to furnaces in southern Ohio. Ferrosilicon—iron and silicon used in separation of certain industrial materials by flotation—was the end product. Small mines opened throughout the hills south and northeast of Shoals, but talk of restarting the Ironton mill led nowhere.

### House Rock, Jug Rock, and Sandstone Cliffs

Vertical cliffs 20 to 50 feet high are common where the Mansfield formation is exposed in the deep valley of the East Fork White River at Shoals. House Rock and Jug Rock have attracted visitors since the early 1800s. House Rock is on the east bank of the river, north of U.S. 50 and Shoals. Two sets of intersecting fractures in the sandstone created the grotto in the high cliff. Jug Rock is west of the river, north of U.S. 50, near the bridge. It is shaped like a giant mushroom. Erosion along fracture surfaces separated it from the main cliff. Jug Rock was part of an early town park and the site of many weekend outings; it is now a state nature preserve.

Overlook Park west of Jug Rock provides an excellent view of the valley of the East Fork White River. The town of Shoals got its name from the riffles where the river crosses a particularly hard bed of sandstone in the Mansfield formation.

*Jug Rock, an erosional remnant of the Mansfield formation along the East Fork White River at Shoals.*

### Health Spas in the Hills of Martin County

Indian Springs, 8 miles north of Shoals, seep from the west bank of Sulphur Creek, producing water with dissolved sulfates from the underlying gypsum beds. The water issues from fractures in the Sample sandstone. According to some accounts, commercial health resorts began in 1814 and continued into the late 1800s.

Trinity Springs, 3 miles southeast of Indian Springs near Indian Creek, resemble Indian Springs. They produce sulfurous water loaded with minerals but without sulfates. The resort hotel operated from the 1840s until it burned in 1863. Today, an old road leaves Indiana 450 on the south side of the bridge over Indian Creek and leads east to a pond that covers the old springs. Weeds and brush hide sandstone ledges covered with the graffiti of countless visitors.

La Salle Spring, with sulfate waters, was 2 miles northeast of Trinity Springs on the north bank of the East Fork White River. A hotel stood on the bluff above the river in the early 1900s. Elliott Springs, north of Willow Valley, also produced sulfate water, which its owner bottled and sold.

### Early Clay Mines of Martin County

Clay was mined less than 1 mile south of the old Indian Springs Hotel around the turn of the century. An entrance in a cliff of Pennsylvanian rocks featured a tram system for removing the clay, which was used to make pottery. Cheaper and better sources of clay put this mine out of business before 1904. Other mines operated at Dover Hill before 1900.

*An early view of the mineral spring area at Trinity Springs.* —Mark J. Camp Collection

# U.S. 150
## New Albany—Shoals
### 59 MILES

U.S. 150 begins in the Ohio River valley and ends on bedrock hills in the unglaciated region of south-central Indiana. The eastern half of the route crosses the drainage basins of small creeks that flow directly south to the Ohio River. The western half of the route crosses the basins of the Patoka and Lost Rivers, which flow west.

Between the Ohio River and the area 4 miles to the west, U.S. 150 shares its roadway with I-64. They pass from a terrace of glacial outwash at the edge of the river valley to the bedrock hilltops of the Norman upland, formed from rocks of the middle Mississippian Borden group of formations. The steep slope is the Knobstone escarpment. U.S. 150 continues across the Norman upland for 7 miles between I-64 and the area 1 mile west of Galena.

U.S. 150 angles across 39 miles of bedrock hills in the Mitchell plain between the area 1 mile west of Galena and that around Prospect. The

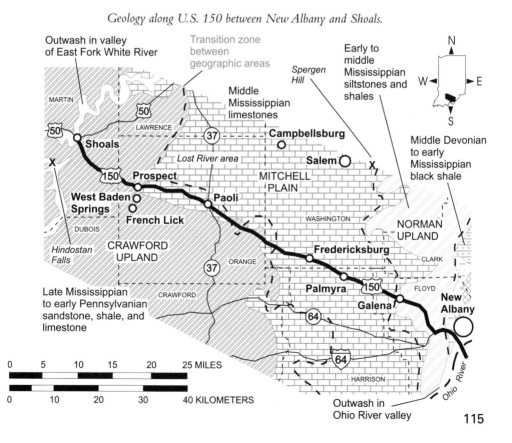

*Geology along U.S. 150 between New Albany and Shoals.*

bedrock is limestone deposited during middle Mississippian time, parts of the Sanders and Blue River groups of formations. Sinkholes are locally abundant, especially between Palmyra and the Blue River valley at Fredericksburg.

The flat valley floor at Prospect is evidence of the outwash fill in the waterways that once drained the melting glaciers. A short side trip south of Prospect leads to West Baden Springs and French Lick, an area famous for its mineral springs.

U.S. 150 crosses 9 miles of bedrock hills, part of the Crawford upland between Prospect and Shoals. They are eroded in sandstones, shales, and limestones deposited during late Mississippian and early Pennsylvanian time. Just west of Prospect, U.S. 150 twice crosses the Lost River valley. At Shoals, the highway enters the East Fork White River valley.

### Salem—Early Quarries, Spergen Hill, and Caves

A side trip north from Palmyra on Indiana 135 leads to Salem, a center of early stone quarrying. The first quarry opened on the west side of the Blue River. It provided stone for the Washington County courthouse in Salem, the state house in Georgia, the New Jersey capitol, and the Cincinnati courthouse, among many other important structures.

The quarry of the Salem Lime and Stone Company never looked much like its counterparts in the Bloomington-Bedford belt because no piles of discarded limestone blocks surrounded it. The company thriftily used all this material to make lime. The old kilns still stand.

A nearby quarry produced crushed stone, mainly for railroad ballast. It came from the Harrodsburg limestone below the Salem limestone. This quarry spread into the original quarry. Indiana 135 crosses another old quarry on the south edge of town. A quarry that opened in 1974 to produce crushed stone from the Ste. Genevieve limestone is 7 miles west of Salem on Indiana 56.

Spergen Hill, a famous fossil-collecting locality of the late 1800s, is 4 miles east of Salem at Harristown. A cut along the former New Albany & Salem Railroad, later the Monon Railroad, exposed a sequence of 15 to 20 feet of rocks that belongs to the Sanders group. As usual, the Salem limestone is full of fossils.

*Generalized surface profile along U.S. 150.*

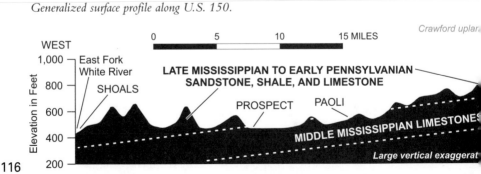

James Hall of the New York Geological Survey collected more than seventy-five species of minute brachiopods, clams, snails, worms, blastoids, and foraminifera at Spergen Hill during the 1850s. All the specimens were tiny examples of their kind and were then interpreted as dwarf animals that grew in an environment somehow not conducive to normal shell growth. Their small size is now attributed to the sorting action of waves in the shallow Mississippian sea. Earlier workers apparently did not notice an abundance of small fragments of larger animals.

The countryside around Salem abounds in caves and springs, typical karst terrain. Even so, water supply has been a recurring problem for Salem. The first municipal system got its water from Morris Springs west of town beginning in 1885. A pipe laid to Indian Springs northwest of town in 1910 supplemented that supply. In 1930 additional water was obtained from springs in Henderson Park, also northwest of town. Each of the springs flowed from a cave and all were the sites of gristmills in the early 1800s. Two reservoirs have been dug since then to satisfy the needs of a growing community.

You can see cave springs at Cave River Valley Park, 3 miles north of Campbellsburg, off Indiana 60. This area is also called Clifty and was the site of an early mill. It contains six explored caves, most notably Endless and River Caves, and has a deep valley with steep limestone walls. Becks Mill, southwest of town, drew its power from water flowing from the mouth of Clicks Cave. The old mill, built in the 1860s, still stands.

### The Home of Pluto Water

French Lick began as a health resort to exploit mineral springs and is still the most impressive resort in the state. The springs flow from the contact where the Mansfield formation overlies formations of the West Baden group. The name French Lick came from French explorers who noted that the natural salt licks attracted an abundance of wildlife. In the late 1830s, people came to drink and bathe in the supposedly curative waters. The popular key to a healthy life was to drink plenty of mineral water and exercise daily. By 1908 two railroads brought visitors to the growing area.

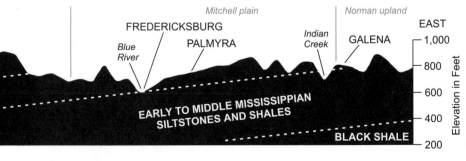

*Clicks Cave lies in the hillside behind Becks Mill, southwest of Salem. Water is flowing from the mouth of the cave.*

The first hotel opened around 1836 and burned in 1897. A competing hotel, erected in 1852 at West Baden Springs, burned in 1901. Both were rebuilt in sumptuous fashion. French Lick's hotel still serves visitors; West Baden Springs's architectural wonder has been partly restored to its former glory. Visitors still come in large numbers, and the local tourist railroad offers many scenic views.

Pluto Springs, the largest of those in the neighborhood, is near the hotel. In the early 1900s, a bottling operation made Pluto Water a household name to the health-conscious Midwesterner. The water is rich in the sulfates of calcium, sodium, and magnesium, the last of which is better known as epsom salt. The bottling operation expanded in the 1940s, but declining sales led to its demise in the 1970s. You can still get Pluto Water if you bring your own container. Similar waters flow from many springs nearby.

### Whetstones and Grindstones

Lower Pennsylvanian rocks yielded whetstones from a rock called Hindostan stone, named after the town of Hindostan Falls in Martin County. Hindostan stone is a siltstone about 60 to 100 feet above the base of the Mansfield formation. Whetstone manufacturers also used the uppermost sandstone of the West Baden group, the Elwren formation. Coarse whetstones came from the layers with the lightest color.

The best whetstone rock comes in layers as much as 3 feet thick. The preferred stone was pale, but gray, rust, orange, and banded varieties also found wide use. The reddish siltstones were carved into knickknacks sold in the French Lick Creek valley. Sledgehammers and chisels were used to split slabs of whetstone from cliff faces and break them into rough pieces. Teams of horses drove gang saws that trimmed the rocks. The rough whetstones were hauled 15 miles on wagons or flatboats down the Lost River to a finishing mill at Hindostan Falls on the East Fork White River. The finished whetstones went by flatboat to New Orleans and by ship to Europe.

Whetstones were later made in four mills near French Lick, where teams of horses turned large cast-iron wheels covered with coarse sand and water that ground the raw stone smooth. The Braxton Brothers, who operated one of the larger quarries in the French Lick Creek valley, also ran a steam mill in Paoli. Another steam mill was in Orangeville. At least six quarries and many seasonal pits worked the whetstone layers in the French Lick area during the 1890s.

Operations at Moore's Quarry in the valley of French Lick Creek revealed the fossil trunk of a Pennsylvanian tree fern preserved in its original vertical position to a height of at least 6 feet. It is tempting to suppose that the tree was buried suddenly in a catastrophic dump of sediment, perhaps during a flood. The Dougherty and Osborn Quarries also yielded plentiful plant fossils, so many that they led to early abandonment of the Dougherty Quarry. Braxton Quarry near French Lick yielded two fossil insect wings. The numerous trace fossils on the bedding surfaces include the tracks of amphibians, the earliest land vertebrates.

It seems likely that the whetstone beds record intertidal deposition along the western coastline of the land mass that existed in the Appalachian area during Pennsylvanian time. This part of Indiana was then a shallow inland sea that accumulated sediment layers with each rising tide. Some of the layers appear to have been above sea level long enough for land plants to grow. A careful study of the thin siltstone layers may someday provide information about the tides of Pennsylvanian time.

### Other Orange County Quarries

U.S. 150 passes quarries southwest and northwest of Paoli that expose the Blue River and West Baden groups. The quarries produce crushed stone from the Paoli and Ste. Genevieve limestones. Crushed stone is also the major product of a quarry east of town. An old underground mine there is now used for storage.

An abandoned quarry at Abydel once supplied ground limestone from the St. Louis formation to a glassworks in Harrison County. Another quarry still operates nearby. A quarry beside Indiana 550 southwest of Shoals produced sandstone and conglomerate from the Mansfield formation for use as refractory sand.

### Hindostan Falls

Indiana 550 leads to the Hindostan State Fish and Wildlife Area, once the site of Hindostan Falls, a former Martin county seat. At low water, a fractured ledge of sandstone of the Pennsylvanian Mansfield formation stretches nearly across the channel just below the arcuate falls. Look for the square holes in the rock that once anchored the foundation timbers of the whetstone mill. The mill and town became history when an epidemic nearly wiped out the people during the 1820s.

The sandstone ledge also contains many more-or-less cylindrical potholes that the modern stream eroded. Rippled bedding surfaces are souvenirs of the original depositional environment back in Pennsylvanian time.

# Indiana 37
## Indianapolis—Tell City
**153 MILES**

Indiana 37 crosses a few miles of outwash and till near Indianapolis, then passes onto unglaciated bedrock for most of its route to the Ohio River. The long route between Indianapolis and northern Crawford County is in the drainage basin of the White River. The highway crosses the basins of several small streams that flow directly to the Ohio River between northern Crawford County and Tell City.

Indiana 37 crosses 28 miles of glacial deposits laid down during the Wisconsinan ice age between I-465 at Indianapolis and the area 4 miles south of Martinsville. The glacial deposits are between 50 and 150 feet thick, the deepest portions being filled valleys. Most of the route parallels the West Fork White River along the east side of its valley, which floods of meltwater eroded and filled with outwash. The road also crosses a few areas of sand dunes blown against the valley wall, now so covered with vegetation that no open sand is visible.

The hills a few miles southwest of I-465 are actually kames, mounds of sand and gravel. They were deposited as outwash on the glacier, then let down onto the landscape as the ice melted. Several rise as much as 120 feet above the valley floor. These are as large and impressive as any kames anywhere.

The dividing line between the Tipton till plain to the north and the Norman upland to the south is 4 miles north of Martinsville. Glacial till completely covers the bedrock north of the line. Till covers some of the hilltops in the Norman upland but does not obscure the eroded bedrock landscape.

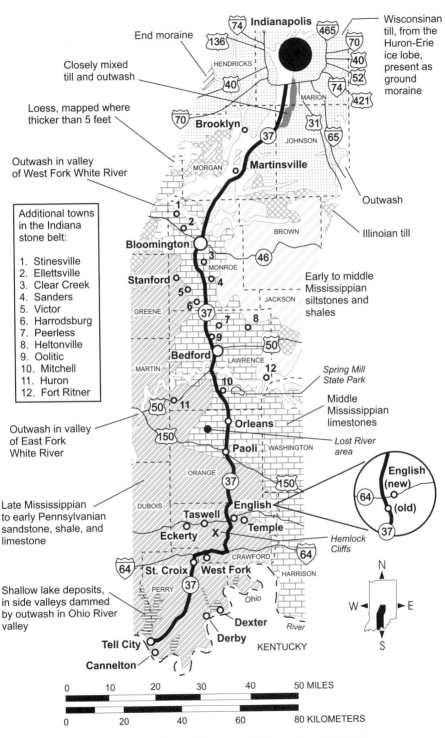

*Geology along Indiana 37 between Indianapolis and Tell City.*

*An abandoned quarry in the Salem limestone on the north side of Bloomington.*

Between the area 4 miles south of Martinsville and that just south of Paoli, Indiana 37 winds across 62 miles of bedrock hills, most of which never felt the scrape of glacial ice.

Most of the rocks in southern Morgan and northern Monroe Counties are siltstones and shales of the middle Mississippian Borden group. The landscape eroded on them is part of the Norman upland. Watch just south of Martinsville, where Maxwell Hill west of the highway and Thacker Ridge east of the highway provide the first view of the Norman upland. A few small patches of Illinoian till cover some of the upland areas in extreme southern Morgan County. The thin till cover was once much broader but is mostly lost to erosion.

The landscape between northern Monroe County and the Paoli area is eroded in limestones of the middle Mississippian Sanders and Blue River groups. This area is part of the Mitchell plain. Watch for sinkholes and

*Generalized surface and bedrock profiles along Indiana 37.*

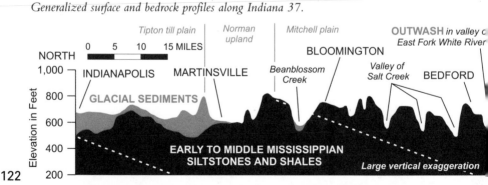

dimension stone quarries. A few miles north of Bloomington, Indiana 37 crosses the valley of Beanblossom Creek with its fill of glacial outwash.

The quarries along the roadside at the junction with Indiana 46 work limestones in the Sanders group of formations. They are at the northern edge of the great building-stone belt in the Bloomington-Bedford area. Other quarries abound along and near the highway, especially near Oolitic, just north of Bedford.

Areas north and west of Oolitic, south of Bedford, southeast of Mitchell, and around Orleans have some of the finest sinkhole landscapes in the world. Reddish terra rossa soils, the weathered accumulation from clay impurities in limestones, become conspicuous a half-mile south of the junction with Indiana 48.

A roadcut in the St. Louis limestone on the southern outskirts of Bloomington shows a small flexure, perhaps due to differential settling of the original sediments. Watch a bit farther south for roadcuts that expose the Salem limestone and the underlying Harrodsburg limestone. A long roadcut north of Harrodsburg exposed almost the entire thickness of the Harrodsburg limestone, with a cap of Salem limestone. The road to Monroe Lake (Monroe Reservoir) passes through excellent roadcuts in the Sanders group, some of which contain well-preserved crinoid fossils. The same sequence of rocks appears just south of the line between Monroe and Lawrence Counties.

An excavation in soil that filled a crevice in the bedrock 3 miles south of the line between Monroe and Lawrence Counties disclosed a trove of Pleistocene mammal bones. They included bones and teeth of dire wolves, saber-toothed tigers, and a panther. The animals probably fell into a cave.

More than 50 feet of glacial lake sediments lie beneath the flat valley floor of Salt Creek just north of Oolitic. Deep deposits of glacial outwash in the West Fork White River impounded its tributary, Salt Creek, to make the lake.

Indiana 37 crosses the East Fork White River on the south side of Bedford. Torrents of meltwater poured through this valley as the great glaciers were melting. They entrenched the river at Bedford some 150 feet below the surface of the Mitchell plain, then left its floor deeply filled with outwash.

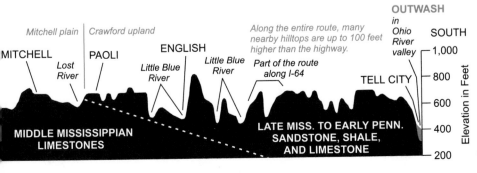

123

*Roadcut in St. Louis limestone, Indiana 37 between Oolitic and Bedford.*

Indiana 37 crosses 63 miles of upper Mississippian and lower Pennsylvanian sandstones, shales, and limestones between the area 1.5 miles south of Paoli and Tell City. The landscape eroded in them is the Crawford upland. It ends at the Chester escarpment. A view to the northeast from the top of the escarpment shows the Mitchell plain with its rash of as many as one thousand sinkholes per square mile.

Hilands Overlook, 1.5 miles south of English, offers a good view of the Crawford upland and its numerous small stream valleys. This landscape is entirely the work of stream erosion, with no help from glaciers.

High rock walls at the interchange with I-64 offer excellent exposures of the rocks from the Sample sandstone at the base through the Hardinsburg formation at the top. South of I-64, Indiana 37 crosses late Mississippian rocks of the Raccoon Creek group at St. Croix. An abandoned quarry near West Fork, on Indiana 62 east of St. Croix, exposes 40 feet of Tar Springs formation and 39 feet of Glen Dean limestone.

No solid bedrock appears along the road between St. Croix and Tell City. Occasional deeply eroded roadbanks in many colors suggest the presence of soft and easily erodible Pennsylvanian rocks. Elevations of the hilltops decline southward from 830 feet near Paoli to 600 feet at Tell City.

At Tell City, Indiana 37 descends the bedrock uplands into the Ohio River valley. A good exposure of the Mansfield formation appears along Indiana 66, behind the commercial strip. Tell City stands on a terrace of glacial outwash sands and gravels at an elevation of 400 feet. The outwash is more than 100 feet thick.

## Edges of the Great Ice Sheets—the Martinsville Area

Interpreting the soil and glacial sediments around the town of Martinsville and the West Fork White River is like trying to complete a jigsaw puzzle that lacks most of its pieces. Both the Illinoian and Wisconsinan ice sheets stalled against the Knobstone uplands of south-central Indiana. The ice split into two lobes that passed on either side of south-central Indiana.

Areas that were between ice lobes are invariably hard to study because the tills and outwashes are generally mixed. That happened at Martinsville, where various combinations of tills, outwashes, and recent stream sediments plaster the hills and fill the valleys. The glacial sediments locally approach 120 feet in thickness.

Glacial till and Borden shales exposed in the hillside just east of the plant provided raw material for the Adams Brick Company, one of the largest soft clay brick operations in Indiana. The yellowish clay and shale were mixed one part clay to two parts shale and fired to make a daily quota of about forty thousand bricks in 1904. The Martinsville Brick Company opened next to the Adams company in 1909. Shipments of Pennsylvanian clay came from pits near Brazil and later Switz City. The brick business declined in the 1970s. Its remnants are along Blue Bluff road, north of Martinsville. Another brick plant operated near Brooklyn and one continues production near Mooresville.

Martinsville was known around the turn of the century for its mineral waters and health resorts. A well drilled for gas in 1887 produced salty artesian water instead. Several sanitariums promptly went into business, nearly doubling the population of Martinsville between 1890 and 1900. Five resorts were in operation by the turn of the century, all within easy carriage ride of the railroad depot, and all complete with physicians and piped mineral water.

## Leesville Anticline—An Oil and Gas Trap

The long arch of the Leesville anticline stretches from northern Monroe County to northern Orange County. It is 1 to 2 miles west of the Mt. Carmel fault and more or less parallel to Indiana 37. Five folded domes along this trend probably formed as the younger rocks sagged over buried Silurian reefs. They inspired a search for oil and gas.

If any oil or gas exists in rock, an anticline or dome will probably trap it. Petroleum is lighter than water, so it floats up through pore spaces within the rocks until it reaches an impermeable layer, generally shale. Then it continues to move beneath the shale until it reaches a fold that blocks any further rise. Three of the domes along the Leesville anticline did yield oil or gas.

The Ohio Oil Company discovered the Unionville gas field in 1929. The gas came from a middle Devonian limestone at a depth of some 750 to 900 feet. The field produced an estimated 1.5 billion cubic feet of gas before

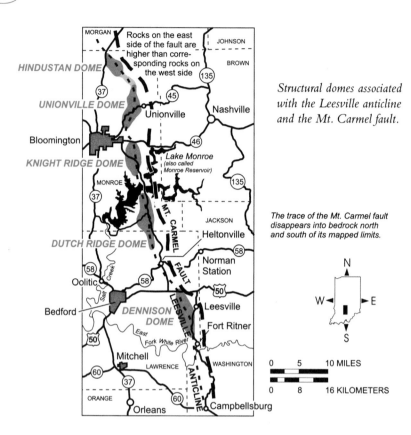

*Structural domes associated with the Leesville anticline and the Mt. Carmel fault.*

The trace of the Mt. Carmel fault disappears into bedrock north and south of its mapped limits.

it was converted to a gas storage reservoir in 1954. A depleted gas field provides a much safer place to store gas than surface tanks. Two wells drilled through the gas reservoir and into the deeper Trenton limestone of Ordovician age began producing small amounts of oil in 1987.

The Dutch Ridge dome was first drilled in 1910, but the early wells were not profitable. Deeper drilling later found oil in the Trenton formation. The Bartlettsville pool began production in 1951, and pumping continues. Production of natural gas from Devonian limestones at the Dennison dome began in the 1920s, but the field later became a gas storage reservoir. Hindustan dome, which Indiana 37 crosses in northern Monroe County, connects to the Unionville dome to the south, and the two operate as one storage field.

### A Spelunker's Delight—The Bloomington-Bedford Region

Many sinkholes pit the countryside west of Indiana 37, between Bloomington and Bedford. Where sinkholes abound, so do caves, most of which become sinkholes when they ultimately collapse.

The better-known caves in the Bloomington area include Coan's, Eller's, Goode's, Grotto, Keyhole, Saltpeter, and Wayne's, all along Indiana 45 between Bloomington and Stanford. Dog Hill, Donnehue's, Ramsey, Shiloh, and Sullivan's caves are among the better-known caves in the Bedford area. Sullivan's Cave contains one room that is 50 feet high and 100 feet wide, one of the largest in the state. Most of the caves are either within the St. Louis limestone or at its contact with the overlying Salem limestone.

## Virginia Furnace

A small mound of rubble in the southwestern corner of Monroe County, on the floodplain of Indian Creek south of Stanford, is all that remains of the earliest blast furnace in southern Indiana, the second oldest in the state. The Randolph Ross & Sons' Virginia Iron Works fired it up in 1839, then abandoned it five years later. The company made pig iron from iron-oxide cemented sandstones of Pennsylvanian age. Farmers collected the ore from deposits near the village of Cincinnati in Greene County and hauled it to the furnace. Flux came from local limestone. Some of the iron was cast into kettles and other household implements. The difficulty of shipping the pig iron over poor wagon roads all the way to New Albany and Louisville contributed to the demise of the enterprise. Even today the site is remote.

## Clear Creek Valley–Victor–Sanders Building Stone District

Numerous quarries that dot the countryside between Clear Creek and Harrodsburg worked the Salem limestone, which is at the surface and as much as 50 feet thick. Solution cavities that reach deep into the formation make the upper part unfit for use.

Quarrying began in the Sanders district in 1888, when the Oolitic Stone Company of Indiana started a pit just northwest of Sanders. By 1905 this company had opened other quarries and was using the latest technology. They used compressed air to drive channelers, new machines that required fewer workers. Compressed air also enabled the derricks to hoist stone all the time, without having to also lower coal to power them. The company was also the first to use hoses to strip loose overburden and clean off exposed ledges. In 1905 the firm employed a workforce of about one hundred men at the quarries and mill.

During the decades just before and after 1900, at least fourteen companies started quarrying dimension stone in the general area of the Clear Creek valley, Sanders, and Victor. Most of those quarries are now closed, filled with water, and overgrown, but a few remain in business. Watch for quarries and mills along Tapp and Rockport roads east of the Indiana 37 bypass.

*Quarry in Salem limestone along Tapp Road east of Indiana 37, south side of Bloomington.*

### Quarrying around Bedford

The area around Bedford rapidly became the center of the southern part of the building-stone belt. Few quarries are within the city, but several surround it. The most successful ones are to the northwest on Buff Ridge, west of Salt Creek, and in Dark Hollow, west of Oolitic.

Quarries in the Buff Ridge district opened in 1879 and operated through the late 1880s. The quarries of the original Hoosier Stone and Perry Matthews & Buskirk Stone companies developed into the largest in the stone belt. The Hoosier Quarry opened in 1879, just north of Oolitic. Different colors and textures of stone were available among the many pits. The quarries crushed the waste rock and sold it for road and railroad ballast. The Oolitic Mill was the largest in the state, one of the largest in the country.

The quarry of the Perry Matthews & Buskirk Stone Company opened ten years after the Hoosier Quarry and a half-mile east of it. It began as several small quarries that coalesced into a huge pit. Kilns at its center produced lime from the waste rock. This quarry supplied the stone facing for the Empire State Building.

The Dark Hollow district began to produce Salem limestone in 1878. The first quarry was on the south side of Dark Hollow valley, near its junction with Salt Creek. It furnished the stone for the state house in Indianapolis. Many quarries started, but most closed within a few years.

A number of other quarries started at several places around Bedford. North of town, operations near Reeds Station and Peerless continued through the 1890s and into the early 1900s. The Blue Hole Quarry on the east side of Bedford opened in 1850. It was one of the first in the region and became a major operation in 1878, finally closing in the 1920s. Quarries were also located at Walner, northeast of Bedford, and at Heltonville.

*A historical marker in downtown Oolitic.*

A number of quarries on the south side of Bedford, along the old Monon Railroad, closed by the 1890s. These are thought to be some of the earliest quarries because they show no sign of machine channeling. The stone must have been worked by hand. Kilns burned all the waste rock to make lime, leaving no piles.

Southwest of Bedford were the quarries of the Spider Creek district, along the former Milwaukee Railroad. The first opened in 1888. Quarries once operated southeast of Bedford along Tanyard Creek, in Mitchell Hollow, in the Fort Ritner area, and along Rock Lick Branch. The first opened in 1860. For many years all the stone was quarried by hand, then hauled in wagons to the Fort Ritner railroad depot for shipment to nearby towns. The Tanyard Creek quarries blossomed in the early 1890s when a railroad opened to Bedford.

Only a few quarries still operate around Bedford, and they are idle during the winter months. The glory years of the stone industry passed with the early decades of the twentieth century, but the old pits will probably remain for millions of years.

## Mitchell and Spring Mill State Park

A modern cement plant on the northeast side of Mitchell uses Salem limestone and the overlying St. Louis limestone. Both come from a quarry that has operated since 1902 when it opened as property of the Lehigh Portland Cement Company of Allentown, Pennsylvania. Shale mined from Borden group rocks at nearby Blue Lick provides the clay.

Spring Mill State Park is a few miles east of Mitchell off Indiana 60. The road crosses the Mitchell plain, passing numerous sinkholes. They are easiest to see when the trees are bare.

An abandoned quarry and lime kiln along Mill Creek near the Spring Mill Lake dam are the remains of a cement plant. Salem limestone is the oldest rock in the park; the overlying St. Louis limestone is exposed in the upland areas. An old lime kiln stands on the hill above the pioneer village.

Water flowing from Hamer's and Donaldson's Caves supplies Mill Creek, which drains north into the East Fork White River. A village grew up around the gristmill as early as 1815. The entrance to Hamer's Cave is west of the restored pioneer village. A stream flows from the mouth of the cave and through a flume to the reconstructed gristmill made of blocks of St. Louis limestone.

Donaldson's Cave is at the end of a rocky gorge in the center of the park. Another stream emerges from it and flows into Mill Creek. Sets of perpendicular fractures in the St. Louis limestone controlled development of Donaldson's Cave, explaining its many parallel passages and right-angle bends. Bronson's and Twin Caves are openings into Donaldson's Cave that formed where its roof collapsed. Steps that descend into a deep sinkhole lead into Twin Caves, where an underground stream flows from one cave, across the bottom of the sink, and into another cave in the opposite wall. Creation of the park in the 1920s required damming Mill Creek to make Spring Mill

*A small sinkhole across from the entrance to Spring Mill State Park, Indiana 60.*

*Donaldson's Cave in Spring Mill State Park. Bring a flashlight to explore part of this cave along the elevated boardwalk.*

Lake for recreational use. Most of the drainage is through caverns, which manifest themselves in a series of springs and swallow holes east of Spring Mill Lake and in the sinkholes south of Mill Creek valley.

### Quarrying in the Orleans Area

The Mississippian Ste. Genevieve limestone was quarried near Orleans and Orangeville in the 1870s. The rock was called firestone because so much was used in hearths. The Orangeville Mill used millstones made from chert concretions from the Ste. Genevieve limestone and the overlying red clay in its early days.

The abandoned sandstone quarry of the Hindostan Whetstone Company is west of Orleans. The sandstone caps some of the hills around Orleans. A quarry in the Ste. Genevieve and Paoli limestones northwest of Orleans closed in 1983 after thirty years of operation. It supplied limestone for use in the scrubbers that strip sulfur dioxide from the stack gases at the power plant at Petersburg. A newer quarry is just south of the former pit.

### Lost River

South of Orleans, Indiana 37 crosses the dry channel of Lost River, which lost its flow to caverns. Lost River and its tributaries drain an area of more than 350 square miles, starting at the junction of two small creeks near

*Ste. Genevieve and Paoli limestones form the walls of this quarry on the northwest edge of Orleans.*

Smedley in Washington County. The north and south forks join near Claysville to become a stream that flows across part of the Mitchell plain, where a layer of impermeable clay keeps the water on the surface. Beginning 1 mile east of Indiana 37, Lost River sinks through swallow holes into caverns. Its dry channel meanders for 22 miles west of Indiana 37, then again acquires a stream near Orangeville. Most of the water from Lost River follows a nearly straight route from swallow holes along the upper river to a big spring south of Orangeville, a distance of 8 miles.

Below the spring, Lost River flows through a deeply entrenched valley that winds to the East Fork White River in Martin County. During times of excessive rainfall, water flows along the normally dry streambed because the caverns below are completely full. A tributary to Lost River surfaces as another, more accessible spring at the crossroads in Orangeville, but it is not part of the main channel. Known as Orangeville Rise, this spring is a National Natural Landmark.

Wesley Chapel Gulf is a sinkhole that covers a third of an acre and is about 350 feet deep. The cavern collapse that opened it revealed a network of passageways dissolved into the Ste. Genevieve limestone. Part of the water from Lost River rises in the southeastern corner of the sinkhole, where floating debris often covers it. The water flows along the southern edge of

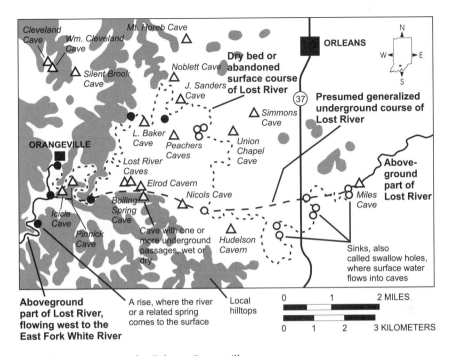

Cleveland Cave
Wm. Cleveland Cave
Mt. Horeb Cave
Silent Brook Cave
Noblett Cave
J. Sanders Cave
**Dry bed or abandoned surface course of Lost River**
ORLEANS

N
W ◄──►E
S

Simmons Cave

37
**Presumed generalized underground course of Lost River**

ORANGEVILLE
L. Baker Cave
Peachers Caves
Union Chapel Cave

**Above-ground part of Lost River**

Lost River Caves
Elrod Cavern
Nicols Cave
Boiling Spring Cave
Icicle Cave
Pinnick Cave
Cave with one or more underground passages, wet or dry
Hudelson Cavern

Miles Cave

Sinks, also called swallow holes, where surface water flows into caves

**Aboveground part of Lost River, flowing west to the East Fork White River**

A rise, where the river or a related spring comes to the surface

Local hilltops

| 0 | 1 | 2 MILES |
|---|---|---|

| 0 | 1 | 2 | 3 KILOMETERS |
|---|---|---|---|

*The Lost River in the Orleans-Orangeville area.* —Modified from Powell, 1961

*The dry channel of the Lost River between Orangeville and Indiana 37.*

*Orangeville Rise, where water from a tributary to the Lost River comes back to the surface.*

the sinkhole, then disappears underground at Wesley Chapel Gulf Cave. The entrance to Elrod Cave is in the northwest wall of the same sinkhole. It opens into a large room and another connection with the Lost River system.

## Paoli Mineral Springs

The Paoli Mineral Springs was actually a well drilled in 1892 that produced warm mineral water instead of oil. The water was so salty and loaded with calcium sulfate that it tasted bad, so people naturally concluded that it must have some medicinal value. The water was bottled as well as piped to the Mineral Springs Hotel. In 1895 another well drilled along Lick Creek furnished enough water to enable the hotel to grow to 100 guest rooms and several baths. It operated with amazing longevity into the 1950s. The old three-story brick and stone Mineral Springs Hotel still stands on the south side of the public square.

## Hemlock Cliffs

Hemlock Cliffs is in the Hoosier National Forest, west of Indiana 37 between Grantsburg and I-64. Take Union Chapel Road and follow the signs.

*The Mineral Springs Hotel, a former health spa, in Paoli.*

The Big Clifty sandstone of Mississippian age eroded into overhanging cliffs that make shelter caves arranged around a box canyon. Archaeological excavations show the area was well known to the Indians. Many similar scenic spots lie hidden in the hills of Crawford County. Look closely along Indiana 37 south of Union Chapel Road for small caves eroded in rocks of the West Baden group along a tributary to the Little Blue River. When the trees are bare, watch for a table rock of sandstone known locally as Salt Shake Rock.

The limestones are full of fossils, mostly segments of crinoid stems, brachiopods, and blastoids. Some of the bryozoans are the usual lacy fans, others are shaped like big screws. Look on the bedding surfaces in the sandstones for trace fossils, mostly tracks and trails of tiny footprints.

### The English Area

English originally stood where Camp Fork, Bird Hollow, Brownstown, and Dog Creeks join to become the Little Blue River. Flooding was part of the local lifestyle. After a series of especially disastrous floods in the 1990s, the town moved northeast to higher ground along Indiana 64.

Elk Springs, on the north side of town, inspired the construction of a large hotel and sanitarium in 1885. It burned in 1889, and later the spring

*Small shelter caves in West Baden group rocks along the Little Blue River, north of Sulphur.*

*Mississippian Glen Dean limestone overlies the Hardinsburg formation in this quarry north of Eckerty along Indiana 145.*

dried up. A well drilled in the public park in 1899 produced artesian mineral water.

The abandoned Hill Quarry and mill of the French Lick Sandstone Company is west of English on Indiana 64, just east of Taswell. They produced colorful Pennsylvanian sandstones for veneer and ornamental uses in the 1960s. The Spring Valley Sandstone Company operated a similar quarry at Westall.

A nature preserve just southeast of Taswell, off the road to Mifflin, features a natural bridge that formed as most of a cave collapsed, leaving just a remnant of its roof standing. A nearby cave yielded more than 100,000 animal bones, including those of a peccary and a dire wolf, which lived in this area during the ice ages.

A large quarry along Fleming Creek, 2.5 miles north of Eckerty, is in the Glen Dean and Hardinsburg limestones. It also includes an underground limestone mine that reaches the Haney limestone. Another quarry, at Temple, reaches formations of the Blue River group. Crushed stone is the main product.

### Derby-Dexter Area—Quarries and a Meander Scar

The Ohio River town of Derby is a short side trip east on Indiana 70, which descends from a terrace of glacial outwash. Quarries and roadcuts near Derby expose limestones, sandstones, and shales of the Stephensport group, from the Beech Creek limestone through the Glen Dean limestone. The large quarry west of town operated from 1954 to 1982, when it was converted to stone storage. Three underground mines worked the Ste. Genevieve, Haney, and Glen Dean limestones.

Upriver, along Indiana 66 just north of Dexter, is a prominent arcuate meander scar, once a tight bend of the Ohio River. The Ohio River took a shortcut across the neck of the bend, then deposited sediments that converted the bend into a lake, now long since filled. Sand blown from the floodplain built a ridge that extends to the river south of Dexter. Indiana 66 north of Dexter crosses the former island that stood within the abandoned meander loop.

### First Coal West of the Alleghenies

Indiana 37 ends at Tell City on the floodplain of the Ohio River. Tell City and adjacent Cannelton are on the eastern edge of the Wabash lowland and of the coal beds of southwestern Indiana.

Nicholas J. Roosevelt, the great-uncle of Theodore Roosevelt and an associate of Robert Fulton of steamboat fame, discovered a coal seam in the Ohio River bluff while surveying the river from a flatboat. That was in 1809. He foresaw that coal would eventually replace wood as the fuel for steam engines and persuaded local settlers to pile some coal on the riverbank.

He returned in 1811 on the maiden voyage of the steamboat *New Orleans*, picked up the coal, and bought the property that contained the seam. But the site never became a mine because more and better coal was available elsewhere. Today, this coal seam is nearly hidden along the railroad tracks south of town.

By the 1820s settlers intent on mining coal were moving into the region. In 1837 eastern investors organized the American Cannel Coal Company. They purchased more than 6,000 acres of coal lands and platted a company town called Coal Haven. It was partly built and then mostly destroyed in a fire two years later. Reorganization in the 1840s led to the development of another town, eventually known as Cannelton. Cannel coal is rare, even in this place where it named a town. But bituminous coal was plentiful and brought prosperity to the river cities.

By the 1870s stoneware, fruit jars, and sewer pipe were produced from thick clay seams within the same formations that contained coal at Cannelton and Tell City. Clay seams at Troy furnished the raw material for the popular Troy Ware.

Quarries in the Mansfield formation at Cannelton furnished sandstone for locks on the Green River in Kentucky and many local buildings, includ-

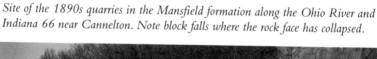

*Site of the 1890s quarries in the Mansfield formation along the Ohio River and Indiana 66 near Cannelton. Note block falls where the rock face has collapsed.*

*Crossbedded sandstone of the Mansfield formation at Lafayette Spring.*

ing the historic Cannelton cotton mill. Three companies extracted Mississippian sandstones during the 1890s for use in bridge piers and building foundations.

The massive overhanging cliffs above the Ohio River southeast of Cannelton on Indiana 66 expose the Mansfield sandstone. Park at the Cannelton Locks observation area for a great view of the river and its surroundings. The shale beds at the base of the cliffs contain trace fossils, mainly trails and burrows; the overlying sandstone also contains plant fossils and more trace fossils. Look for huge fallen blocks of Mansfield sandstone.

Lafayette Spring flows from the base of the same sandstone cliff farther east on Indiana 66. Springs commonly flow from the base of a thick layer of sandstone. Pore spaces between the sand grains store water, which cannot seep farther down if a layer of impervious shale is beneath the sandstone. So the water leaks out of the base of the sandstone.

# Indiana 46
## Columbus—Spencer
**51 MILES**

Indiana 46 between Columbus and Spencer is rather like a pair of geological bookends—it begins and ends on partly glaciated hills, with a long stretch of unglaciated hills in between. This part of the highway is completely within the greater White River drainage basin, going from the East Fork to the West Fork White River.

Columbus is within the valley of the East Fork White River, which is part of the Scottsburg lowland and has glacial outwash in its floor. The valley is 5 miles wide at Columbus and the outwash is 50 to 100 feet deep. Those floods of meltwater must have been truly massive. Indiana 46 crosses 2 miles of the valley west of Columbus.

Indiana 46 crosses 29 miles of mostly unglaciated bedrock hills between the area 2 miles west of Columbus and that 2 miles east of Bloomington.

*Geology along Indiana 46 between Columbus and Spencer.*

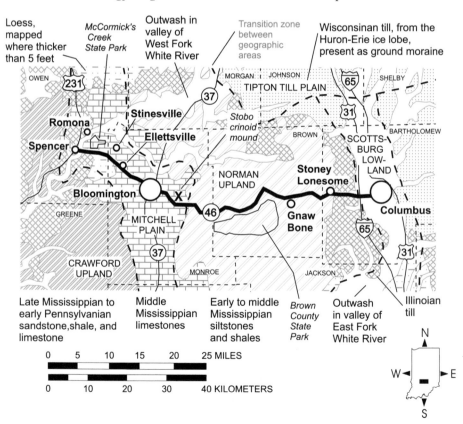

The Illinoian glacier lapped onto the eastern edge of this area. Erosion has removed almost all the Illinoian till.

Bedrock layers between the area west of Columbus and the area east of Bloomington are siltstones and shales deposited during middle Mississippian time. The landscape is in the Norman upland. The highway crosses the valley of the North Fork Salt Creek in the 5 miles east of Nashville and the 6 miles centered on the line between Monroe and Brown Counties. The broad flatness of the valley floor is a clue that it contains a fill of outwash sands and gravels. Its headwaters begin about where the Illinoian ice stopped.

Indiana 46 crosses 20 miles of bedrock hills in the Mitchell plain between the area 2 miles east of Bloomington and Spencer. The bedrock is limestone that was deposited during middle Mississippian time. Most of the building stone quarries and caves are farther south.

Hilltops with a thin cap of till show that Illinoian ice covered the old bedrock landscape as far south as the area 6 miles east of the West Fork White River. A stretch of chaotically mixed glacial till and outwash 2 miles wide lies mostly south of the highway near the White River valley. The highway crosses 4 miles of windblown silts east of the mixed till and outwash and again south of the highway, all deposited as the last ice age was ending.

At Spencer, the highway crosses the West Fork White River valley at its narrowest point for many miles, only one-third mile wide. Farther upstream and downstream, the valley is between 1 and 4 miles wide. The constriction at Spencer is where the stream cut through hard bedrock at the edge of the Crawford upland.

### Mineral Springs and Health Resorts

Mineral water exists throughout Bartholomew County. A well drilled for gas at Columbus in 1893 produced water rich in common salt, calcium carbonate, and various sulfates. The Columbus Sanitarium Company followed the next year. In 1900 a hotel with twenty rooms was added. The water was bottled and sold.

Azalia Mineral Spring produced water rich in iron, but a sanitarium never opened, even though the terrible flavor of such water would normally have persuaded some people that it had curative value. A spring at the base of the Knobstone escarpment near Mt. Moriah produced mineral water, bottled under the label "Blue Mountain Laxine Water." Perhaps the name is a hint that epsom salt was the principal medicinal ingredient.

### An Ancient Channel

The junction with I-65 is on the eastern edge of the Norman upland. Seven miles west is a long roadcut that exposes siltstones and shales of the Borden group. A brown gravel conglomerate as much as 2 feet thick marks the base of an ancient stream channel cut down into the sediments of the

Borden delta. Streams eroded some parts of the delta while they deposited sediments in other parts; an area accumulated fine sediments for a while, then received coarse sediments as streams shifted channels. This happens on all growing deltas. Look above the brown conglomerate to see crosscutting layers of sandstones, siltstones, and shale. They record the dynamic cutting and filling of the streams that deposited the sediments on the growing delta.

Indiana 46 passes numerous other exposures of Borden delta rocks between Stoney Lonesome and the area just east of Bloomington. A series of roadcuts in the Spickert Knob formation exposes siltstone, shale, and sandstone between Stoney Lonesome and Gnaw Bone, near the entrance to Brown County State Park.

### Glacial Lakes along Beanblossom Creek

Five miles north of Nashville on Indiana 135 lies the valley of Beanblossom Creek. This wide and terraced valley lies at the southern edge of Illinoian glacial tills, some 8 miles south of the Wisconsinan till. Glacial sands, silts, and clays fill its floor, in places to depths of 50 feet. Two buried layers of sediments that contain shells of land and freshwater snail and plant fossils record warm intervals between ice ages.

Beanblossom Creek is one of three streams that flow all the way across the unglaciated uplands of south-central Indiana; the other two are the much larger East Fork White River and the Ohio River. Geologists have known since the late 1800s that glacial lakes flooded the valley at various times. Before the Wisconsinan ice age, lobes of a great ice sheet covered both the mouth and source areas of Beanblossom Creek, impounding a lake between them. Considerable thicknesses of laminated clays accumulated in this lake and in a later lake that formed during the Wisconsinan ice age. Outwash dumped in the East Fork White River valley during the Wisconsinan glaciation blocked Beanblossom Valley to the west.

*Generalized surface and bedrock profiles along Indiana 46.*

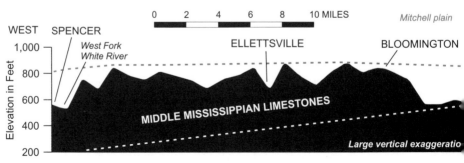

An old railroad cut just south of Trevlac and banks along Lake Lemon are good places to see the complex glacial deposits.

### Brown County State Park

Brown County State Park is typical of the Norman upland. You can see beautiful views, especially when the foliage is gone, from Hohen Point, Limekiln Ridge, Weedpatch Hill, and Hesitation Point. Watch for the rather symmetrical ridges with their flat tops and the dendritic stream networks.

Most of the rocks in the park belong to the Spickert Knob and Edwardsville formations, members of the Borden group. Resistant sandstones in the upper part of the Borden group support the tops of many ridges. The highest point, Weedpatch Hill, has a cap of Sanders group rocks. They are the source of the geodes that people love to find in the streams.

Sand and gravel deposits along the bluffs of Salt Creek are glacial outwash. They show that the stream carried meltwater from the Wisconsinan ice north of the park. Sand and gravel once filled the valley to a much higher elevation than the present floodplain. As the glacier melted back to the north, the flow of meltwater down Salt Creek valley diminished and Salt Creek began to erode deeply into the valley fill, isolating remnants of the outwash as flat terraces above the floodplain. A good example is in Salt Creek valley near the north entrance. Hesitation Point, 2 miles from the west entrance gate, is a good place to get a broad view of the Salt Creek valley.

Brown County State Park opened in 1929. A few years later, the Civilian Conservation Corps built the dams for Strahl and Ogle Lakes and planted trees on slopes that lumbering and mining activities had left barren and eroding. Those trees have since grown into a beautiful forest. The sandstone used in the park buildings and shelters came from an old quarry in the eastern part of the park.

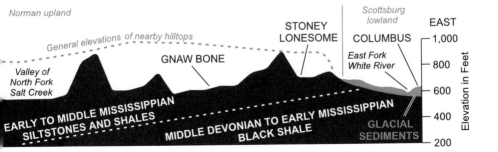

### Brown County Dimension Stone

Formations of the Borden group in Brown County sporadically provide dimension stone. Fieldstone and siltstone slabs from the Edwardsville formation find use as building veneers and ornamental stone throughout the region, especially in the Nashville area.

### Mounds of Sea Lilies—The Stobo Crinoid Mound

Watch a few miles east of Bloomington, north of the highway, for a low cut in gray limestone. It is in a wide valley just east of the junction with Gettys Creek Road. The rock consists mostly of small fossils shaped like disks, fragments of crinoid and blastoid stems.

Crinoids are small animals that stand on long and flexible stems made of disks stacked like coins. Most of the animal lives in an enclosed capsule with many feathery arms perched on the top of the stem. They are members of the large group of animals with five sides that includes starfish, sea urchins, and sand dollars. Blastoids, which are now extinct, were similar to crinoids in most respects.

Crinoids thrived most abundantly during Devonian, Mississippian, and Pennsylvanian time. Many limestones deposited during those periods are full of their stem segments, little disks shaped like coins with a hole through the center. Crinoids nearly disappeared in the great extinction of late Permian time, 245 million years ago. Only a few species live now, mostly in rather widely scattered groups on seafloors.

The rock in the roadcut is part of a resistant mound of crinoids built up in the lower part of the Edwardsville formation of Mississippian age. In addition to crinoids and blastoids, other sea animals, including brachiopods

*Fossil crinoid stems from the Stobo crinoid mound. Stems average one-half inch in diameter.*

*Skeletons of crinoids and blastoids formed a compaction-resistant mound along Indiana 46 east of Bloomington.*

and bryozoans, also flourished. The crinoids and blastoids lived in groups that built mounds of stem fragments. The weight of the sediments that buried the mound flattened some of the stem fragments and stretched others out into ovals. If you crave crinoid stems, the Stobo mound is just the place.

### Indiana Geological Survey

In 1837 the legislature authorized the governor to appoint a state geologist. David Dale Owen of New Harmony received the job of surveying the state for mineral resources that could attract industry. He traveled the state on horseback and eventually drew up a geologic map that showed most of the rock formations exposed at the surface. Owen correctly distinguished the Mississippian and Pennsylvanian rocks; he recognized rocks that would later be assigned an Ordovician age in 1879. He described most of the economically valuable rocks and minerals except gypsum and petroleum, which were below the surface.

Legislatures were as fickle then as now, so the state geologist had no assurance of a long term in office. Little geologic work was done in Indiana between 1839 and 1859. The next two state geologists were also former residents of New Harmony. The position of state geologist expanded to a department by the 1870s.

The focus of the geologic work changed over the years from county geologic histories to county soil surveys to oil and gas exploration. The office of the state geologist moved to Bloomington in 1919, with the appointment of a combination state geologist and geology professor. The growing geological survey eventually occupied a number of scattered offices, finally united when the survey wing of the geology building was completed in 1964.

Today the Indiana Geological Survey is a team of specialists in geophysics, geochemistry, economic geology, environmental geology, hydrogeology, stratigraphy, and other fields of geology. It is ready and anxious to serve the populace, industry, schools, and educational groups.

### Bloomington Buildings, Building Stones, and Quarries

Bloomington masons cut the Salem limestone as early as the 1850s, but serious quarrying did not begin until 1891 when the Hunter Stone Company found 25 to 40 feet of good quality building stone in the Hunter Valley district northwest of town. Laying of a railroad spur and construction of a stone mill accompanied the opening of quarries. At least four other companies soon joined the Hunter Stone Company. Three finishing mills located on the south side of town.

Indiana University buildings show how use of the limestone changed over the last one hundred years, from a reliance on artistic carvings to flat milled panels. Campus buildings built largely of Salem limestone include the Fine Arts Building, Geology Building, Lilly Library, Memorial Union, Psychology Building, School of Business, Showalter Arts Center, and Student Building. A former quarry at the southeastern edge of the campus first became the site of a sunken garden about 1930, and later became the site of Jordan Hall in the 1950s.

### Ellettsville-Stinesville Quarries

The Ellettsville-Stinesville area, halfway between Bloomington and Spencer, was once home to a number of dimension stone quarries. One of the earliest quarries in the Salem limestone opened in 1827 just south of Stinesville along the bluffs of Jack's Defeat Creek. The first large commercial quarry opened in 1855 after the railroad came to Stinesville. The operators blasted large blocks of limestone from the rock ledges west of town and hauled them on wagons drawn by three-ox teams to the mill where they were slabbed. This White River stone began to supplant the marbles, actually limestone, of the southeastern part of the state.

Even though it failed in 1868, this first quarry paved the way for other operators in the Stinesville area. All the Stinesville area quarries required a large amount of stripping to expose the stone. The railroad along Jack's Defeat Creek to Ellettsville passes many old quarries that opened in the 1860s and 1870s. One mile north of Ellettsville, the Matthews Brothers Quarry opened in 1862 and used the first steam channeling machine in the

*Discarded blocks of Mississippian limestone form a mountain on the edge of Ellettsville.*

state in 1875. The nearby Perry Brothers Stone Company was another successful Ellettsville firm.

The bustle of the early days is long gone, but overgrown pits and scattered limestone blocks tell of busier times. The only surviving dimension stone operation is on the north side of Ellettsville. An underground mine, opened in 1988, produces ground limestone from the Salem and Harrodsburg formations near Stinesville.

### Flatwoods

A mile and a half northwest of Ellettsville, Indiana 46 enters an extremely flat area of the Mitchell plain enclosed by bluffs of Mississippian limestones of the Blue River group. Glacial Lake Flatwoods once flooded this area while ice blocked the drainage outlet to the north. The lake covered an area of 8 square miles and extended its fingers south down the valley of Raccoon Creek to Freeman and Whitehall. As the ice melted to the north, the area around Raccoon Creek opened up and Lake Flatwoods drained. Underground drainage resumed after sinkholes and swallow holes clogged with glacial debris finally cleared. Forests covered the former lakebed until early settlers cleared them for their farms. You can drive around the edge of the former lake, now a flat lake plain.

### McCormick's Creek State Park

McCormick's Creek State Park is just west of the intersection with Indiana 43. The park is high above the West Fork White River, among the forested hills of the Crawford upland.

The first loop road off the main road, about 0.2 mile into the park, leads to the head of a trail to the overgrown State House Quarry. The rock is

*McCormick's Creek falls over the resistant St. Louis limestone in McCormick's Creek State Park.*

heavily crossbedded Salem limestone, near the mouth of McCormick's Creek Canyon. Contractors building the capitol in Indianapolis used stone from this site in 1878 and 1879, but the quarry closed because it could not supply enough good stone. The rest of the stone in the capitol came from the Dark Hollow district near Bedford.

The main park road crosses the deep canyon of McCormick's Creek. A short walk brings you to a waterfall where the creek cascades over outcrops of the St. Louis limestone. The waterfall started on the east flank of the White River valley as the Illinoian ice melted but has since eroded its way

*Litten Natural Bridge, or Twin Bridge, is a remnant of a former cave that collapsed after groundwater sought deeper passageways through the Mississippian limestone.*

upstream. It left in its wake the narrow chasm below the falls that is nearly 100 feet deep in places. The creek may have pirated the waters from glacial Lake Flatwoods.

A large percentage of the drainage in the park area was certainly underground before the glaciers came. Sinkholes dot the uplands, particularly north of McCormick's Creek. A number exist northeast of the canyon and along Litten Branch in the northeast part of the park. Litten Natural Bridge formed as parts of a cave passage collapsed, leaving remnants of its roof as natural bridges.

Wolf Cave displays an earlier phase of cavern collapse. This dry passageway is no longer growing because the water table has dropped far below its level. Caverns are now forming mostly at the level of McCormick's Creek and the West Fork White River.

## West Fork White River Valley and Romona District

Just west of McCormick's Creek State Park, Indiana 46 crosses the broad valley of the West Fork White River, filled with outwash. Numerous sand and gravel plants have operated in these sands and gravels over the years.

Just up the river from the Indiana 46 bridge is the northernmost concentration of quarry operations in the Salem limestone. Taking a side road off U.S. 231 north of Spencer will bring you to Romona, the center of the Romona dimension stone district. The Gosport Stone and Lime Company opened a quarry on the north side of town in 1868. Its successor, the Romona Oolitic Stone Company, made history in 1895 by operating the first and, for a time, the only diamond saw in the building-stone belt. The diamond saw

*Wolf Cave is in an early stage of cavern abandonment. It may someday look similar to Twin Bridge.*

was more useful in cutting large blocks while the common band saw was more efficient in cutting slabs. Most of the stone from this quarry went into bridge piers and foundations. Its coarsely crystalline texture was not suitable for buildings. The White River Stone and Lime Company opened the large quarry on the south edge of town in 1870 and operated it for more than one hundred years.

*Abandoned limestone quarry in Salem limestone, south of Romona.*

# Southwestern Indiana
## CLAY AND COAL

### THE PENNSYLVANIAN WORLD

Pennsylvanian formations are the bedrock throughout the southwestern and west-central parts of the state, from the Ohio River north to Warren County. Within these bounds are coal mines, vestiges of a once flourishing clay industry, oil fields, famous fossil occurrences, and an early center of learning. The region, named the Wabash lowland, slopes toward the Wabash River, the boundary with Illinois south of Terre Haute.

*Raccoon Creek Group.* The Raccoon Creek group of Pennsylvanian age surfaces in outcrops along the eastern part of the Wabash lowland. The Raccoon Creek group and later Pennsylvanian units accumulated along a fluctuating shoreline that featured repeating depositional episodes called cyclothems. Sandstones, siltstones, underclays, coal seams, and limestones of varying thicknesses typify these sequences.

*Crossbedded sandstone of Pennsylvanian Mansfield formation, part of the Raccoon Creek group, Portland Arch State Nature Preserve.*

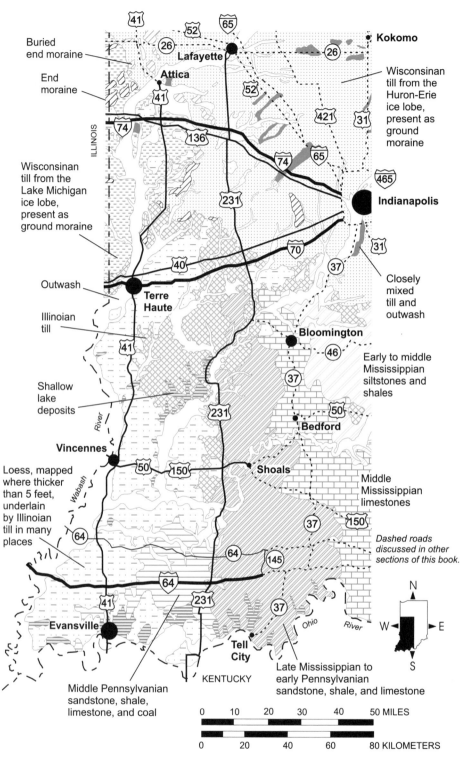

Buried end moraine

End moraine

Wisconsinan till from the Lake Michigan ice lobe, present as ground moraine

Outwash

Illinoian till

Shallow lake deposits

Vincennes

Loess, mapped where thicker than 5 feet, underlain by Illinoian till in many places

Kokomo

Wisconsinan till from the Huron-Erie ice lobe, present as ground moraine

Lafayette

Attica

ILLINOIS

Indianapolis

Closely mixed till and outwash

Terre Haute

Bloomington

Early to middle Mississippian siltstones and shales

Bedford

Middle Mississippian limestones

Shoals

*Dashed roads discussed in other sections of this book.*

Middle Pennsylvanian sandstone, shale, limestone, and coal

Evansville

KENTUCKY

Tell City

Late Mississippian to early Pennsylvanian sandstone, shale, and limestone

River

Wabash

Ohio River

N
W    E
S

| 0 | 10 | 20 | 30 | 40 | 50 MILES |

| 0 | 20 | 40 | 60 | 80 KILOMETERS |

*Highways and geology of southwestern Indiana.*

Most of the time this area was land crisscrossed by rivers and streams flowing west to the inland sea. The water offshore was shallow, and coastal lagoons nestled behind barrier islands. At other times, seawater flooded that landscape, the forests drowned, and a sequence of marine sediments, including limestones, accumulated.

The Mansfield formation is the oldest of the Raccoon Creek group and can be seen mainly in south-central Indiana. The Brazil formation, above it, surfaces locally in a northwest band that trends from Spencer to Warren County. The Brazil formation, like the underlying Mansfield formation, is quite irregular in thickness, 40 to 90 feet, and many of the individual layers do not continue far. The formation contains, in ascending order, the Lower Block, Upper Block, and Minshall-Buffaloville coals.

The Lower and Upper Block coals got their names from the way they break along a pattern of vertical cracks. Their seams range in thickness from 9 inches to almost 6 feet. Gray underclay lies beneath them, gray shale above.

*Indiana was the site of vast swamp forests during Pennsylvanian time. Giant insects, some of the first reptiles, amphibians, and fernlike plants (some as tall as 100 feet) lived there.*

The Staunton formation is the youngest of the Raccoon Creek group. It consists of 75 to 150 feet of cyclothem sequences with at least eight coal seams. Only the Seelyville coal, in the upper part of the formation, is thick enough to mine.

**Carbondale Group.** The Carbondale group, which is above the Raccoon Creek group, contains four of the five most productive coal seams in the state. Its outcrop belt across southwestern Indiana outlines the largest area of strip mines. The Linton formation, from 43 to 162 feet thick, is the lowest part. The Colchester and Survant coals mark consistent levels within the Linton formation.

The Petersburg formation lies on the Linton formation. It is 70 to 190 feet thick and includes the Houchin Creek and Springfield coal seams. The Springfield coal, at the top of the formation, is the most widely mined seam in the state, accounting for about half the annual production.

The Springfield coal contains coal balls—limestone nodules that yield fossils of plants—and marine animals. Botanists especially prize the limestone coal balls because their plant fossils are not compressed, evidently because the nodule solidified before the weight of the sediments accumulating above could squash the soft sediments in which it formed. Paleontologists can pull the nodules apart in microscopically thin layers and reconstruct a model of the original plant.

The Dugger formation is the youngest, with four limestones and four coal seams. It is between 73 and 185 feet thick. Sea level was higher and the area more persistently flooded than earlier. The upper two coal seams, the Hymera and Danville coals, have supplied many large mines. The lower two are too thin to mine.

**McLeansboro Group.** The four formations of the McLeansboro group were laid down during late Pennsylvanian time. They account for more than half the thickness of all the Pennsylvanian rocks. They are at the surface along the Wabash Valley, typically beneath a thick cover of windblown silt. As many as fourteen coal seams exist in the McLeansboro group, but they have escaped much mining.

The Shelburn formation, 50 to 250 feet thick, is the oldest of the McLeansboro group. It surfaces in a band between Evansville and Vermillion County.

Above the Shelburn formation lies the Patoka formation, another rather monotonous sequence of sandstone, shale, limestone, and coal. It is the thickest of this group, ranging from 100 feet in Sullivan County to 310 feet in Posey County.

The overlying Bond formation ranges in thickness from 100 feet in the north to 250 feet in the south. The Fairbanks coal is as much as 4 feet thick in the Fairbanks area, where it was mined on a small scale.

The Mattoon formation is the youngest of the Pennsylvanian formations. Erosion destroyed most of it. The most notable exposures are near Merom in western Sullivan County and in the Mumford Hills of northwestern Posey County.

## TILL AND WINDBLOWN SILT

Illinoian ice advanced into Indiana from the north and northeast. Ice that flowed south from the area of Lake Michigan left the Glasford till, remnants of which plaster hilltops in Parke, Vermillion, and Vigo Counties, generally west of the Wabash River and Raccoon Creek. Ice that entered from the northeast left the Jessup till plastered on hilltops farther east. Geologists distinguish tills mainly by identifying the rocks they contain.

Wisconsinan ice also left two distinctive till sheets. Ice from the Lake Michigan area left the Wedron till across much the same area as the Illinoian Glasford till. The Huron-Erie ice lobe plastered the Trafalgar till virtually everywhere else.

Meanwhile, meltwater swept tremendous volumes of silt, sand, and gravel away from the former areas of ice and deposited them as outwash in almost every valley. Geologists can generally assign an age to an outwash deposit by following it upstream to its associated till sheet. The volume of outwash across Indiana is so enormous that it boggles the imagination. The meltwater floods that deposited it are even harder to believe.

And the wind never tires. Wherever wind blows across barren land surfaces, it raises clouds of silt and blows them for miles before they finally settle. It also sweeps sand into dunes and marches them along until something stops them. The strong westerly winds that blew across Indiana back then dumped windblown silt across most of the state, most deeply in areas downwind of the larger rivers. The sand dunes are piled along eastern valley walls and are so covered with plants that they are hard to see.

## OHIO AND WABASH RIVERS

The Ohio and Wabash Rivers in southwestern Indiana were important avenues for the settlers from the late 1700s until the coming of the railroads. Once a canal bypassed the Falls of the Ohio at Louisville, navigation on the Ohio River became a simpler matter of avoiding sandbars on the meander loops. Major centers of river commerce in southwestern Indiana in the early 1800s included Evansville, Mt. Vernon, Newburgh, Rockport, and Troy.

The Wabash River originates in northwestern Ohio, then curls across northern Indiana to Attica, where it turns south. It joins the Ohio River 15 miles southwest of Mt. Vernon in a setting of unspoiled natural beauty. Hovey Lake State Fish and Wildlife Area, south of Mt. Vernon, is an excellent place to see point bars, meander scars, sloughs, oxbow lakes, and natural levees.

Other major tributaries to the Ohio River in southwestern Indiana include Little Pigeon Creek, east of Newburgh, and Pigeon Creek and the

*The Wabash River covers its floodplain during major floods. Here the railroad depot at Covington lies unusable during the 1913 flood.* —Mark J. Camp Collection

Green River at Evansville. The Wabash River receives water from Sugar Creek and Raccoon Creek in Parke County and the White and Patoka Rivers at East Mt. Carmel.

Both rivers and their tributaries were major meltwater streams when the great Pleistocene glaciers were melting. The terraces that rise like broad steps from the floodplains are made of outwash sluiced from the melting ice and deposited by the meltwaters. After the major meltwater floods filled the valleys with deep outwash, the dwindling streams scoured away large areas, leaving remnants either along valley walls as terraces or as isolated hills. Some of these isolated hills include Oak Hill Cemetery in Evansville, the Mumford Hills at Griffin, Gordon Hills at East Mt. Carmel, and the Orrville Hills at Orrville.

### COALFIELDS

Coal has been dug from southwestern Indiana since the 1830s, when small mines operated in Perry and Warrick Counties. Miners dug coal from thin seams exposed along stream banks, then hauled it in wheelbarrows and wagons to the Ohio River. Steamboats and blacksmiths used most of it. The first coal company of record was the American Cannel Coal Company of Coal Haven, later Cannelton.

The discovery in 1851 of the Lower and Upper Block coals east of Terre Haute launched another coalfield in northern Clay County. Mines scattered from Warren County on the Wabash River south to the Ohio River produced 100,000 tons annually by 1860.

The rising demand for coal forced companies to dig underground mines. The first one opened in 1850, near Newburgh. Underground production increased until 1910 when a series of labor, economic, and supply problems

*Lattes Creek Mine in the early 1900s, near Jasonville.* —Mark J. Camp Collection

cut production. The introduction of mechanical loaders in the 1920s helped increase mine productivity, as briefly did the Second World War. By 1954, 90 percent of the mines used mechanical loaders. Continuous mining machines appeared in the 1950s, but underground mining continues its decline, yielding to strip mining.

Underground mining minimizes waste rock production and damage to the environment, but strip mining is much more economical where the coal is near the surface. Strip mining has grown steadily since 1920 and now accounts for most of the production. Miners used horse- or mule-drawn scrapers in early strip mines, then turned to steam shovels in the early 1900s. Electric, gasoline, and diesel shovels and draglines replaced steam shovels by the late 1930s. The late 1960s brought gigantic draglines with bucket capacities up to 176 cubic yards. Dump trucks that can carry 170 tons are now standard.

*Ayrshire Mine, east of Evansville. The dragline, in the background, can remove more than 175 cubic yards of earth and rock with each swipe across the landscape.*

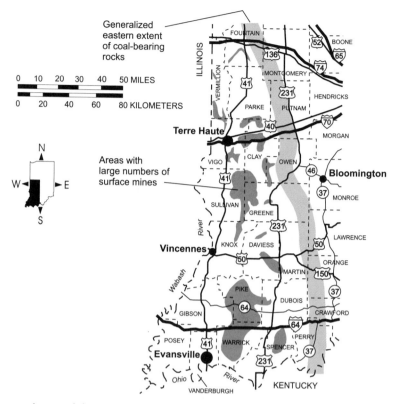

Generalized eastern extent of coal-bearing rocks

0  10  20  30  40  50 MILES

0  20  40  60  80 KILOMETERS

N
W ◄ ► E
S

Areas with large numbers of surface mines

*Areas with large numbers of surface coal mines in southwestern Indiana.*

Greene, Knox, Pike, Sullivan, Vigo, and Warrick Counties produce the most coal because they have middle Pennsylvanian formations near the surface. Little coal comes from early and late Pennsylvanian rocks because their seams are thin and full of impurities.

## MINING AND RECLAMATION

Early miners operated with little consideration for the environment. Indiscriminate strip mining destroyed the plant cover, increased soil erosion, choked streams with sediment, and generated acidic drainage from spoil heaps.

The first attempt to combat spoil heaps came in 1918, when forty-seven hundred fruit trees were planted at Clay City. Other companies followed suit, especially after 1921 when Indiana enacted tax advantages for owners of forested land. Some firms offered their mined acreage for use as game and forest preserves and parks.

In 1941 the Indiana legislature required companies to plant trees on spoil banks, but the law contained no provision that the trees would survive. Ten years later, revision of the law allowed planting of crops and grasses for pasturage. Companies then had to replant each year an area the same size as had been mined. Permit fees were increased and larger bonds required, but nothing in the law demanded that revegetation succeed. A 1963 amendment required that rocks likely to generate acid waters as they weathered be buried and that reclaimed areas designated for farming be leveled.

Further revision of the law in 1967 required mining companies to develop reclamation plans that followed stringent state guidelines before they could begin mining. Repayment of bonds was withheld until the area was properly revegetated.

Federal support for reclamation came with the passage of the Surface Mining Control and Reclamation Act of 1977. Although scars remain, the hills of southwestern Indiana are slowly healing.

## CLAY INDUSTRY

The Pennsylvanian rocks of southwestern Indiana contain a variety of clays. Early settlers soon found that some of the clays exposed along the hillsides of southwestern Indiana were soft, workable, and fired well. Potteries at Troy on the Ohio River produced stoneware as early as 1834. By 1869 at least eleven potteries were in operation in the southwestern counties. Most were small operations that served local demands.

Flower pots are the lowest grade of earthenware fired at low temperatures and left porous and unglazed. Almost any clay can be used. Stoneware, the next grade, uses better clay and differs in being glazed and fired at higher temperatures. Yellow ware and white ware, the higher grades of pottery, were made only at Troy and Evansville. Other potteries operated at Annapolis, Brazil, Clay City, Huntingburg, and Selvin.

*Reclaimed coal lands at Ashboro along Indiana 46.*

Ordinary brick and drain tile could be made with little technical skill from most clay deposits. Itinerant masons traveled throughout the state in the 1800s, making bricks and tile from local deposits. Most towns had a brick and tile yard by 1900. They produced many ceramic products including dry pressed brick, paving brick, fire brick, hollow block, sewer pipe, roof tile, ornamental products, terra-cotta, and refractories. The raw material came from underclays and shales, and from combinations of surface clays, underclays, and shales. Major plants were at Brazil, Cayuga, Evansville, Huntingburg, Mecca, Montezuma, Newport, and Terre Haute. Some coal companies in southwestern Indiana still sell raw underclay.

Vitrified paving brick was a big industry in the early 1900s. Major producers in southwestern Indiana were at Brazil, Cayuga, Clinton, Crawfordsville, Evansville, Terre Haute, and Veedersburg. The clay or shale was ground, sieved, mixed with water and perhaps other clays, pressed through auger machines, cut to size, dried, and kiln fired.

## PETROLEUM INDUSTRY

The early settlers knew of oil seeps but focused their attention on clay and coal. That changed in 1889 when Indiana oil production began on the eastern edge of the Illinois Basin, the same year oil was discovered farther east in the Trenton field. As early as 1865 a well drilled for water found oil in downtown Terre Haute. Another well drilled in Terre Haute in 1889 struck oil that made a small pond around the derrick and then blew 50 feet into the air when the drill stem was pulled. Despite more drilling, oil production remained limited.

A number of small oil fields were found during the 1920s in Daviess, Gibson, Knox, Pike, and Sullivan Counties. Major discoveries at Clay City, Illinois, and Griffin, Indiana, in the late 1930s inspired more drilling. Most of the petroleum came from old stream channels in sandstones of late Mississippian and Pennsylvanian age, at depths between 1,500 and 3,000 feet.

Production from southwestern Indiana slowed by the late 1940s. Deeper drilling in 1950 at Plainville found more oil in Mississippian and Devonian rocks, mostly in places where they were draped over reefs in the underlying Silurian rocks. A larger discovery made in 1969 at Plummer produced oil from the Salem limestone. These two fields produced more than 9.1 billion barrels of oil by 1989. Oil companies knew of more than one hundred other reef pools by 1990.

Water flooding is the main method of wringing more oil from an old field. The operator pumps water into the reservoir through some of the old wells to displace the remaining oil that floats on the water and is pumped out through other wells. Secondary production of the larger reservoirs is now declining in most of the old fields.

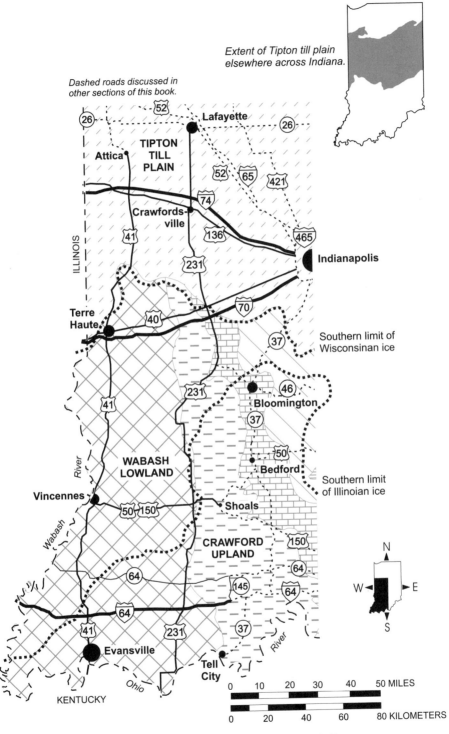

*Highways and geographic regions of southwestern Indiana.*

*Typical Wabash lowland landscape along Indiana 66, east of New Harmony.*

## GEOGRAPHIC REGIONS

*Wabash Lowland.* The Wabash lowland extends from the Ohio River north to near the Parke-Vigo county line and from the Wabash River east to the edge of the Crawford upland. It ranges from 30 miles wide in the north to 65 miles wide in the south. Elevations range from 500 feet on the eastern upland areas down to 320 feet along the lower Wabash and Ohio Rivers, the lowest point in Indiana.

The Wabash lowland includes low hills eroded in middle Pennsylvanian sandstones, shales, limestones, and coals—a less rugged landscape than that in the Crawford upland. The Wabash lowland includes the Wabash Valley, a former meltwater channel filled with outwash to a depth of between 50 and 150 feet.

Illinoian and Wisconsinan ice left till over the northern two-thirds of the Wabash lowland. It is generally thin because it was laid down near the southern end of the glaciers. Deposits of sand and silt were blown from the outwash plain of the Wabash Valley. Till and windblown sediments are between 50 and 100 feet deep just east of the Wabash Valley.

# Interstate 64 and Indiana 64
## Indiana 145—Illinois Line
### 60 TO 71 MILES

Interstate 64 and Indiana 64 continue the scenic journey westward across southern Indiana that they began at New Albany. Most of I-64 passes across the upper basins of three streams that flow directly into the Ohio River and of two that head into the Wabash River. The western part of I-64 and all of Indiana 64 pass along the southern edge of the basin for the Patoka River, on its way toward the Wabash River.

Between Indiana 145 and the area around Indiana 162, I-64 and Indiana 64 cross 5 miles of the western edge of the Crawford upland eroded in upper Mississippian and lower Pennsylvanian bedrock.

Near Indiana 162, the highways pass into the Wabash lowland for the remaining 55 to 66 miles of their journey to the Wabash River, I-64 having the longer route. The hills were carved from middle Pennsylvanian sandstone, shale, limestone, and coal. The coal seams have been and still are

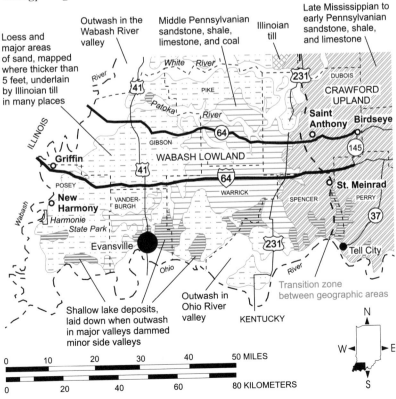

*Geology along I-64 and Indiana 64 between Indiana 145 and the Illinois line.*

extensively mined across this area. Views from the main roads and most side roads show every stage from current operations to the aftermath of mining.

Small oil fields exist in the southwest corner of Indiana. Their returns are small but consistent. More than six thousand wells have been drilled since the early 1900s.

A persistent blanket of windblown silt covers the region and thickens toward the Wabash River valley. Strong westerly winds blew the silt off the broad outwash plain in the river valley shortly after the last ice sheets melted. Scattered areas of sand dunes exist along the east side of the Wabash River valley, blown against the hills by the same winds that carried the smaller silt particles farther east. The unconsolidated deposits adjacent to the Wabash River valley, including the underlying Illinoian till, are 50 to 150 feet thick. The outwash fill in the valley is 100 to 150 feet thick.

### Birdseye

Birdseye was the site of the Birdseye Brick Company, which supplied most of the brick in the older buildings in town. The clay was dug from a Pennsylvanian underclay. The nearby Mansfield formation supplied sandstone for other buildings in Birdseye.

Coal from the Raccoon Creek group was mined for use by blacksmiths. A silver and gold mining enterprise briefly worked conglomerates of the Mansfield formation in the late 1800s.

The town became the center of a brief oil boom when drilling revealed petroleum under portions of Dubois and Crawford Counties around 1900. The oil comes from the underlying Mississippian Blue River group, the Aux Vases formation, and the Harrodsburg formation. Birdseye became a boomtown as many wells yielded close to 100 barrels each day. Many old fields no longer produce, but new pools are still being discovered, usually in deeper Mississippian layers.

### Sandstone from St. Anthony

One mile west of St. Anthony is the old Lyne Quarry, which opened in the Pennsylvanian Mansfield formation in 1887. A massive layer of sand-

*Generalized surface and bedrock profiles along I-64 and Indiana 64.*

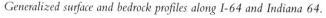

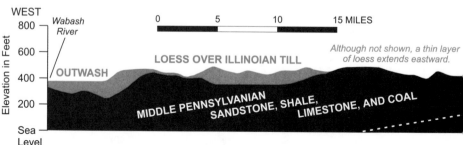

stone 10 to 16 feet thick provided excellent dimension stone. Two smaller sandstone quarries were worked during the late 1890s and early 1900s.

### St. Meinrad Archabbey and Its Sandstone Quarries

The St. Meinrad Archabbey is south of I-64, just off Indiana 62. The archabbey is famous for its church, with twin steeples 168 feet high, built of Mansfield sandstone between 1899 and 1907. The stone came from quarries near Ferdinand and Monte Cassino, which were in operation by 1870. The sandstone was first used in 1868 in the foundation of the present building at the Shrine of Our Lady of Monte Cassino, just northeast of town.

North of Monte Cassino and just south of I-64 is a flooded quarry that the archabbey worked from 1941 to 1970. The uniformity of grain size of the Mansfield sandstone at this site made it useful for exterior and interior use in many structures. Wire saws were used in removing the slabs; little blasting was needed. The stone was finished at the abbey's mill on Ferdinand Road, 1 mile east of Ferdinand. A century of quarrying by the archabbey produced more stone from the Mansfield formation than any other operation in Indiana.

### Coal Mining around Evansville

The Springfield Coal member of the Petersburg formation has been mined extensively in Pike, Vanderburgh, and Warrick Counties, where it may reach 12 feet in thickness. Particularly in Warrick County, ancient stream channels commonly split this coal into two or more seams.

Numerous shafts opened in the mid-1800s around the growing city of Evansville. The Ingleside Mine at the foot of Reitz Hill, started in 1858, was one of the earliest operations. At the time of its abandonment in 1918, it extended completely under the Ohio River into Kentucky. Other underground mines were along the Pigeon Creek valley. By 1908 twenty-three companies were in business, but most closed their Evansville mines by the late 1930s. Abandoned mines now underlie Helfrich and Mesker Parks. At least six mines opened around Chandler and Newburgh in the 1890s and early 1900s.

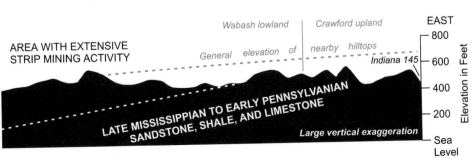

*An oil well pumps atop Monte Cassino near St. Meinrad. The Shrine of Our Lady of Monte Cassino in the background was constructed of local Mansfield sandstone in 1868.*

Surface mines gradually displaced the underground mines as coal seams became depleted. The spreading metropolis of Evansville also pushed out the mining interests. Strip mining dominates Pike and Warrick Counties, between Petersburg and the Ohio River. Not only is the Springfield coal mined but also the overlying Hymera and Danville coals of the Dugger formation.

### Wabash Valley Fault System

The northern edge of the Wabash Valley fault system lies underground just west of the Indiana 65 interchange with I-64. The Owensville fault extends 5 miles north to Owensville. The parallel New Harmony fault lies under the Griffin interchange near the Wabash River. This steeply inclined fault shows a vertical displacement of 450 feet and can be traced more than 30 miles. Five parallel faults break the rock into slices at the line between Posey and Gibson Counties. The projected trace of the Ribeyre Island fault extends into Illinois 1.5 miles west of the New Harmony fault. Geologists believe these faults extend several thousand feet below the surface, into the ancient rocks of the continental basement.

The faults moved sometime between the deposition of Pennsylvanian rocks and Pleistocene glaciation. No earthquakes have been recorded, so they are probably dead. The maximum displacements of the Wabash Valley faults occur in southwestern Indiana, and displacements decrease and eventually disappear in northwestern Kentucky. Therefore, no direct connection appears to exist between the Wabash Valley faults and those of the New Madrid faults in southeastern Missouri, which caused the largest earthquakes of historic record in the United States during 1811 and 1812.

The Wabash Valley fault system offsets numerous coal seams and requires that coal geologists study its structure carefully. Petroleum, natural gas, and other mineral deposits have been presumed to exist in the area for years, but no major deposits have yet been located, except for an oil field at Griffin.

### Griffin Oil Discovery

Griffin was the site of an important petroleum discovery in 1938. Drilling revealed a series of oil pools in the underlying Pennsylvanian strata; more were found in the underlying Mississippian rocks. The field yielded more than 80,000 barrels of oil by 1990. The Griffin discovery spurred new interest in drilling the flanks of the Illinois Basin, and oil prospecting has been more or less continuous there ever since. Notable oil fields near I-64 are at Fort Branch, Haubstadt, Owensville, St. Wendell, Stewartsville, and near Lynnville. Oil fields also exist near Indiana 64 at Francisco, Oakland City, Patoka, and Princeton.

### New Harmony—Birthplace of Indiana Geology

New Harmony was an early center of learning in Indiana. Harmonists, a group of Lutheran dissenters originally from Germany, built a colony there in 1814 they called Harmonie. The site was sold eleven years later to Robert Owen and William Maclure who wanted to establish a utopian community. Respected scientists from Europe and throughout the United States received membership invitations.

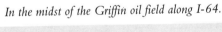

*In the midst of the Griffin oil field along I-64.*

167

Overall the utopian experiment failed, and few scientists and educators remained by the early 1830s. David Dale Owen, one of Robert Owen's sons, set up residence there in 1833. His interests in chemistry were slowly supplanted by geology, and he was appointed Indiana state geologist in 1837. He traveled extensively, mapping Indiana's mineral resources as then known and correlating them to deposits in other states. David Dale Owen accepted employment with the federal government in 1839 but was invited back as Indiana state geologist in 1859. Remaining professional obligations required him to have his brother Richard take his place. David Dale Owen died the next year; his brother was retained until 1861 when state funding expired.

New Harmony survives through historical preservation and tourism. David Dale Owen's last residence at Main and Church Streets, his third geological laboratory and museum on Granary Street, and his fourth laboratory between Main and West Streets still stand. His geological specimens went to Indiana University, the Smithsonian, and the American Museum of Natural History. The Workingmen's Institute Library and Museum, at the corner of West and Tavern Streets, was founded in 1838 by William Maclure, who hoped to make science accessible to laborers. It also contains early New Harmony manuscripts and geological specimens.

*Former geological laboratory of David Dale Owen, built in 1859 at New Harmony.*

### Indiana 69 to Harmonie State Park

Geologists call the ridge of windblown dust along Indiana 69 on the south side of New Harmony the Atherton formation. It probably records several episodes of steady, strong winds blowing down and across the valley, spreading silt from glacial outwash deposits to the north and west. David Dale Owen brought the renowned Sir Charles Lyell to this site in 1846 during the British geologist's visit to New Harmony. Owen's grave site, and those of other members of the Owen family, are in the cemetery at the top of the hill. Harmonie State Park, farther south off Indiana 69, provides opportunities to observe the restless Wabash River. Note the steep cutbanks where the river sweeps toward the banks and the sandbars where it veers away.

## Interstate 70 and U.S. 40
### Indianapolis—Illinois Line
#### 72 MILES

Interstate 70 and U.S. 40 parallel one another across western Indiana's till plain and bedrock hills capped with till. They cross side streams in the drainage basin of the West Fork White River between Indianapolis and northern Clay County. The routes between northern Clay County and the Illinois line cross the drainage basin of the Wabash River.

The highways cross Wisconsinan ground moraine deposited by the Huron-Erie ice lobe between Indianapolis and southeastern Putnam County. This area is in the southern part of the Tipton till plain that extends across most of Indiana north of these two highways.

The nearly flat deposits of Wisconsinan glacial debris pass into gently rolling Illinoian till along U.S. 40 near U.S. 231, and 4 miles east of U.S. 231 along I-70. The Illinoian till is no more than 50 feet deep, so the buried bedrock terrain asserts itself in the landscape. The windblown silt that covers the area is locally more than 5 feet thick near U.S. 231.

Across Hendricks County and eastern Putnam County, the bedrock is Mississippian siltstone and shale. I-70 passes 3 to 5 miles north of the line between the southern part of the Tipton till plain and the northern part of the Norman upland.

The highways cross bedrock hills eroded in middle Mississippian limestones to middle Pennsylvanian rocks between U.S. 231 and Terre Haute. Thin remnants of Illinoian till cap these hills; windblown silt exceeding 5 feet thick also blankets the area. Technically, these rock units underlie the far northern parts of the Mitchell plain, Crawford upland, and Wabash lowland,

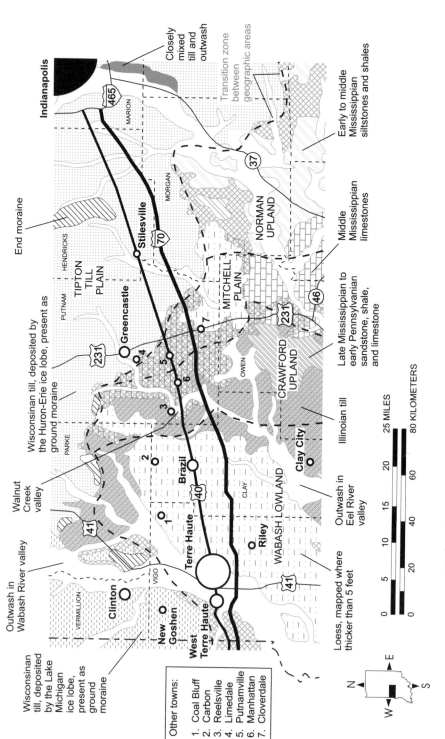

*Geology along I-70 and U.S. 40, between Indianapolis and the Illinois line.*

but the look of the landscape does not change. At Terre Haute, the two highways cross the valley of the Wabash River, 5 miles wide and filled with glacial outwash to a depth of more than 100 feet.

Between the west side of the Wabash Valley and the Illinois line, the highways converge across 4 miles of bedrock hills capped with Illinoian till called the Glasford formation. Rocks within the till show it was deposited by ice from the Lake Michigan area, rather than from the northeast. Wind-blown silt also covers most of these hills.

### Putnam County Mineral Resources

At least twenty quarries have worked the St. Louis, Ste. Genevieve, and Paoli limestones of the Blue River group within Putnam County since the early 1830s.

Dimension stone quarrying began near Putnamville, where several quarries operated south and west of town. The Lee Quarry opened in 1838 to produce blocks of Ste. Genevieve limestone for use in bridges, culverts, canal locks, and buildings, including many along the National Road (now part of U.S. 40), the Wabash and Erie Canal, and steps for the first building of Indiana Asbury College, now Depauw University, at Greencastle. The upper 3 feet of the formation provided slabs of flagstone; the lower part provided the more massive dimension stone.

Another early quarry opened at Greencastle Junction, now Limedale, in the 1850s. By the 1860s it was working a face 25 feet high in the Ste. Genevieve limestone. A large lime kiln was in operation by 1880. In 1919 the Indiana Portland Cement Company began blending Beaver Bend, Paoli, and Ste. Genevieve limestones with local Mississippian, Pennsylvanian, and Pleistocene clays to make a fine grade of portland cement. Lone Star Industries purchased the plant in 1925 and built a new plant in 1969 in the quarry area east of Limedale. At least six other quarries operated between Greencastle and Oakalla Station in the late 1800s.

A quarry opened around 1917 at the Indiana State Farm, a prison facility near Putnamville, to make bricks, tile, and drainpipe. The inmates began producing lime in 1924 in a brick beehive kiln. Another quarry opened south of U.S. 40, exposing the Sample through St. Louis formations, as well as the buried erosion surface of the Mississippian rocks on which the Pennsylvanian rocks were deposited. The Indiana State Farm stopped making ceramics in 1972.

Fern Cliff, a delightful glen of sandstone cliffs covered with ferns, moss, and dripping springs, exists 5 miles southwest of Greencastle. Excursion trains stopped at the scenic picnic grounds until the Root Glass Company of Terre Haute bought the property in 1910. In 1913 their quarry shipped its daily production of more than 100 tons of crushed sandstone mined from the Mansfield formation to their bottle factory in Terre Haute. The

*A small dimension stone quarry in the Ste. Genevieve limestone still operates near Manhattan.*

quarry is abandoned now and the site is a national natural landmark. Ask locally for directions.

Other quarries dot the hills near Cloverdale, Manhattan, and Stilesville. The main products are crushed stone, pulverized limestone for animal feeds, and agricultural lime from the Blue River group. A small quarry near Manhattan supplies dimension stone.

### Mineral Waters of Putnam County

A well bored in search of oil at Reelsville in 1865 penetrated four saltwater horizons in Mississippian and Devonian rocks, then tapped a strong flow of sulfurous artesian water at a depth of 1,240 feet. Although no oil was

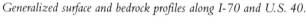

*Generalized surface and bedrock profiles along I-70 and U.S. 40.*

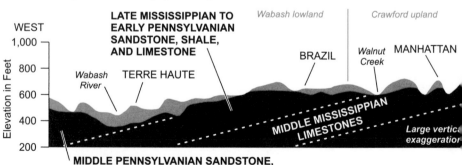

*An abandoned coal mine near Carbon.*

struck, the water fountained 20 feet into the air and then continued to flow until Big Walnut Creek flooded in 1875 and covered the site with mud. The well seeped for another twenty years but never became commercially valuable.

McLean's Springs, between Greencastle and Limedale, issued from the contact of Mississippian and Pennsylvanian strata. Bottles of the water sold locally during the 1880s and 1890s, as did some at nearby Mahan's Spring.

## *Clay County Coal Mines*

Strip mines and draglines dot the Wabash lowland between the Clay and Putnam county line and the Wabash River. Town names like Carbon, Clay City, and Coal Bluff speak of the area's history.

Block coals, up to 5 feet thick, were low in sulfur and ash and burned without caking. Mines quickly multiplied north and east of Brazil along South Otter Creek, between Brazil and Clay City, and west to the Vigo County line as these coals became popular for domestic heating, blacksmithing, and iron smelting. By the late 1800s, the coals were mined out in the eastern part of Clay County where they were within 100 feet of the surface. Mining then followed the coal seams into the subsurface toward the Vigo County line.

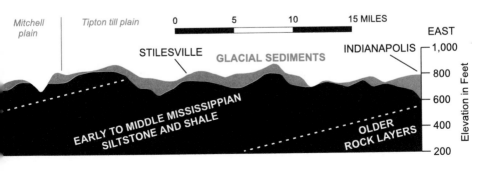

*A dragline rusts away at Saline City south of I-70 in Clay County.*

Many of the early mines were family enterprises with short life spans. Mergers became rampant as the coalfields developed, making corporate histories complex. Mines still operate near Brazil and Clay City, producing from the Lower and Upper Block and Minshall coals. The Chinook State Fishing Area occupies reclaimed coal land along I-70.

### Clay County Ironworks

Iron production began in Clay County after the Civil War, and five blast furnaces were in operation by 1869. The Indianapolis Rolling Mill Company erected their Planet Furnace 1 mile northeast of Harmony in the summer of 1867. In the first year or so, iron came from Pennsylvanian strata near Eaglesfield. Depletion of this deposit made it more economical to ship in the plentiful and higher grade Missouri ores. The pig iron went to Indianapolis to become rails.

The Central Iron & Steel Company built the largest blast furnace in this region, the Brazil Furnace, in 1867, towering 60 feet high. The Western Iron Company built a furnace at Knightsville in 1867 and added a second in 1868. In 1875 the company moved to Cleveland. The Lafayette Iron Company fired up its Lafayette or Masten furnace along South Otter Creek, 1.5 miles north of Brazil, in May 1869.

Each of the companies owned its coal mine or bought block coal from nearby mines. Limestone for flux came from nearby quarries at Hamrick's Station and Greencastle Junction, now Limedale. Iron ores arrived from Iron Mountain, Missouri, and from the Lake Superior district. Changes in the iron industry and advances in shipping across the Great Lakes gradually favored industrial development along the lakeshores farther north. The furnaces in Clay County finally cooled in the 1890s.

### Clay Plants of Clay County

The ceramic industry in Clay County began in the 1860s with a brick plant along South Otter Creek, north of Brazil, where a fair grade of fire clay came from below the Block coals. The coal was used for kiln fuel and the raw clay became fire bricks and terra-cotta products, molded by hand and stamped "Brazil."

By 1869 three potteries were in business around Brazil and Harmony producing a popular bluish gray stoneware. The raw material was the underclay beneath the Upper Block coal.

The Weaver Clay and Coal Company, established in 1872 on the northeast side of Brazil, was the first of several large clay plants erected in the 1890s and early 1900s. Its plant produced hollow rock-face building blocks, drainpipe, and its famous clay water well pumps. The company leased 80 acres of land a half-mile north of its factory, from which it stripped underclay and mined Upper Block coal from a slope mine. A 486-foot well bored in 1903 outside the company boiler house provided a supply of brine to minimize cracking in the clay.

The Indiana Paving Brick & Block Company opened its plant on the west side of Brazil in 1891. A gray Pennsylvanian shale quarried north of town was mixed with surface clay and underclay from the Upper Block coal. The brick pavers were widely used throughout Indiana and eastern Illinois. At least nine other ceramic plants opened in the 1890s and early 1900s around Brazil, including the Standard Pottery Company, which became the largest stoneware manufacturer in Indiana in 1900.

### Terre Haute Mineral Resources

Companies worked the Seelyville and Springfield coals around Riley and Seelyville as early as the 1830s. By the 1850s, mining spread to the west side of the Wabash Valley and underground mines started to replace surface and slope mines. Mines in the Seelyville, Survant, and Springfield coals spread from West Terre Haute to New Goshen and into Vermillion County.

The Trenton oil and gas boom of 1886 in northeastern Indiana led to drilling around Terre Haute. Oil and gas plays were small, but the exploratory wells yielded valuable information about the positions and thicknesses of deep coal seams. Some twenty-eight mines operated in Vigo County by the early 1900s. Underground mining, mainly of the Survant and Springfield coal seams, peaked between 1909 and 1922.

West of the Wabash River, the Dresser and Viking Mines were underground operations opened in 1926 and 1949, respectively, to supply adjacent electric power plants. By 1935 tunnels extended under the Wabash

River to tap the coal under the eastern floodplain. The Dresser Mine closed in 1954 after a new power plant was built to the north. The Viking Mine exploded in 1961 and closed in 1964. The last underground mine in Vigo County, the Mt. Pleasant Mine near Riley, closed in 1973.

Several large strip mines along U.S. 150 between West Terre Haute and the Vermillion County line are all that remain of a mining district in the Springfield coal. The Sugar Creek Mine, later Vandalia Mine No. 82, was the first, opening in 1902. The onset of World War I led to a boom, but many of the mines closed after the war and others during the Great Depression.

The Vigo Iron Works blast furnace, south of the intersection of Washington and Sixteenth Streets in Terre Haute, began operation in 1870, the last furnace built to use the Lower and Upper Block coals. The plant used local Pennsylvanian ironstones, but eventually most of the iron ore came from southeastern Missouri. A number of related iron firms opened in Terre Haute in the late 1800s, but a combination of exhaustion of the Missouri ores, low quality of Indiana iron deposits, and rapid development of Great Lakes ports killed the industry. The Vigo blast furnace closed in about 1895, the last of its breed in western Indiana.

# Interstate 74 and U.S. 136
## Indianapolis—Illinois Line
**72 MILES**

Interstate 74 and U.S. 136 cross ground moraine of the Tipton till plain and five areas of glacial outwash in their course across western Indiana. Between Indianapolis and southwestern Boone County, the highways cross tributaries to the West Fork White River. From southwestern Boone County to Illinois, the roads pass over streams that flow directly to the Wabash River.

About 2 miles west of I-465 at Indianapolis, I-74 and U.S. 136 pass near and within the valley of Eagle Creek, filled with more than 100 feet of outwash. The valley is one of many former channels for glacial meltwaters in this part of the state.

Between the west side of the Eagle Creek valley near Clermont and the line between Fountain and Montgomery Counties, I-74 and U.S. 136 angle across 50 miles of Wisconsinan ground moraine, the Trafalgar formation. The glacial cover is thickest across northern Hendricks County, up to 250 feet, where it fills a buried bedrock valley. Farther west, the glacial sediments thin to less than 50 feet.

Two areas of outwash deposits cut across this expanse of till. One is a subtle zone of closely mixed till and outwash about 3 miles wide at the line between Boone and Hendricks Counties. The second area has two parts:

one east of Crawfordsville, in the valley of Little Sugar Creek, and the other northwest of Crawfordsville, in the larger valley of Sugar Creek and its gradation westward into a large outwash plain.

Interstate 74 and U.S. 136 cross 14 miles of Wisconsinan ground moraine between the boundary of Fountain and Montgomery Counties and the area 1 mile east of Covington. It is part of the Wedron till deposited from the Lake Michigan ice lobe. The glacial cover is generally less than 50 feet thick, so the buried bedrock terrain begins to exert its influence.

Across the Wedron formation, the highways intersect two relatively narrow areas filled with outwash. One is north of Hillsboro and about 2 miles wide. Difficult to see because the surface is only slightly lower than the surrounding areas, it is a sort of backwater of the much larger outwash plain farther south of Attica. The second area is the deep valley of Coal Creek, just east of Veedersburg. The Coal Creek valley was the outlet channel for part of the meltwater that deposited the wide outwash plain south of Attica. Lower Pennsylvanian strata of the Mansfield formation surface along parts of Coal Creek. Windblown silt covers this landscape, in many places to a depth of 5 feet.

Interstate 74 and U.S. 136 cross 4 miles of outwash in the Wabash River valley. Sand dunes lie along the east side of the river just south of Covington.

*Geology along I-74 and U.S. 136 between Indianapolis and the Illinois line.*

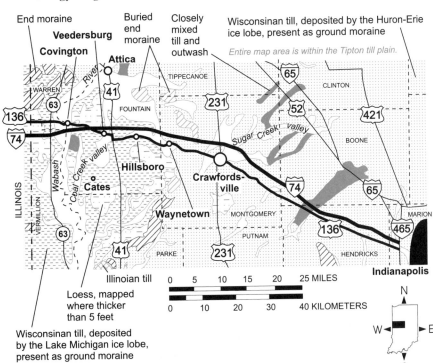

Between the west side of the Wabash River valley and the Illinois line, the routes cross 4 more miles of ground moraine deposited from the Lake Michigan ice lobe. Thick layers of windblown silt also cover this area.

Near Indiana 63, watch for shallow valleys that trend from north to south and look like slight undulations in the land surface. These defunct channels carried water that flooded out of the main river valley and scoured its way across higher ground.

### Crawfordsville Crinoids

Professor Edmund O. Hovey, who taught natural science at Wabash College, discovered siltstone slabs covered with crinoid stems in 1836 in the deeply incised valley of Sugar Creek at the north edge of Crawfordsville. He collected samples and showed them to his classes as well as sharing them with other paleontologists, including James Hall of New York. In 1842 Hovey's young son, Horace, found a crinoid head, the first reported from this site. For the next thirty years, numerous paleontologists and collectors combed the strata and collected an impressive fauna of corals, bryozoans, brachiopods, mollusks, blastoids, and crinoids. Most of the specimens came from a gray siltstone within the Borden group, probably part of the Edwardsville formation.

Corey's Bluff, a cliff some 60 feet high just west of where the old Monon Railroad bridge spans Sugar Creek, yielded many specimens. Many collectors worked the Crawfordsville site in the 1870s and 1880s, supplying specimens to many collections including those of the Berlin and British museums. Collectors and organizations purchased much of the land and quarried tons of rock. Most of the activity ceased in the early 1900s.

Some fifty crinoid species occur in the Crawfordsville strata. Early collectors did not keep detailed notes on the enclosing sediments, position in the stratigraphic sequence, and associated fossils, so their collections are not as valuable as they might be. The abundance of crinoids originally led to the belief that these were colonies, but closer study showed that currents might have carried them in from places higher on the delta.

*Generalized surface and bedrock profiles along I-74 and U.S. 136.*

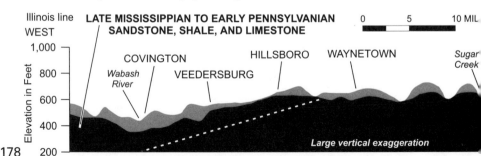

*Looking down Sugar Creek, just west of the famous crinoid collecting sites at Crawfordsville.*

## Bricks from Fountain and Montgomery Counties

The same formations that yielded the famous crinoids also provided the raw material for paving brick. The first brickyard opened there in 1880 and produced one million pavers per year over the next seven years. The Poston Paving Brick Company opened later in 1901. Its nine kilns had a capacity of six hundred thousand paving bricks per month. Production of face bricks began in 1904. Poston family members also established brick plants in Attica and Martinsville. Three other brick companies opened in Crawfordsville during the 1890s and early 1900s. They made construction bricks from Borden shales. The last closed in the 1970s.

West of Crawfordsville, the Mississippian rocks give way to the Pennsylvanian Raccoon Creek group of formations. Surface clays, underclays, and shales within the Raccoon Creek group were in high demand for ceramic

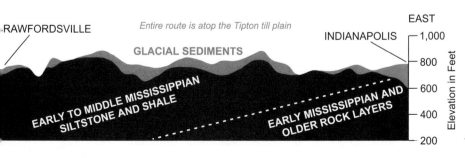

*Delicate arms and ornate features of the head, or calyx, of this Crawfordsville crinoid are nicely preserved. Calyx is three-fourths inch across.*

materials. A company at Hillsboro made bricks out of surface clay in the late 1800s, then closed by the turn of the century.

Two brick companies operated at Veedersburg around 1900. Shale pits were along Coal Creek, south of Veedersburg, and north of town along the railroad. In 1904 the Wabash Clay Company with its twenty-five beehive kilns was the largest plant of its kind in the state. Coal for the kilns came from mines at Cates and Mecca. Veedersburg still has many ornate brick sidewalks. Bricks from Veedersburg were the original paving of the Indianapolis Motor Speedway, sometimes called the Brickyard.

### Coal Creek Quarries and Mines

Quarries in the Ste. Genevieve limestone, of the Mississippian Blue River group, worked along the banks of East Fork Coal Creek 3 miles west of Waynetown in the early 1870s. Limestone suitable for building is scarce in this area, so the quarries prospered.

*The Veedersburg Paver and Culver Block were trade names of bricks fired in Veedersburg brick plants.*

180

Many small strip mines have dotted the countryside southwest of Coal Creek since the middle 1800s. The Block Coal is thin and highly discontinuous. Few mines lasted more than a few years before running out of coal. A shaft sunk 84 feet on the west side of Veedersburg in 1872 encountered both Block Coals, but a strong flow of water closed it.

# U.S. 41
## Attica—Evansville
**167 MILES**

U.S. 41 crosses a combination of young glacial landscapes and old bedrock terrains that are just beginning to show through at the surface as erosion strips the cover of glacial deposits.

U.S. 41 crosses the southern edge of the Tipton till plain for 38 miles between Attica and the area just south of Rockville. South of Attica, it passes over 8 miles of an outwash fan whose sands and gravels, generally less than 50 feet deep, were deposited as spillover from the Wabash River valley.

The highway crosses 23 miles of Wisconsinan till between the area 2.5 miles north of I-74 and that east of Bloomingdale. The Lake Michigan ice lobe deposited this till, the Wedron formation. Windblown silt caps the entire landscape, more than 5 feet thick in many places. The total thickness of glacial deposits here is 100 to 150 feet.

The hilly parts of the landscape between I-74 and the Bloomingdale area indicate the bedrock topography is beginning to show through the thinning till cover.

U.S. 41 crosses 6 miles of Wisconsinan Trafalgar till between Bloomingdale and the area 1 mile southwest of Rockville. The Huron-Erie ice lobe deposited it as ground moraine. The hills are the result of the glacial cover thinning over the buried bedrock surface. The glacial sediments are 50 to 100 feet thick.

The highway crosses 5 miles of Illinoian Glasford till on the uplands southwest of Rockville and on the hillside west of the Raccoon Creek valley. At Raccoon Creek, the road drops about 150 feet into a large valley that holds a small stream. Meltwater floods eroded the valley to its present size, then left it partially filled with about 50 feet of outwash.

U.S. 41 curls for 4 miles over a peninsula of hills between the valleys of Raccoon Creek and the Wabash River. The hills are bedrock with a cover of some 50 feet of the southernmost till deposits of the Glasford and Wedron formations. The vegetation obscures any differences between the two kinds of till.

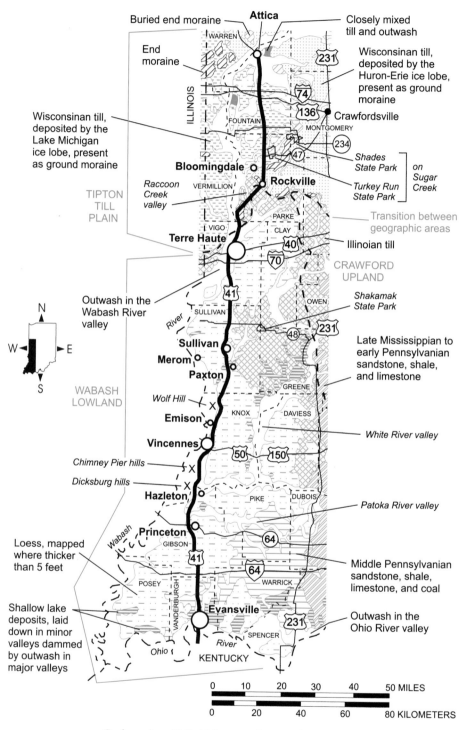

*Geology along U.S. 41 between Attica and Evansville.*

The highway crosses 17 miles of outwash and windblown deposits between Lyford and the southern edge of Terre Haute. The outwash and windblown deposits range between 100 and 150 feet deep. Most of the landscape is an outwash terrace, with sand dunes against the valley walls east of the river.

Between the southern edge of Terre Haute and the east side of Vincennes, U.S. 41 crosses 54 miles of nearly flat to locally hilly uplands. The highest portion is along the line between Vigo and Sullivan Counties. Illinoian ice left till on these hills and later windblown silts capped the till. The windblown deposits are as much as 100 feet thick near the Wabash valley, but thin to less than 50 feet farther east.

Two small areas of outwash deposits interrupt this upland tour: One is the subtle valley of Busseron Creek between Sullivan and Paxton. The other is the more sharply defined mouth of the Maria Creek valley near Emison. A large sand and gravel pit produces from the 100-foot-thick deposit of outwash west of the highway. Watch about 1 mile west of U.S. 41 for Wolf Hill, an isolated bedrock hill with a cap of windblown silt. It once stood as an island in the great floods of meltwater that poured off the glaciers as they melted at the end of the last ice age.

U.S. 41 crosses 14 miles of flat outwash deposits along the Wabash River valley between the southeast side of Vincennes and the hillside south of the White River west of Hazleton. The Wabash River is 2 to 6 miles to the west.

The Chimney Pier Hills rise out of the outwash plain 1 mile west of the highway, roughly halfway between Vincennes and the White River. They are bedrock capped with windblown silt standing like islands in a sea of outwash, similar to Wolf Hill farther north. On the north bank of the White River, U.S. 41 passes between two rises in the Dicksburg Hills, more hills that stand above the outwash.

At the White River, U.S. 41 crosses an outwash plain about 1 mile wide that holds the meandering river channel just above its junction with the Wabash River a few miles to the west. Watch for the flood control levee parallel to the White River.

Between the White River and Evansville, U.S. 41 crosses another 35 miles of hilly bedrock uplands with a thick cap of windblown silt. The narrow valley of the Patoka River, nearly filled with sediment, and the subtle valley of Pigeon Creek are the two major breaks in this terrain. Watch for oil wells. South of Princeton, the highway crosses the drainage divide that separates waters flowing west to the Wabash River from those flowing south toward the Ohio River. At Evansville, U.S. 41 leaves the diminishing bedrock uplands and enters the valley of the Ohio River, nearly filled with outwash.

## Springs, Mud, and Bricks

Springs along the Wabash River, now within Ravine Park, first attracted Indians and later drew the first settlers to Attica. A reservoir held the spring

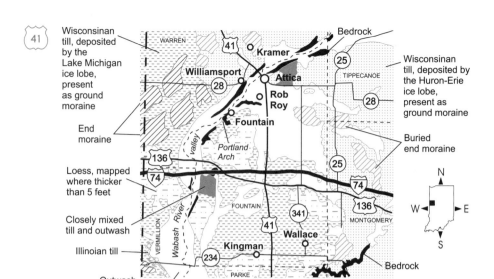

Wisconsinan till, deposited by the Lake Michigan ice lobe, present as ground moraine

End moraine

Loess, mapped where thicker than 5 feet

Closely mixed till and outwash

Illinoian till

Outwash

WARREN

41 Kramer

Williamsport
28
Attica

Rob Roy

Fountain

Portland Arch

valley

136

74

VERMILLION

Wabash River

FOUNTAIN

41

Wallace

Kingman

234

PARKE

Bedrock

25

TIPPECANOE

28

Wisconsinan till, deposited by the Huron-Erie ice lobe, present as ground moraine

Buried end moraine

25

74

136

MONTGOMERY

341

N

W ◄ ► E

S

Bedrock

*Detailed geology of the Fountain County area showing towns associated with mineral springs and quarries.*

water as early as 1835. Log pipes carried the water from the reservoir to the town. Parts of these pipes were aboveground, so people could pull one of the wood plugs to get a drink. Iron pipes and hydrants replaced those pioneer pipes in the 1870s. In 1901 the city sank deep wells into the Wabash floodplain to tap the groundwater in the outwash.

Four health spas, Lithia Springs in Attica, Mudlavia and Hunter Mineral Springs at Kramer, and Kickapoo Magnetic Spring northeast of Attica opened between 1889 and 1905. People drank the waters and soaked in muds for their supposed curative powers. Except for Mudlavia, the hotels were gone by the 1920s.

A ravine in what became Ravine Park was the source of the clay used to make the first building bricks in Attica, which survive in some of the older buildings. It was the Poston brick plant that brought fame to Attica. That plant lies in ruins now, but you can see its products in many of the older buildings on the campus of Purdue University.

*Generalized surface and bedrock profiles along U.S. 41, south of Attica.*

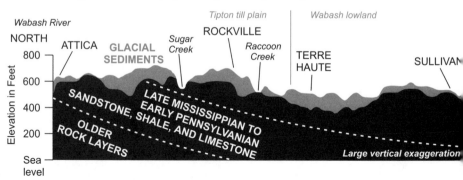

Wabash River

*Tipton till plain*

*Wabash lowland*

NORTH

ATTICA   GLACIAL SEDIMENTS

*Sugar Creek*

ROCKVILLE

*Raccoon Creek*

TERRE HAUTE

SULLIVAN

800

600

400

200

Elevation in Feet

SANDSTONE, SHALE, AND LIMESTONE

LATE MISSISSIPPIAN TO EARLY PENNSYLVANIAN

OLDER ROCK LAYERS

*Large vertical exaggeration*

Sea level

## Sandstone Products near Rob Roy and Coxville

The Pennsylvanian Mansfield formation makes cliffs along many streams in Fountain, Parke, and Warren Counties. It supplied sandstone used in building Attica, Fountain, and Williamsport. Some went into locks on the Wabash and Erie Canal.

In the early 1900s, the Western Silica Company of Danville, Illinois, mined glass sand from a layer about 15 feet thick along the south side of Shawnee Creek, 1 mile west of Rob Roy. The Acme Glass Sand Company of Terre Haute quarried 40 feet of sandstone exposed along Raccoon Creek at Coxville.

Specifications for glass sand have become much more stringent since those quarries operated. It must now be almost completely free of iron, which imparts a green color to the glass. The sand in the Mansfield formation is still used for foundry sand to make molds for casting metal into odd shapes that cannot be machined economically. A small quarry southwest of Attica produced limited quantities of foundry sand.

## Portland Arch

Portland Arch State Nature Preserve is west of U.S. 41 just southeast of Fountain. A trail leads to Bear Creek valley, a rocky canyon eroded in the Mansfield formation. The high vertical walls show crossbedding and pebble layers, souvenirs of strong scouring currents in the streams that flowed here in Pennsylvanian time. The trail leads to a natural arch eroded through a narrow ridge of sandstone. Another erosional remnant, Devil's Tea Table, looms as a pedestal in the forest.

## Kingman and Wallace Area

The country around Kingman and Wallace contains coal mines and sandstone quarries. Turn east on the first road north of Indiana 234 to see trenches of the Kingman Mine north of the road. The mine closed in the 1950s and is now full of water.

Abandoned quarries along Sugar Mill Creek just south of Wallace provided dimension stone for local buildings. A clay tile plant operated just south of the intersection of Indiana 234 and Indiana 341, south of Wallace.

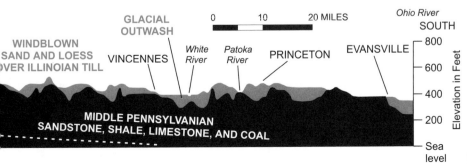

185

*Tributaries to the Wabash River cut through a resistant Pennsylvanian sandstone ridge at Portland Arch State Nature Preserve near Fountain. Note the crossbedded layers of Mansfield formation.*

### Shades State Park

Turning east on Indiana 234 also brings you to Shades State Park, developed in 1947 along Sugar Creek. Here, Sugar Creek and its tributaries have carved deep valleys and rocky canyons into the Pennsylvanian Mansfield formation and underlying Mississippian Borden group. The preglacial drainage changed as meltwater floods enlarged and deepened some stream courses and meanders formed in others that emptied into temporary proglacial lakes. Indian Creek, in adjacent Pine Hills Nature Preserve, follows a winding course before entering Sugar Creek. Apparently its ancient meanders eroded into Pennsylvanian bedrock, creating an entrenched valley 75 to 100 feet below the ridgetops. Hike back to Devils Backbone, east of Indiana 234, to see a good example. Pedestal Rock, along the north bank of Sugar Creek in Pedestal Rock Nature Preserve, is of similar origin. The lower part of the pedestal is less resistant strata of the Borden group of formations.

Shades State Park began as a resort in the late 1800s situated around mineral springs flowing from the contact of basal sandstone of the Mansfield formation and underlying siltstone and shale of the Borden group. The Garland Dells Mineral Springs Association eventually acquired the property, including the springs. They erected a forty-room hotel near the Devil's Punch Bowl, a scour basin hollowed out of the Mansfield formation. The hotel is gone now, but the natural wonders remain.

Hike the trails for spectacular views of Sugar Creek valley. Note the wide gravel bars, some of which now support trees. Follow Trail 1 for a

*Cliffs of Mississippian Borden group siltstones and shales mark the outside of a meander along Sugar Creek at Shades State Park.*

scenic view of Devil's Punch Bowl, the crossbedded Mansfield formation rich in colorful iron oxides, shelter caves, seeping springs, and the unusual Silver Cascade. The lower, main part of this waterfall is a bulging mass of Borden siltstone. The surface is convex because of internal expansion of the rock due to freezing during the winter. Silver Cascade marks the unconformable contact of the Mississippian and Pennsylvanian rocks. Fossilized crinoid stems dot the surface of gray limestone that forms the upper cascade and also serves as the trail path.

### Turkey Run State Park

A short side trip on Indiana 47 leads to Turkey Run State Park, one of the most beautiful in the state. We owe the preservation of its rocks and wildlife to a visionary son of the Lusk family who moved there in the 1820s. John Lusk died in 1915 and the family home became Indiana's first state park.

The name Turkey Run came from the flocks of wild turkeys that frequented the sandstone cliffs in the early days. The park is mostly flat uplands with a thin mantle of till. Sugar Creek flows through a narrow canyon eroded in the Mansfield formation. Two major and many secondary tributaries to Sugar Creek have dissected the upland into steep canyons eroded along vertical fractures in sandstone layers. Layers of weaker shale and silt-

*Small tributaries cut deep valleys as they flow into Sugar Creek at Shades State Park.*

stone appear as indented zones on the cliff faces and explain some of the overhanging cliffs and shelter caves.

Layers of rounded pebbles in the rocks tell of times 300 million years ago when torrents of water swept gravel down streams. A number of potholes may be seen in the walls of the canyons as well as on their floors. These mark areas where hard cobbles were swirled about by the stream water, abrading and gouging holes. Intersecting inclined beds, or crossbeds, are prevalent in the rocks too.

Thin layers of rusty nodules are the source of the reddish brown iron oxide stain seen on weathered surfaces of the Mansfield formation. These nodules are common. They were once mined as iron ore at various localities in southwestern Indiana.

Steep cliffs eroded in the Mansfield formation appear at many sites south of Sugar Creek, and even more are across the suspension bridge. Near that bridge are many canyons, potholes, and unusual weathering features that follow the fracture patterns in the rocks. A thin seam of Block Coal along Trail 4 was mined in the late 1800s as fuel for iron smelting.

### Parke County Coal

The date of the first coal mining in Parke County is unknown. The first mines worked at the surface, but underground mining expanded as the easy

*Sugar Creek meanders through the scenic terrain of Turkey Run State Park. This creek is responsible for much of the Parke County landscape.*

surface coal disappeared. Most of the earliest mines exploited the Minshall and Seelyville coals of the Brazil and Staunton formations.

Coke Oven Hollow, west of Annapolis, was the site of a coal mine by about 1835. A nearby iron furnace used coke made at this location, and some was shipped to Cincinnati. Many other small mines opened along the tributaries to the Wabash River from the 1850s to 1860s. Coal mining became big business in the late 1800s, when it centered around Caseyville, Lyford, Mecca, Minshall, Nyesville, Rosedale, and Roseville. This correlated with railroad construction and the appetites of the steam locomotives.

The Sand Creek Coal Company opened a slope mine along Sand Creek in 1872, the eventual site of Nyesville. Meanwhile, the Parke County Coal Company worked in the Rosedale area. Eight mines eventually worked the Minshall coal and Rosedale became a typical boom-and-bust town of the coal belt. The Parke County Coal Company also opened three mines southeast of Catlin at the former site of Minshall. Minshall made history in the 1880s when the state militia was called in to quell a violent strike.

Roseville and Caseyville have similar boom-and-bust histories. The Brazil Block Coal Company opened a mine at Roseville in 1885, completely exhausted the coal, and closed it before the First World War. Other companies operated mines at Caseyville, now Diamond, from the 1890s to the early 1900s. It is hard to believe that around twelve hundred people once lived there.

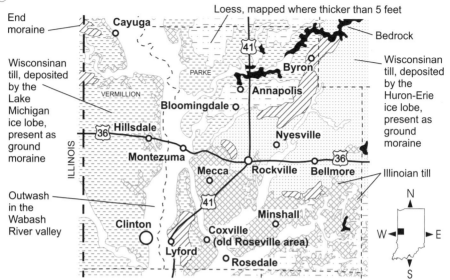

End moraine

Loess, mapped where thicker than 5 feet

Cayuga

Bedrock

Wisconsinan till, deposited by the Lake Michigan ice lobe, present as ground moraine

PARKE

VERMILLION

Byron

Annapolis

Bloomingdale

Hillsdale

Nyesville

Wisconsinan till, deposited by the Huron-Erie ice lobe, present as ground moraine

ILLINOIS

Montezuma

Mecca

Rockville

Bellmore

Illinoian till

Outwash in the Wabash River valley

Clinton

Coxville
(old Roseville area)

Lyford

Minshall

Rosedale

N
W — E
S

*Detailed geology and towns associated with coal and clay mining in Parke and Vermillion Counties.*

On the west side of Parke County, coal mines opened in the Seelyville coal at Lyford and Mecca in the 1890s. All were abandoned by 1912. Mines operated in Parke County sporadically into the 1970s, but most of the easy coal is gone.

### A Ghost Arch in the Mansfield Area

A side trip east along U.S. 36 at Rockville and then south on Indiana 59 brings you to the small community of Mansfield. The surrounding area contains the remnants of a natural bridge and old sandstone quarries.

Perhaps the most spectacular natural arch in Indiana stood along a tributary to Raccoon Creek between Ferndale and Mansfield. The span was 60 feet long and 20 feet wide, with a 6-foot passageway underneath. The arch may have formed as meltwaters eroded a sandstone ridge of Pennsylvanian Mansfield formation during the last ice age. For many years the arch was known only to locals and geologists. Unfortunately, it was on the edge of a sandstone quarry, which destroyed it in the early 1950s.

This sandstone quarry was just one of many small quarries that once operated in eastern Parke County. The first ones opened in the late 1800s to quarry the Mansfield Brownstone, a coarsely granular upper part of the Mansfield formation. The stone was used for foundations and bridge abutments. The L. L. Wolf Quarry, just north of Mansfield, was the best known. It shipped stone to many places in Indiana, Illinois, Kentucky, Ohio, and

Nebraska during the late 1800s. Competition from other building-stone belts gradually drove these small firms out of business by the early 1900s. A need for face stone from the 1940s to the 1960s led to a temporary revival.

### Brick, Pottery, and Tile

The glacial soils and Pennsylvanian formations of Parke County provided clay for making stoneware as early as the 1820s. Annapolis, Bloomingdale, Coke Oven Hollow, and Rockville all had pottery shops by the 1830s. Completion of the Wabash and Erie Canal in the 1840s opened trade routes to the south and northeast.

Seven clay plants once did business in Hillsdale and Montezuma, west along U.S. 36. The Burns and Hancock Fire Brick Company at West Montezuma was the pioneer of Indiana fire brick manufacturers, making its first bricks in 1872 from local underclay. The Marion Brick Works of Montezuma was the largest facility making ordinary brick in the state around the turn of the century. Pennsylvanian shales stripped from nearby hillsides provided the raw material. The plant site is south of U.S. 36 just east of the railroad viaduct east of town. The scarred hills north of the highway mark the location of the National Drain Tile Company plant.

A brick factory, now gone, operated around 1900 in Byron. Two homes made of its brick still stand in town. A plant at Bellmore made drainage tile. One of the more recent companies, Dee Clay Products, established in 1937, sold bricks and drainage tile from an eight-kiln plant in Bloomingdale.

Cayuga was a center of brick manufacture in Vermillion County. Bluffs along the Wabash River there expose Pennsylvanian shales, clays, and coals. Three companies made bricks. At Clinton, a paving brick company quarried shale beginning in 1893.

### Montezuma Mineral Waters

Mineral waters are common in the Pennsylvanian rocks. A sanitarium and hotel opened on the east bank of the Wabash River on the south side of Montezuma in the 1890s, attracting customers who wished to partake of the curative waters. As in several other cases, the mineral waters appeared during the search for oil and gas.

### Mecca Sewer Pipe

In 1896 William E. Dee launched the heyday of Mecca, just west of U.S. 41, when he opened a sewer tile factory. Fire clay and shale from the Raccoon Creek group rocks provided the raw material which was fired in thirty-four kilns. The Great Depression finally closed the factory, and just a few crumbling remnants survive in the woods northwest of town. The Indiana Sewer Pipe Company began business at Mecca in 1907, but now only huge drain tiles and towering smokestacks remain.

## Sharks in Indiana

The fossilized fin of a Pennsylvanian shark was discovered in a black shale near Mecca in 1950. The find was significant because of its extreme rarity. Sharks have no bones, only cartilage, so their teeth are the only parts that commonly survive as fossils. Chicago's Field Museum opened a small quarry in the 1950s and collected fossil skeletons of many more fish. Prospecting the hills for similar shales led to the discovery of a partial shark fossil about 12 feet long near Annapolis.

## Sullivan and Greene County Coal Mines

By 1870 small mines worked the Hymera coal of the Carbondale group of formations near Shelburn. They shipped coal to Terre Haute for coking and blast furnaces, sold some to blacksmiths and some for heating homes. Underground mining of the Hymera coal and underlying Springfield and Survant coals was an important industry in eastern Sullivan County, especially near Bucktown, Dugger, Hymera, Shelburn, and Wilfred. The same coals were mined from the 1890s to the 1920s between Jasonville and Linton in western Greene County and near Coalmont in southwestern Clay County.

*Strip-mined areas and towns associated with coal mining and oil in Sullivan, Greene, and Knox Counties.*

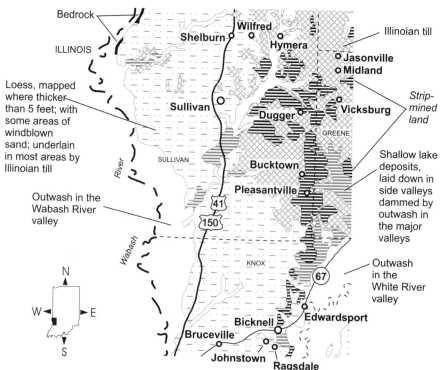

Strip mining from the Danville and Hymera seams expanded in the early 1900s and after the Second World War. The Minnehaha Mine stretches north of Indiana 54 between Dugger and Sullivan. The Hawthorn Mine at Pleasantville offers similar views. Huge draglines strip three or four coal seams at once, something unheard of in the early 1900s.

The Coal Museum on Main Street in Dugger displays historical photos and artifacts, keeping alive the colorful history of coal in this part of Indiana.

## Shakamak State Park

Shakamak State Park is east of U.S. 41, along Indiana 48 between Hymera and Jasonville. It covers mined land as does the neighboring Minnehaha State Fish and Wildlife Area. The scars of coal mining are thinly disguised as ponds and piney hills. Trail 2 passes an abandoned mine.

## Merom—A Great View of the Wabash River

The bluff that rises 100 feet above the Wabash River in western Sullivan County became the site of Merom in 1817. The town rapidly developed into a trading center, then declined when the railroad bypassed it in 1854. The old commons is now Merom Bluff Park. It offers an excellent view across the Wabash Valley and Lamont Prairie of Illinois. The bedrock is the Mattoon formation of the McLeansboro group. The Merom sandstone is exposed along the bluff and was quarried for use in the old college buildings at Merom.

## Sullivan County Oil Field

Oil was discovered in the Pennsylvanian bedrock 2 miles west of Sullivan in 1906. By 1914 more than four hundred wells dotted the countryside there and west of Shelburn. The field still produces small quantities of oil, but some now comes from Devonian limestones some 2,000 feet deeper.

## Bicknell Coal Mines

Indiana 550 and Indiana 67 lead east from U.S. 41 to Bicknell, the center of another important coal district. The first mine opened in the 1870s. Many others followed, tapping the Danville, Hymera, Bucktown, and Springfield coals of the Dugger formation. Mines also operated at Bruceville, Edwardsport, Johnstown, and Ragsdale. The American No. 1 Mine at Ragsdale became known as the Million Ton Mine in the 1920s for its record production in the days before mechanization. This part of Knox County still has coal mines, but they are not as productive as they once were.

## Energy Under Princeton

In 1891 gas exploded from a well on the east side of Princeton. Other wells also produced gas and revealed a series of coal beds underneath the town, some mineable.

*An early oil field near St. Francisville, Illinois, neighboring Knox County, Indiana.* —Mark J. Camp Collection

The systematic search for petroleum began in 1902. The next year a well found oil in Pennsylvanian sandstone and started a rush. Sixteen companies were active by the fall of 1903. More than 150 wells perforated the country-side west of U.S. 41 between Princeton and Patoka by 1907. Pumps now raise oil from nine horizons as deep as the Mississippian Harrodsburg formation, nearly 2,700 feet below the surface.

# U.S. 50 and U.S. 150
## Shoals—Illinois Line
**46 MILES**

These two routes share a common roadway across bedrock terrain mostly capped with glacial deposits and windblown silt and sand. The route crosses parts of the basins of the East and West Forks of the White River and a small part of the Wabash River basin.

West of Shoals, U.S. 50 and U.S. 150 cross 5 miles of bedrock hills eroded in sandstones, shales, and limestones deposited from middle Mississippian through late Pennsylvanian time. This short route also passes near the deep valley of the East Fork White River, partly filled with glacial outwash.

The Shoals Overlook, just west of town, offers a spectacular view of a meander loop entrenched in the valley floor, some 250 feet below. Small

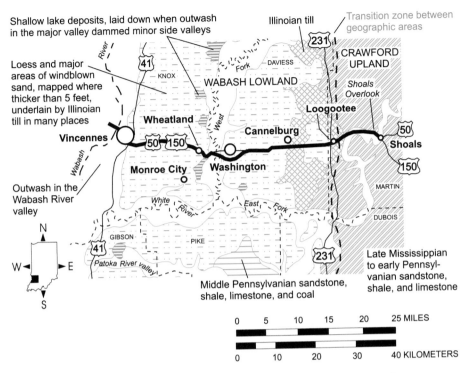

*Geology along U.S. 50 and U.S. 150 between Shoals and the Illinois line.*

areas of sand at the bases of the western sides of the ridges are part of the great blanket of windblown sediments that spreads across western Indiana.

The highways cross the western edge of the Crawford upland and the eastern edge of the Wabash lowland between Shoals and Loogootee. Despite the name, the Wabash lowland is hilly. Between the area 1 mile east of Loogootee and Vincennes, the highway crosses 34 miles of hills eroded in sandstones, shales, and limestones with numerous coal seams, all deposited during middle Pennsylvanian time. Illinoian ice covered this area and left behind till deposits, but erosion has since removed all but a thin cap on the ridge crests.

Strong winds deposited thick layers of silt on the uplands. Winds also added large deposits of dune sand, more than 50 feet thick in places, to the valley walls east of the West Fork White River and the Wabash River.

At the West Fork White River, the highways cross a meltwater valley about 3 miles wide with more than 100 feet of outwash in its floor.

At Vincennes, U.S. 50 curls north around the city and crosses 4 miles of outwash in the Wabash River valley before entering Illinois. Although not

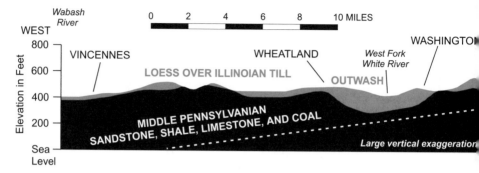

*Generalized surface and bedrock profiles along U.S. 50 and U.S. 150.*

described here, U.S. 150 shares the roadway with U.S. 41 north to Terre Haute, before turning west to Illinois.

### Loogootee–Clay and Glass Products

Kilns fired local clay as early as 1844 at a site that later became the Loogootee Clay Products Company. The plant produced bricks, clay blocks for basements, and tile. A number of potteries also operated in Loogootee during the late 1800s.

Glass factories appeared on the west side of Loogootee shortly before 1900. At least five used the local natural gas to make glass from the local sandstones of the Pennsylvanian Mansfield formation.

### Coal Mines of Daviess and Knox Counties

By 1870 more than fifteen coal mines operated around Washington and Cannelburg. Cannel coal has a distinctly waxy look and feel. It commands a

*A modern coal mine near Wheatland.*

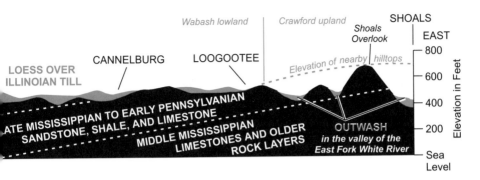

high price because it burns very well and leaves little ash. Many other small mines dotted the countryside on either side of the highway. A few underground mines still produce coal near Wheatland and Monroe City.

### Indiana Furnace

A blast furnace began operation along Brouilletts Creek west of Clinton in 1840. The raw ore delivered to the furnace for smelting was iron carbonate, or siderite, exposed above the Danville coal. The eventual lack of wood for charcoal and the isolated location finally closed the operation in 1861. Later strip mine operations removed all evidence of its existence.

# U.S. 231
## Lafayette—Kentucky Line
### 192 MILES

U.S. 231 crosses ancient bedrock, old and young glacial till and outwash, and windblown sand and silt. It passes through three drainage basins: a small part of the Wabash River basin between Lafayette and the area south of Crawfordsville, the west side of the greater White River basin between central Putnam County and southern Dubois County, and several minor creeks between northern Spencer County and the Ohio River. North of Lafayette, U.S. 231 parallels I-65 to Gary; the description for that interstate applies equally well to U.S. 231.

U.S. 231 crosses the Tipton till plain for 57 miles between Lafayette and its intersection with U.S. 40. Wisconsinan till, the Trafalgar formation, lies beneath this generally flat countryside. It was deposited by the Huron-Erie ice lobe. The till is generally 50 to 100 feet thick here, but a buried valley east of the highway in southern Tippecanoe County contains as much as 300 feet of undifferentiated glacial fill. Another buried valley with 100 to

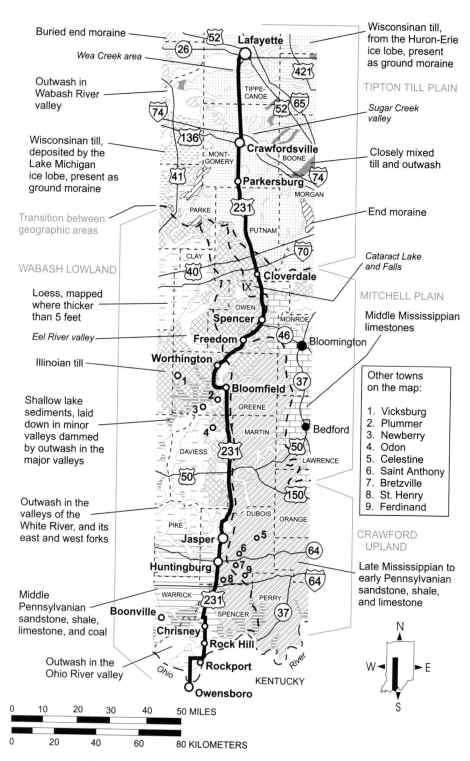

*Geology along U.S. 231 between Lafayette and the Kentucky line.*

200 feet of till lies along the line between Montgomery and Putnam Counties.

U.S. 231 crosses 4 miles of a shallow valley filled with outwash at Lafayette just south of its intersection with Indiana 25. The highway passes into another shallow valley filled with outwash about 5 miles north of Crawfordsville.

U.S. 231 crosses Sugar Creek on the north side of Crawfordsville. The creek eroded a gorge about 50 feet deep in rocks of the Borden group, deposited during Mississippian time. Downtown Crawfordsville stands on tens of feet of outwash deposits along the south edge of the Sugar Creek valley.

Windblown silt covers much of the Tipton till plain between Crawfordsville and Parkersburg. It is generally between 20 and 40 inches thick but is more than 60 inches thick in the area between New Market and Parkersburg. The Tipton till plain becomes increasingly hilly as the glacial cover thins and the buried bedrock terrain asserts its presence between Parkersburg and U.S. 40.

Between U.S. 40 and the area about 1 mile south of Spencer, U.S. 231 crosses 21 miles of hills eroded into middle Mississippian limestone. This is the northernmost portion of the Mitchell plain. Illinoian till and windblown silt cap the hills. The silt cover is thickest, slightly more than 5 feet, southeast of Cloverdale. Isolated bedrock hills just west of Cloverdale are the Raccoon Creek group of Pennsylvanian formations.

South of Spencer, U.S. 231 approaches the bedrock valley of the West Fork White River, where that river runs through the narrowest chasm along its entire length.

Between the area 1 mile south of Spencer and 1 mile north of Huntingburg, U.S. 231 crosses 73 miles of the Crawford upland. The bedrock is sandstones, shales, and limestones deposited during late Mississippian and middle Pennsylvanian time. A thin covering of Illinoian till, the Jessup formation, tops these hills. A blanket of windblown silt more than 5 feet thick in many places covers the till.

About 5 miles north of Worthington, the highway makes a short jaunt across river bottomland in an abandoned meander loop of the West Fork White River.

Between Worthington and the west side of Bloomfield, U.S. 231 curls across 9 miles of the West Fork White River valley filled with outwash. Practically every side valley in this stretch is layered with lake sediments that accumulated in shallow waters impounded behind outwash in the main river valley. At least eight such areas are known. This short segment of U.S. 231 also crosses two low bedrock hills, capped with Illinoian till, isolated by erosion in this meltwater valley. Almost any back road leads to active and abandoned strip mines.

U.S. 231 crosses the deep valley of the East Fork White River at the line between Martin and Dubois Counties. It has glacial outwash as its floor. Watch near Portersville for cliffs about 120 feet high in the Mansfield formation and shelter caves. Excavations at Kitchen Rock, Raven Rock, and Rock House yielded animal and human bones, burned and blackened hearth stones, and artifacts.

Between the area 1 mile north of Huntingburg and the Ohio River, U.S. 231 crosses 41 miles of hills, along the eastern side of the wide Wabash lowland. The rounded hills, eroded from sandstones, shales, and limestones deposited during middle Pennsylvanian time, include numerous coal seams. The coal was mined from both strip and underground mines. Any side trip to an area about 10 miles west of the highway takes you into strip-mined countryside.

The cap of windblown silt thickens to about 5 feet in the hills west of Chrisney. Strong winds swept it off the outwash plains of the Wabash and Ohio Rivers.

In the shallow valley south of Chrisney, U.S. 231 approaches the Ohio River valley across 2 miles of shallow lake sediments. They were deposited when glacial outwash in the floodplain of the Ohio River ponded a tributary stream. Similar lake sediments exist in at least fifteen small valleys on the Indiana side of the Ohio River.

Between Rock Hill and Rockport, U.S. 231 cuts across outwash in the Ohio River valley. West and south of Rockport, the highway angles across low bedrock hills capped with a thick cover of windblown silt. The road returns to the valley filled with outwash on the way to the bridge to Owensboro, Kentucky.

### Clinton Falls

Clinton Falls is southwest of the junction of U.S. 231 and U.S. 36. Little Walnut Creek falls about 8 feet over strata of the Mississippian Blue River group. Look for potholes on the exposed ledges.

*Generalized surface and bedrock profiles along U.S. 231.*

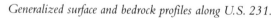

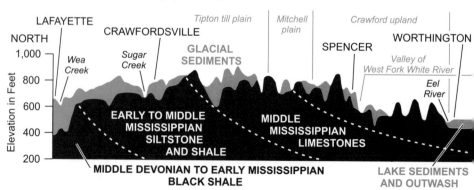

## Cataract Lake—Evidence of Multiple Glaciations

Rocks exposed along the emergency spillway of Cataract Lake, west of U.S. 231, provide evidence of changing environments in Pennsylvanian time and of multiple glaciations in Pleistocene time.

The spillway exposes rocks of the Raccoon Creek group and shows the gentle trough of an ancient stream valley filled with crossbedded sandstone. A coal seam above the sandstone shows that the area became a swamp and a layer of decaying vegetation accumulated. The fairly rapid change in rock types from the bottom to the top of this section nicely illustrates the migration of streams through the Pennsylvanian coastal swamps and the resulting changes in deposition.

The Pleistocene sediments that overlie the Pennsylvanian rocks include the first Kansan glacial sediments discovered in Indiana. They are much older than the Illinoian till that covers large parts of the state. Three feet of brownish silt, full of fossil snails, lie on top of the Pennsylvanian rocks. The silt records a time when the area was free of ice and land snails thrived. Some of the snails occur only in sediments of Kansan age. Although not visible in the spillway cut, nearby Kansan glacial sediments reach some 27 feet in thickness; Illinoian ice left 23 feet of its own till.

## Cataract Falls State Recreation Area

Cataract Falls State Recreation Area is 6 miles west of U.S. 231, just south of Cloverdale, off Indiana 42. Bedrock in this area is Mississippian and Pennsylvanian in age, but the landscape owes its origin mainly to events of Pleistocene time.

While the Illinoian ice melted, the edge of the glacier stagnated in northern Morgan County, covering the former headwaters of Mill Creek. Meltwater ponded along the ice edge and flooded the lower reaches of the creek for some 50 square miles. Layers of fine silt and clay accumulated in Glacial Lake Quincy.

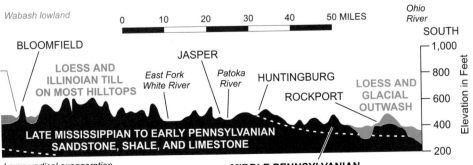

Wabash lowland

BLOOMFIELD

LOESS AND ILLINOIAN TILL ON MOST HILLTOPS

JASPER

East Fork White River

Patoka River

HUNTINGBURG

ROCKPORT

Ohio River

SOUTH

LOESS AND GLACIAL OUTWASH

Elevation in Feet

1,000
800
600
400
200

0 10 20 30 40 50 MILES

LATE MISSISSIPPIAN TO EARLY PENNSYLVANIAN SANDSTONE, SHALE, AND LIMESTONE

MIDDLE PENNSYLVANIAN SANDSTONE, SHALE, LIMESTONE, AND COAL

Large vertical exaggeration

*Raccoon Creek group strata along the emergency spillway at Cataract Lake near Cloverdale.*

*Mill Creek drops over a resistant ledge of Mississippian Blue River group limestones to form Lower Cataract Falls just off Indiana 42, southwest of Cloverdale.*

*Numerous potholes lie in the bed of Mill Creek at Cataract Falls State Recreation Area.*

After the ice was gone, Mill Creek resumed its former course and eroded through the soft lake sediments. Prominent terraces that flank the creek are remnants of the lake plain. As the creek entrenched its channel, it exposed bedrock of the Mississippian Blue River group near the western margin of the lake plain. Upper and Lower Cataract Falls cascade across those rocks as Mill Creek drops some 80 feet in less than 1 mile. Many potholes in the rock appear at low water, evidence of the swirling eddies that stir the stream.

### Unconformity at Freedom

A low roadcut on U.S. 231, 1 mile south of Freedom, exposes an unconformity where the Pennsylvanian Mansfield formation lies on a buried erosion surface developed on the Mississippian Beech Creek limestone. The intervening formations of the Stephensport and Buffalo Wallow groups are missing, presumably because they were eroded.

### Greene County Coal Mines

U.S. 231 follows the West Fork White River valley through most of Greene County. Coal mines have operated for more than a century in the area west of the highway. Underground mining began around Linton in the 1890s, spreading north, south, and west; then it slowly died as strip mines began to dominate in the 1930s. Large strip mines lie northwest of Worthington, at the junction with Indiana 54, and on either side of Indiana 59 near the line

*The Pennsylvanian Mansfield formation unconformably overlies the Mississippian Beech Creek limestone along U.S. 231, just south of Freedom.*

between Greene and Sullivan Counties. They produce from the Brazil, Staunton, Linton, Petersburg, and Dugger formations.

### Richland Furnace

The Pennsylvanian Mansfield formation surfaces along the West Fork White River valley where U.S. 231 passes through Greene County. It has yielded good building stone and mediocre iron ore. Sandstone quarries operated northwest of Worthington and along Plummers and Richland Creeks near Mineral City in the late 1860s. Sandstone slabs were used in foundations, steps, and trim pieces of buildings in Bloomfield and Worthington.

Nothing remains of the Richland Iron Furnace that once operated south of Bloomfield. In 1841 it began to produce iron for plows and other ironware from ore mined from the Mansfield formation, but the operation closed in the 1850s. Most of the products were shipped downriver to southern markets.

### Plummer Oil Field

Although Greene County bedrock was used for several underground gas storage sites, a major oil field of more than one hundred wells escaped discovery until 1969. The Plummer field is west of U.S. 231 on the west side of

*Atlas No. 8 Coal Mine near Linton, circa 1910.* —Mark J. Camp Collection

the West Fork White River between Newberry and Plummer. The discovery was in middle Devonian rocks; later wells also produce from the much younger Ste. Genevieve and Salem limestones of Mississippian age. The wells produce from an arch that probably formed as younger sedimentary formations draped over buried Silurian reefs along the edge of the Illinois Basin.

### Strip Mining in Daviess, Dubois, and Spencer Counties

The highway crosses a vast region of strip mines between Greene County and the Ohio River. Many of the early mines worked underground around Washington and Cannelburg. Strip mines came later, and now you can see them in active, abandoned, and reclaimed conditions west of U.S. 231, in a belt between Odon and Alfordsville. They all worked coals from the Mansfield, Brazil, and Staunton formations.

Most of the coal mines in Dubois County produce from the Mansfield and Brazil formations west of the highway between Jasper and Huntingburg. Earlier underground mines were in Reservoir Hill at Jasper, near Bretzville, Celestine, Ferdinand, Portersville, St. Anthony, and St. Henry.

### Glacial Diversion at Jasper

The Patoka River flows through Jasper in a narrow valley carved in a resistant ridge of Pennsylvanian sandstone, but it was not always that way. Before the glaciers came, the ancestral Patoka River flowed about 2 miles

205

*Stages in stream diversion because of glacial ice near Jasper.*

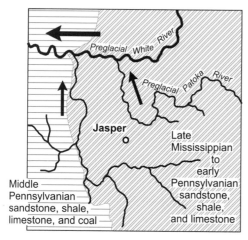

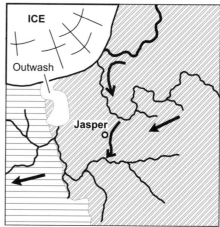

**Preglacial Landscape:** The Patoka River was one of several small, local streams that flowed generally north to the preglacial White River. The future location of Jasper sits on a divide between the small streams.

**Maximum Ice Advance:** During Illinoian time, ice diverted the preglacial White and Patoka Rivers to the southwest, and meltwater carved a new channel at Jasper and farther west. Outwash began filling part of the valleys of some of the former small streams.

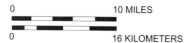

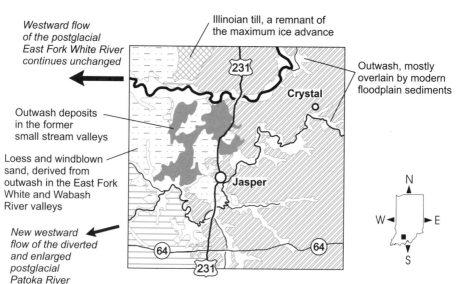

**Modern Landscape:** The Patoka River is now isolated from the postglacial East Fork White River. The former small stream valleys are filled with outwash and modern floodplain deposits.

*Coal stripping operations near Huntingburg.*

north of Jasper in a deep valley to join the East Fork White River. Ice diverted the Patoka River about 4 miles west of Crystal, onto the ridge of sandstone at Jasper. The old channel north of Jasper is now completely filled with outwash and is invisible at the surface. West of Jasper, the river parallels the White River all the way to the Wabash River at East Mt. Carmel, winding among the low hills of the Wabash lowland, in some places on a wide floodplain. The modern Patoka River is an underfit stream, too small for the valley it inherited from the floods of meltwater.

### Mineral Springs near Boonville

Ash Iron Springs, Fairview Springs, and DeGonia Springs long ago lured health-conscious people to central Warrick County. Some visitors stayed at the hotels and used the baths at Fairview Springs and Ash Iron Springs, others simply fetched bottles of the bitter water. DeGonia Springs became the most popular of these resorts because it was on the line of the Southern Railway. The popularity of these spas declined by the early 1900s, and they closed after their hotels burned in the 1930s.

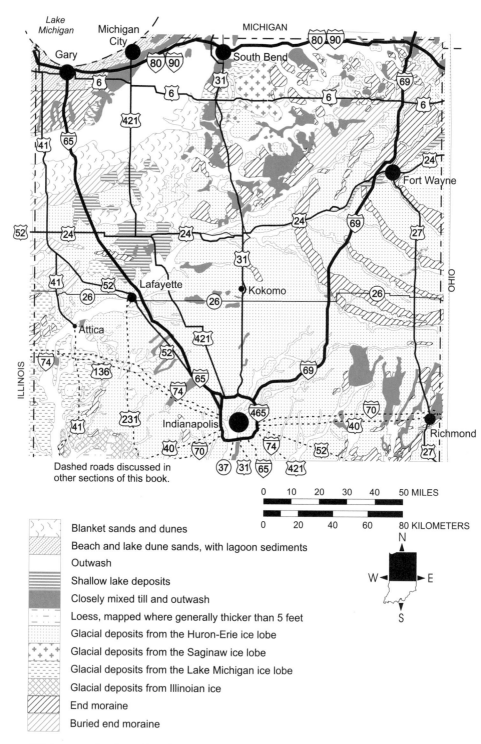

Lake Michigan

MICHIGAN

Michigan City

Gary

South Bend

Fort Wayne

OHIO

ILLINOIS

Lafayette

Kokomo

Attica

Indianapolis

Richmond

Dashed roads discussed in
other sections of this book.

0    10    20    30    40    50 MILES

0        20        40        60        80 KILOMETERS

N
W◄──────►E
S

Blanket sands and dunes
Beach and lake dune sands, with lagoon sediments
Outwash
Shallow lake deposits
Closely mixed till and outwash
Loess, mapped where generally thicker than 5 feet
Glacial deposits from the Huron-Erie ice lobe
Glacial deposits from the Saginaw ice lobe
Glacial deposits from the Lake Michigan ice lobe
Glacial deposits from Illinoian ice
End moraine
Buried end moraine

*Highways and geology of northern Indiana. Map patterns for glacial geology are used on all roadlog maps in the Northern Indiana chapter.*

# Northern Indiana
## GLACIAL PLAINS OVER BEDROCK HILLS

The flatness of the northern half of the state contrasts with the forested hills of southern Indiana. Hills and valleys like those in southern Indiana lie buried under a veneer of ice-age glacial deposits.

### THE LATE ORDOVICIAN AND SILURIAN WORLD

The early Paleozoic sedimentary rocks of northern Indiana were laid down in ancient shallow seas. Regional movements during Ordovician time raised a broad structure known as the Cincinnati Arch, which probably brought new sediments above sea level. The exposed sediments eroded before later seas covered them with more sediments. Meanwhile, the Kankakee Arch rose to the northwest, further separating what would become the Illinois and Michigan Basins. As the subsidence of these basins continued, the pattern of deposition across Indiana changed.

*Whitewater Formation.* The oldest bedrock layers in northern Indiana are the limestones and shales of the late Ordovician Whitewater formation. Their only surface exposure near northern Indiana is in the deeper parts of the river valleys south of the Richmond area. The Ordovician period ended as the newly deposited sediments rose above sea level and eroded.

*Brassfield Limestone and Cataract Formation.* The sea again flooded the northern Indiana area in Silurian time, and deposition resumed with the Brassfield limestone southwest of the Kankakee Arch and the Cataract formation northeast of the arch. The Cataract formation, which is not exposed on the surface in Indiana, is generally gray dolomite with greenish shale in its upper part. It ranges from 10 feet thick along the crest of the arch to 100 feet thick in northeastern Indiana. The Brassfield and Cataract rocks have what geologists call a facies relationship—different kinds of rocks formed in connected areas at the same time. Facies relationships are common between sedimentary rocks in different regions and have long complicated geologists' lives.

*Salamonie Dolomite.* The Salamonie dolomite was laid down next in two units. The lower unit is the Osgood member, generally impure limestone, dolomite, and shale. The upper unit, the Laurel member, is a much purer, whitish fossiliferous dolomite. Along the crest of the Kankakee Arch, the Salamonie dolomite is about 50 feet thick, but thickens to 100 feet in northwestern Indiana and to more than 250 feet in the northeastern part of the state. This formation contains the oldest of the small patch reefs that continued to grow into Devonian time.

*Salina Group.* Silurian deposition north of the Kankakee Arch continued with the Salina group, a large, wedge-shaped unit that ranges from 50 feet thick along the arch crest to 400 feet thick in northwestern Indiana and 500 feet thick in northeastern Indiana.

The lower Salina unit is the Pleasant Mills formation that contains a variety of carbonates. In some places the rock is brownish fine-grained dolomite; in other places it is whitish pure dolomite. The latter type is typical of the patch reefs that were still growing from the earlier starts in the Salamonie dolomite.

The upper Salina unit is the Wabash formation. It is variably colored and mostly ranges from pure limestone to dolomitic limestone to dolomite in the thousands of small patch reefs. This formation also includes interreef sediments like the Mississinewa shale member that ranges from a silty dolomite to a dolomitic siltstone.

Part of the Salina group has facies relationships with other Silurian rocks in southwestern Indiana. The Pleasant Mills formation is related to the Waldron shale and the Louisville limestone. The Wabash formation is not assigned to a group southwest of the Kankakee Arch.

As Silurian time continued, the land rose above sea level and was eroded again. The Wabash formation is missing from southeastern Indiana because of this erosion.

### SILURIAN REEFS IN INDIANA

From 420 to 405 million years ago, Silurian Indiana was a shallow sea dotted with numerous small reefs, in the form of mounds of organic debris—stromatoporoids, bryozoans, crinoids, brachiopods, some types of mollusks, and algae. Early geologists did not understand these mounds, but in 1928 two Indiana geologists correctly identified the mounds as fossil reefs.

These ancient reefs formed as isolated mounds in shallow ocean waters with no particular orientation to any land area. They ranged from only a few feet wide to about 1 mile across, and from a few feet to 75 feet above the seafloor. In contrast, modern reefs tend to be long fringes along coasts. Silurian reefs became tall, narrow columns in the rock record, as much as 800 or more feet high, because most of them continued to grow as sediments accumulated around them. Growth ceased if the reef was buried by sediments.

Most Silurian reefs across Indiana are in two great tracts, the Fort Wayne Bank to the north and the Terre Haute Bank to the southwest. Outcrop

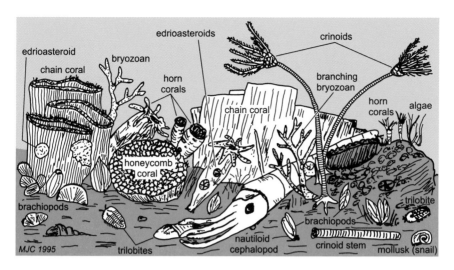

*Typical animals of a Silurian reef. Brachiopods, bryozoans, corals, mollusks, trilobites, and crinoids were common.*

samples and drilling indicate that thousands of mound reefs may exist. These banks developed on the flanks of the Kankakee Arch. More than three hundred other reefs are recorded between these two banks. Most Silurian reefs exposed by erosion are along the Wabash River and the lower stretches of the Mississinewa and Salamonie Rivers. Hanging Rock near Lagro is an easily visited reef site.

Today the Silurian reefs are dolomite—magnesium-calcium carbonate—but they grew as mostly calcium carbonate. Magnesium-rich waters later

*Generalized cross-sectional and oblique views of Silurian reefs.*

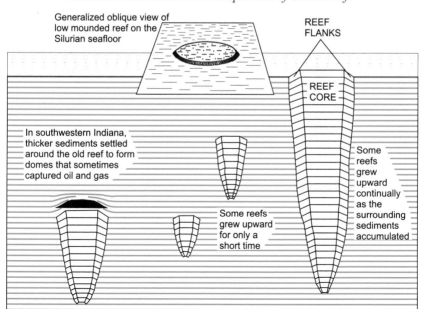

211

replaced some of the calcium with magnesium. This preserves the general shape of the reef and its fossils, but expansion in the new minerals destroys details.

Fewer than thirty quarries produce limestone from reef rock across Indiana. The pioneers mined it for road stone and railroad ballast, also burning

*Silurian reefs across Indiana and nearby states.*

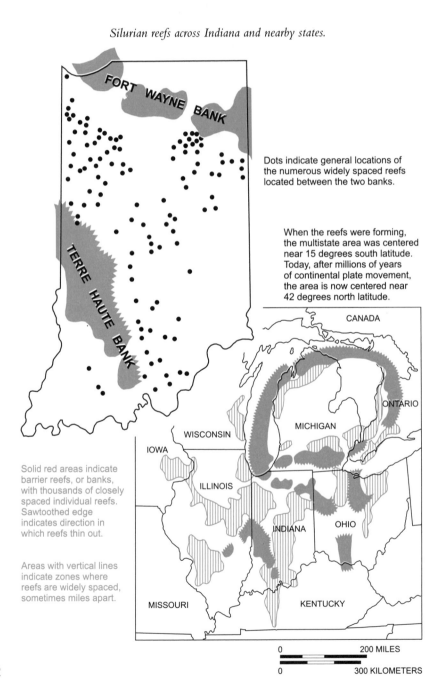

Dots indicate general locations of the numerous widely spaced reefs located between the two banks.

When the reefs were forming, the multistate area was centered near 15 degrees south latitude. Today, after millions of years of continental plate movement, the area is now centered near 42 degrees north latitude.

Solid red areas indicate barrier reefs, or banks, with thousands of closely spaced individual reefs. Sawtoothed edge indicates direction in which reefs thin out.

Areas with vertical lines indicate zones where reefs are widely spaced, sometimes miles apart.

the rock to form lime for mortar, agricultural lime, and whitewash (an early substitute for paint). Limestone and dolomite are still quarried for those uses, but they are also now used as fluxes in blast furnaces, to desulfurize coal, to "scrub" sulfur dioxide gases from power plant smokestacks, to neutralize acidic lakes, and to filter water. The chemical industry also uses high-purity carbonates.

Devonian sediments buried Silurian reefs in southwestern Indiana and formed about ninety-five small domes, sixty-eight of which produced oil and gas. More than 37 million barrels had been pumped from these domes by 1990. A few pumped-out domes are now used for subsurface storage.

## THE DEVONIAN AND MISSISSIPPIAN WORLD

The shallow seas returned in middle Devonian time and continued the pattern of separate types of sediment accumulation on either side of the Kankakee Arch in the still-developing Illinois and Michigan Basins. The units laid down southwest of the arch, but still technically within northern Indiana, are essentially the same as described for southeast and south-central Indiana. The units laid down northeast of the arch are unique to northern Indiana.

*Detroit River Formation.* The Detroit River formation contains sandy and muddy dolomites and limestones, and occasional layers of gypsum or anhydrite, a mineral similar to gypsum except that it contains no water. The formation was deposited during middle Devonian time and contains few fossils. It includes the Tioga bentonite bed, a few inches of clay derived from volcanic ash, which provides evidence of volcanic eruptions in the ancestral Appalachian Mountains to the east. The Detroit River formation is as much as 80 to 160 feet thick along the border between Indiana and Michigan. It thins to the south and west.

*Traverse Formation.* The Traverse formation is the same age as the North Vernon limestone in southern Indiana. It contains limestones, dolomites, and thin shales with fossils of corals, stromatoporoids, brachiopods, and crinoids. In northwestern Indiana, the Traverse formation is missing along most of the Kankakee Arch, but where present, is only about 20 feet thick. In far northeastern Indiana, it reaches its maximum thickness of 120 feet.

*Antrim, Ellsworth, Sunbury, and Coldwater Shales.* The late Devonian Antrim shale is the same age as the New Albany shale. It marks the start of a nearly continuous sequence of shales in northern Indiana. The dark brownish to black shale is between 60 and 220 feet thick.

Two late Devonian to Mississippian shales followed the Antrim shale. The Ellsworth shale, 40 to 200 feet thick, lies on top of the Antrim shale. Alternating brownish and greenish layers dominate its lower portion; greenish layers and some thin beds of dolomite dominate its upper part. The dark

*Middle Devonian bedrock exposed in one of a number of quarries producing crushed stone in the Fort Wayne area.*

brownish Sunbury shale overlies the Ellsworth shale. Slightly more than 10 feet thick in northeastern Indiana, it thins to the west and south and is absent west of Lagrange County.

The Ellsworth and Sunbury shales are in turn overlain by the early Mississippian Coldwater shale, which is as much as 500 feet thick. Mostly gray or greenish, the Coldwater shale also contains layers of red shale, including one distinctive layer 5 to 20 feet thick at the base of the formation. The Coldwater shale exists only in far northeastern Indiana. Fossils show that the Ellsworth, Sunbury, and Coldwater shales of northern Indiana correspond to the upper New Albany shale and lower Rockford limestone in southern Indiana.

## THE PENNSYLVANIAN WORLD

Pennsylvanian rocks exist within a corner of northern Indiana, southwest of the Kankakee Arch, and are much like those in southern Indiana. The major difference is that the early Pennsylvanian formations of northern Indiana are thinner than their counterparts farther south and do not contain nearly as much coal. They are present from the Attica area southward but are not well exposed at the surface because of the glacial sediments covering them.

## TO THE PRESENT

Hardly any sedimentary rocks were laid down in Indiana between the end of Pennsylvanian time and the beginning of the Pleistocene ice age about 2 million years ago. Some 300 million years elapsed without leaving any geologic record of their passing. The old bedrock was uplifted farther and eroded into the hills and valleys that the glaciers covered with debris. None of the plants and animals of those 300 million years left any fossil evidence. In all that time, only a few small faults broke the rocks and moved them short distances.

## KENTLAND STRUCTURE

Kentland sits atop a featureless plain in southwestern Newton County. The Kentland structure, the most complex bedrock feature in Indiana, is beneath that flat landscape, just south of U.S. 24 about 3 miles east of town.

The Kentland structure is a circular dome approximately 4.5 miles in diameter and broken along faults. The rock at the center of the structure is Shakopee dolomite of Ordovician age, about 450 million years old. It is approximately 2,000 feet above its normal elevation in this area. The Silurian, Devonian, and Mississippian rocks are fractured and folded. Their layers tilt sharply down and out from the center in a region where rock layers normally tilt southwest at a very gentle angle. The oldest undisturbed

*Geology of the Kentland structure.* —Modified from Gutschick, 1983

U = Upthrown side of fault.
D = Downthrown side of fault.
*Only the two major area faults are shown. Many small faults crisscross the structure; more than fifteen have been mapped within the quarry.*

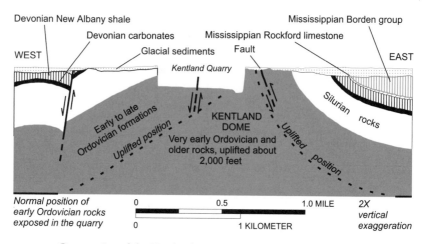

Devonian New Albany shale
Devonian carbonates
Glacial sediments
Mississippian Rockford limestone
Mississippian Borden group
Fault
WEST
EAST
Kentland Quarry
Early to late Ordovician formations Uplifted position
KENTLAND DOME
Very early Ordovician and older rocks, uplifted about 2,000 feet
Silurian rocks
Uplifted position
Normal position of early Ordovician rocks exposed in the quarry

0          0.5          1.0 MILE     2X
                                     vertical
0              1 KILOMETER           exaggeration

*Cross section of the Kentland structure.* —Modified from Gutschick, 1983

bedrock layers are shales and sandstones of the Raccoon Creek group, deposited during Pennsylvanian time, about 300 million years ago.

The Kentland structure was discovered about 1880 when two farmers began to quarry crushed stone from small natural outcrops. Early visitors included George Greene, a paleontologist from New Albany who assisted John Collett, the Indiana state geologist. Greene verified the rock ages by their fossils and described a curious pattern of conical fractures now called shattercones. He and others recognized that something extraordinary had made the structure.

Larger quarry operations after 1900 exposed more of the raised and faulted structure at Kentland. Some early thinkers suggested an ordinary origin, perhaps volcanism. When further excavation revealed no volcanic rocks, proponents of the volcanic theory contended that the quarry was not yet deep enough to reveal them.

Decades later, the shattercones led geologists to believe the Kentland structure is a meteorite impact site. The shattercones range from inches to feet in length, far larger than the small shattercones that charges of dynamite make around the drill holes in a quarry. And the large shattercones all pointed up toward the center of the structure, so the shock came from above. In microscope studies of the rocks, geologists identified quartz crystals with shock fractures and extremely dense variations of natural quartz that could only be formed under high pressure and temperature. The forces necessary to produce shattercones, shocked quartz, and high-pressure quartz are ten to fifty times greater than any generated in volcanoes.

By the late 1960s, it seemed clear that the Kentland structure had formed in the violent impact of a meteorite, but the exact time of the impact is not known—sometime after the rocks formed but before the ice sheets came. It would resemble Meteor Crater in Arizona if it were not so deeply eroded and buried in glacial debris. Some experts still refer to Kentland as a "crypto-explosion" feature because a possible volcanic origin is not explained away completely and a meteor impact origin is not demonstrated conclusively.

## GLACIERS

The earth's climate cooled about 2 million years ago and the latest ice age began. Great sheets of ice formed and began to flow south out of Canada. The ice brought rocks and other debris and dropped them in Indiana. Now Indiana grows lush crops in the soil that Canada lost.

The great ice sheets deposited their sediments in an intricate tapestry of glacial landforms—ground moraine, end moraines, outwash plains, kames, and lake deposits. Blocks of ice incorporated in the glacial sediments melted to leave depressions that became kettle ponds and lakes. The wind blew sand and silt off the outwash plains and spread them across large areas.

The torrents of meltwater that poured off the glaciers as they melted some 12,000 years ago enlarged old valleys and eroded new ones, leaving many filled with outwash sediments. The ice dammed some drainages to make temporary lakes, and in places it completely rerouted streams. Few of the streams in northern Indiana are flowing in channels that existed before the ice came.

Geologists find the ice ages frustrating because they see so much evidence of them in the landscape but understand so little of what happened and when. Detailed studies have allowed geologists to name different tills as the Wedron, Trafalgar, and Lagro formations based on the ice lobe that delivered them to Indiana. These names are applied to the till at the surface, but the same till does not extend all the way to bedrock. Studies show that

*Sand and gravel mined along U.S. 24 near Huntington. Outwash deposits underlie many valleys of northern Indiana.*

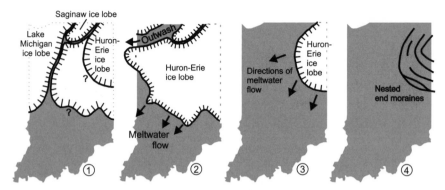

| 1. The Lake Michigan ice lobe advanced southward. As it melted, it left scattered end moraines. The Saginaw and Huron-Erie ice lobes either did not advance very far or were deflected. | 2. The Lake Michigan ice melted, forming two end moraines in northwestern Indiana. The Huron-Erie ice surged westward. The Saginaw ice continued to deflect the Huron-Erie ice. | 3. The Lake Michigan and Saginaw ice lobes melted. The Huron-Erie ice stayed only a short time and melted rapidly across most of Indiana, leaving a wide area of till as ground moraine but no end moraines in western or central Indiana. For either climatic or physical reasons, the rapid melting of the Huron-Erie ice slowed in northeastern Indiana. | 4. The last Huron-Erie ice melted in a stop-and-go fashion, leaving a series of nested end moraines. Each end moraine clearly shows where the melting ice paused. |

*A modern interpretation of how Wisconsinan ice moved across Indiana. Early geologists believed that a single large ice sheet moved southward all at once.*

subsurface layers of glacial sediments are complex and interwoven. Geologists now suspect the glaciers may have advanced and melted more rapidly than anyone dreamed even a few years ago.

## WABASH, MARION-MAHOMET, AND TEAYS VALLEYS

This is the story of three river valleys. The first is a great modern valley that you can see. The second is a buried bedrock valley under part of the visible modern valley. The third is an ancient valley far to the east, often mentioned as being connected with the other two, but now believed to have had little or nothing to do with them.

The Wabash River is the major stream in Indiana. It starts in western Ohio, arcs across northern Indiana, bends southwest near Logansport, bends south near Covington, and finally defines part of the border between Indiana and Illinois as it heads toward the Ohio River. It flows more than 400 scenic miles across Indiana.

The Wabash River valley begins as a comparatively narrow, shallow trench with only minor outwash deposits. Downstream the valley is much wider and deeper, often with great amounts of outwash sands and gravels. The Wabash River valley was cut by meltwater floods from the Wisconsinan ice. The huge torrents of water helped establish the size of the valley and its outwash deposits.

A buried bedrock valley, the Marion-Mahomet Valley, partly parallels the Wabash River and is wider and deeper than the modern valley. It begins in

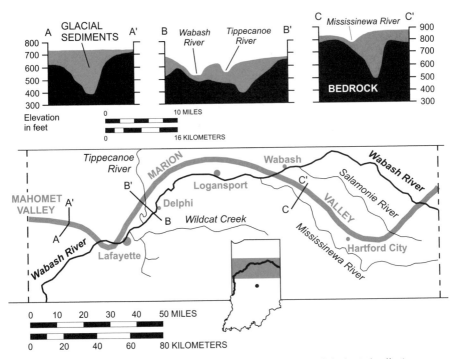

*Three profiles across the buried Marion-Mahomet Valley and the buried valley's location relative to the modern Wabash River.*

western Ohio, enters Adams County at the Indiana line, extends southwest toward Hartford City, then turns northwest into a long arc that takes it just north of the Mississinewa and Wabash Rivers to Lafayette, where it continues straight west into Illinois. It is called the Marion Valley east of Lafayette, the Mahomet Valley farther west. The modern landscape gives no hint that it is there.

Near Lafayette, this buried valley is filled with outwash sands and gravels. The porosity of these deposits enables them to hold a tremendous quantity of groundwater. That groundwater and the idea of the buried valley have long fueled a folkloric belief in a "buried river" flowing under the Lafayette area. In fact, it is just water seeping through the sand and gravel that fill the buried valley.

Modern studies show that the buried Marion–Mahomet Valley is not as old as once thought. Until the last twenty years, the buried bedrock valley was simply presumed to be the preglacial surface, and many geologic studies used it as a model of Indiana before the ice came. Now it seems clear that little of this buried valley existed before the great glaciers came, and this valley and others that join it were enlarged and deepened by the vast floods that followed several glacial advances.

The idea that a major bedrock valley could be eroded during relatively brief glacial times challenged a connection long inferred between the buried valley system in Indiana and the surface valley of the ancient Teays River in Ohio and West Virginia. A large valley meanders from western West Virginia into the hilltops of central and southern Ohio but no longer holds a large river. Early geologists concluded that glaciers diverted the ancient river into the valley of the Ohio River. Because the Teays Valley seemed to

*Preglacial and postglacial drainage patterns across Indiana and nearby states.*
—Modified from Melhorn and Kempton, 1991

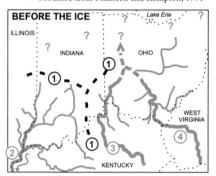

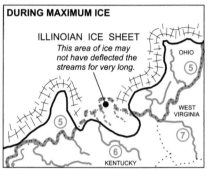

**Before the Ice:** Rivers not present today flowed away from drainage divides (1) that no longer exist. The ancestral Ohio Valley (2) drained to the south. The Kentucky River (3) and Teays River (4) probably drained northward. Preglacial drainages farther north are unknown because of the depth of burial and glacial erosion.

**During Maximum Ice:** The Illinoian ice came the farthest south of all the Pleistocene ice sheets, burying many preglacial valleys. Sediment-laden floodwaters were diverted from their preglacial paths and extended the Ohio River valley (5) much farther east. The diversion of the Kentucky (6) and Teays (7) Rivers aided the extension of the Ohio Valley.

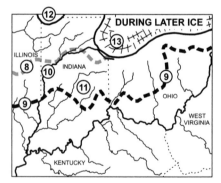

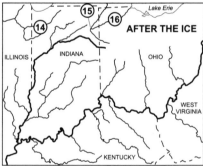

**During Later Ice:** The Illinoian ice melted and formed many of today's river valleys, now draining south. Illinoian and later Wisconsinan glacial deposits reformed the land surface and made new drainage divides. Deposits filled in the Marion-Mahomet valleys (8). The Wisconsinan ice did not advance as far south (9). Meltwaters continued to erode the Ohio River valley and to extend the valleys of the Wabash (10) and White (11) Rivers. Parts of the former Teays Valley no longer held a major stream. The remaining ice occupied the low areas that would become Lake Michigan (12) and Lake Erie (13).

**After the Ice:** Meltwater floods ceased, and modern surface waters began to erode the outwash in the river valleys. Lake Michigan and Lake Erie filled in former basin areas. Several new streams flowed in valleys formed along the edges of the ice or glacial deposits. The Kankakee and Iroquois Rivers (14) flow west in Illinois. The St. Mary's and St. Joseph Rivers join at Fort Wayne (15) to form the northeastward-flowing Maumee River (16).

220

point toward the buried bedrock valley in Indiana, geologists were quick to believe that the ancient Teays River originated on the west slopes of the Appalachians and flowed across Indiana and Illinois to the precursor of the Mississippi River.

New investigations during the last two decades cast doubt on the single river idea. Drill holes and geophysical methods reveal details in the bedrock profile along the buried Marion-Mahomet Valley and in the glacial fill that seem inconsistent with a single long valley. Investigations in central Kentucky and western Ohio reveal old valleys that merged east and north toward western Ohio. Glacial sediments filled these deep valleys where the Licking and Kentucky Rivers now flow into the Ohio River.

It seems clear that the ancient Teays River never reached Indiana but joined the ancestors of the Kentucky and Licking Rivers in flowing north to the Lake Erie lowlands. Most geologists expect that definitive tracing of the Teays Valley will reveal that it leads north, not west. If so, the Marion-Mahomet Valley will no longer be its plausible continuation. As always, we need more data to better understand the old landscape.

## TRENTON GAS AND OIL FIELD

The early pioneers in Indiana found scattered gas and oil seeps, but wells drilled from the 1860s through 1876 yielded little oil and only small amounts of natural gas that were burned off uselessly. The Trenton gas and oil boom started in 1884 near Findlay, Ohio. A well sunk 1,900 feet produced natural gas from the Trenton limestone, a formation deposited during Ordovician time about 450 million years ago. The Trenton limestone changes southward, along the crest of the Cincinnati Arch, from a permeable dolomite to an impermeable limestone to an extremely impermeable shale. When the oil and gas migrated south up the gentle slope of the slightly tilted limestone, they were trapped where they encountered the impermeable rock. Geologists call this a stratigraphic trap.

The Trenton field, once thought inexhaustible, gave out at a pace that warns of the future. Several roads described in this book cross the Trenton area, but only a few scattered wells survive to yield trickles of gas and oil.

Early drilling spread across northwestern Ohio and into Indiana and soon marked the limits of the Trenton field as it is known today. More than thirty-seven thousand wells were drilled, 800 to 1,100 feet deep. The Trenton field covered about 2.5 million acres across twenty-eight Indiana counties. The adjoining Lima field in Ohio covered 550,000 acres.

The early wells in the Trenton field produced only natural gas. Ohio wells began to produce oil in 1885 and wells in Indiana's Wells County yielded oil in 1889, but it was thick, black, rich in sulfur, and hard to refine—crude oil, indeed. A typical Indiana well produced only 25 to 50 barrels per day, with an occasional giant yielding 200 to 300 barrels. But the

*Somewhere in the Trenton field of north-central Indiana, circa 1904.* —Mark J. Camp Collection

*The Trenton gas and oil field across east-central Indiana.*

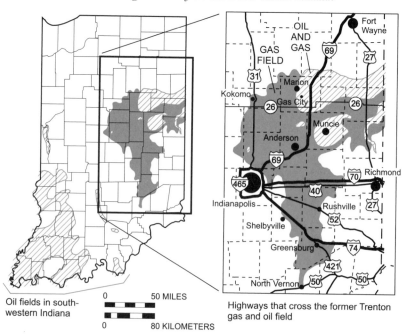

Oil fields in south-western Indiana

0    50 MILES

0    80 KILOMETERS

Highways that cross the former Trenton gas and oil field

sheer quantity of Trenton oil attracted the Standard Oil Company, which built pipelines to carry the oil to midwestern cities.

By 1889 Standard solved the problem of refining the Trenton oil with its high sulfur content. The company established a new subsidiary, Standard Oil of Indiana, to operate a new refinery in Whiting, Indiana, close to Chicago. The Whiting Refinery was the first in the state; it would later become a major refining complex.

City and rural gas companies formed to handle the large supply of cheap fuel that attracted industries. In 1892 one account listed factories making "straw board, straw paper, wood pulp and wood paper; steel works, foundries, nail mills, bar and bolt works and bell foundries; plate glass, window glass, fruit jars and bottle factories; crayon factories, fruit canning factories, excelsior mills, saw mills and flouring mills; brick and tile factories, and many other industries." Towns offered incentives such as free land or reduced gas rates for a factory to locate.

The scale of gas wastage in the Trenton field, between ten and twenty-five times what was sold, would not be tolerated today, and horrified some people in those days. Some gas vented continuously from small wells, some burned in huge torches known as flambeaux. A law was passed in 1891 to prohibit flambeaux but was not enforced until 1898. By this time, the major

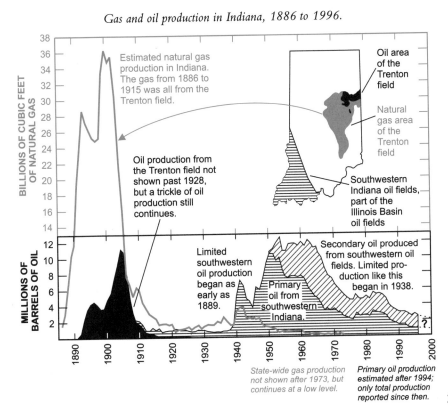

*Gas and oil production in Indiana, 1886 to 1996.*

Estimated natural gas production in Indiana. The gas from 1886 to 1915 was all from the Trenton field.

Oil area of the Trenton field

Natural gas area of the Trenton field

Oil production from the Trenton field not shown past 1928, but a trickle of oil production still continues.

Southwestern Indiana oil fields, part of the Illinois Basin oil fields

Limited southwestern oil production began as early as 1889.

Primary oil from southwestern Indiana.

Secondary oil produced from southwestern oil fields. Limited production like this began in 1938.

BILLIONS OF CUBIC FEET OF NATURAL GAS

MILLIONS OF BARRELS OF OIL

*State-wide gas production not shown after 1973, but continues at a low level.*

*Primary oil production estimated after 1994; only total production reported since then.*

223

damage was done. Had modern practices been observed, the gas in the Trenton field might have served Indiana until the 1960s or later. The peak years were 1900 for gas and 1904 for oil.

By 1910 gas production fell more than 70 percent, oil production more than 80 percent. By 1917 most of the oil companies and operators had moved on. Many of the factories that had come into the Trenton supply area moved or went out of business.

The total volume of oil from the Trenton field was 105 million barrels, a pitifully small portion of the estimated initial reserve of approximately 1 billion barrels. Production from the Ohio part of the field was about 375 million barrels. About 490 billion cubic feet of Indiana gas was sold between 1886 and 1915. Gas sold and wasted amounted to about 1 trillion cubic feet. A few wells still yield some oil, less than 9,000 barrels per year, and a few still produce a trickle of gas.

The Trenton field was mismanaged from the start. Too many wells and unrestricted venting caused the reservoir pressure to drop too quickly. If the Trenton field were discovered today, modern techniques of reservoir management would use fewer wells to produce the oil and gas over a longer period with minimal waste. The Trenton field today is probably too leaky to be repressured. Too many of the wells were not properly plugged, and many of their locations are not known. The unproduced Trenton oil may be inaccessible for all time.

Gas and oil were known to exist in southwestern Indiana before the Trenton boom but were more difficult to develop. About four hundred small, separate oil fields, 1,000 to 4,500 feet deep, are in younger rocks along the eastern edge of the Illinois Basin. Many of these southwestern fields still produce on a small scale.

## MARL AND PEAT

Marl and peat are common organic sediments in the lakes and swamps of the glacial deposits of northern Indiana. They began to accumulate as the last ice age melted and are still being formed. Marls are soft calcareous muds, yellowish white to gray; marls with plant remains are darker. They commonly contain the fossil remains of aquatic creatures such as snails, clams, ostracods, and algae. Most marl deposits are less than 20 feet deep.

Peat is partly decayed plant material, mucky stuff in various shades of dark brown, gray, and black. Buried peat eventually turns into coal. Few peat deposits exceed 10 feet deep and many are less than 5 feet deep. Some peat bogs cover 200 to 300 acres or more.

Marl was used as flux in smelting iron from bog ore in Mishawaka in 1834. People in northeastern Indiana used it to make mortar in the 1860s, but it weathered rapidly. Between 1877 and 1940 three plants in northern Indiana used marl to make cement, but inadequate reserves doomed those

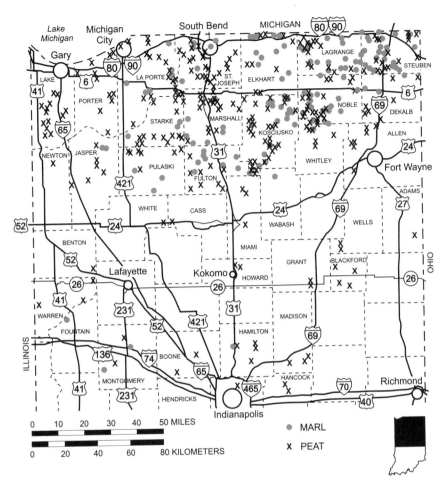

*Peat and marl deposits across northern Indiana.*

efforts. Nearly all the marl mined today is used as agricultural lime to reduce the acidity of soils.

The major use of peat is to improve soils heavy with clay. It opens the soil, improves water percolation, and adds organic matter. Peat is also used as a conditioning agent and filler in some fertilizers, a component in potting soils, packing material for cut flowers, and to grow seedlings, mushrooms, and earthworms. It is becoming useful in such diverse products as cloth, paper, livestock and poultry bedding material, oil-absorbent material, and absorbing and filtering materials for environmental contaminants.

Marl production has steadily declined for years. Peat reserves might last for about 250 years at current rates of consumption. It is unlikely that any new deposits will be found.

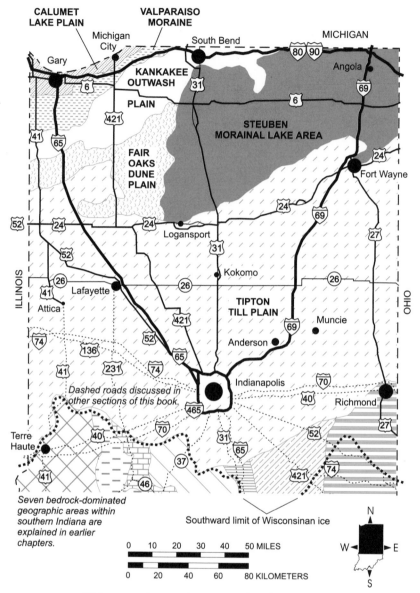

*Highways and geographic regions of northern Indiana.*

## GEOGRAPHIC REGIONS

***Tipton Till Plain.*** The Tipton till plain covers the central third of Indiana. It extends 150 miles across the state and is 60 to 90 miles wide from north to south, almost 12,000 square miles. It includes ground moraine and subtle end moraines, deposited from the Lake Michigan and Huron-Erie ice lobes, as well as outwash deposits in the valleys of the Wabash River and other streams. Large areas of shallow lake deposits and windblown sands exist in its western parts. Elevations average between 900 and 1,000 feet across its eastern third, between 800 and 900 feet across its middle third, and between 700 and 800 feet across the western third.

The thicknesses of the glacial deposits in the Tipton till plain vary from less than 50 feet to as much as 400 feet in one buried stream valley. Most of the province has between 50 and 150 feet of glacial cover. It thins near the southern edge of the region, where the underlying bedrock terrain begins to show through.

*Steuben Morainal Lake Area.* The Steuben morainal lake area includes about 3,500 square miles in northeastern Indiana. It features mixed ground moraine and end moraine expressed mostly as low hills cut by scores of valleys filled with glacial outwash, a heritage of both the Huron-Erie and Saginaw ice lobes. This region contains most of the kettle lakes in Indiana, as well as deposits of marl and peat. The elevations of the hills are about 1,000 feet in the far northeastern corner of the state and decline to about 800 feet to the south and west. Most of the area has between 200 and 450 feet of glacial sediment cover, but this thins southward to about 100 feet and westward to about 150 feet.

*Valparaiso Moraine.* The Lake Michigan ice lobe deposited the Valparaiso moraine in a broad curve across far northwestern Indiana. It is about 60 miles long in Indiana and between 5 and 15 miles wide. The moraine impounded a lake along the edge of the melting ice lobe to the north. Meltwaters overflowed it in places and left mixed till and outwash in large areas across its eastern end and in small linear areas across its western end. The region also contains a few kettle lakes. Elevations range from 650 feet to about 900 feet; the general thickness of the glacial deposits is between 100

*A pile of glacial erratics removed from nearby farm fields. This is part of the Tipton till plain, south of Fort Wayne.*

*Typical landscape of the Steuben morainal lake area, near Brighton circa 1907. Dark objects in field are bundles of corn stalks.* —Mark J. Camp Collection

and 200 feet, although it is more than 300 feet in small areas near Michigan City and LaPorte.

***Kankakee Outwash Plain.*** The Kankakee outwash plain contains sand and gravel that glacial meltwater washed off the Lake Michigan, Saginaw, and Huron-Erie ice lobes. It covers almost 1,200 square miles. Although the meltwaters that deposited it flowed west, some of the modern streams flow west and north. The region includes three islands of closely mixed till and outwash near South Bend. Elevations are between 600 and 700 feet, with the higher areas near South Bend. The glacial deposits are usually less than 100 feet deep in the western half of the area and between 100 and 250 feet deep in the eastern half.

***Fair Oaks Dune Plain.*** The Fair Oaks dune plain is windblown sand from the Kankakee outwash plain to the north and west. The nearly flat area includes hundreds of small dunes, 15 to 40 feet high. The dunes are generally covered with trees, which make them easy to spot. This region extends over about 900 square miles in northwest Indiana. Elevations vary between 650 feet near the Illinois line to 725 feet near the Steuben morainal lake area.

***Calumet Lake Plain.*** The Calumet lake plain is a curved area 4 to 10 miles wide just north of the Valparaiso moraine. It features beach sands deposited when the lake stood at slightly higher levels. Each raised beach has dunes, some large enough to have been mined for their sand, but the best dunes are preserved at Indiana Dunes National Lakeshore and State Park. This region also includes shallow lake sediments deposited in former lagoons behind the beaches. Elevations range from 580 feet at the modern lakeshore to 640 feet near the Valparaiso moraine. The glacial sediments are 150 to 200 feet thick.

# Interstate 65
## Gary—Indianapolis
### 140 MILES

Interstate 65 winds across a sequence of widely varying Wisconsinan glacial deposits. I-65 parallels U.S. 231 between Crown Point and Lafayette, so the route description for I-65 also applies to this section of U.S. 231.

## Calumet Lake Plain

Interstate 65 crosses 7 miles of the Calumet lake plain between Gary and Merrillville. It is an area of old beach sands, dune sands, and shallow water deposits left when Lake Michigan was higher. Beach and dune sands make two sets of low ridges, one in Gary and the other at Ridge Road (old U.S. 6). An island of Wedron formation till, from the Lake Michigan ice lobe, is 2 miles wide, just south of Ridge Road. The remainder of the area is shallow lake deposits. Urban development has covered much of the original landscape. The glacial deposits are 100 to 150 feet thick here. In this area the interstate is within the complex drainage basins of small streams that empty into Lake Michigan.

## Valparaiso Moraine

Between Merrillville and Indiana 2, I-65 crosses the Valparaiso moraine, 14 miles of hilly end moraine of Wedron formation till from the Lake Michigan ice lobe. A few small lakes show where melting ice blocks left depressions in the soggy landscape. The thickness of glacial sediments is between 100 and 150 feet, about the same as in the lake plain to the north. A divide in the northern part of this moraine separates waters flowing to Lake Michigan from those flowing south to the Kankakee River.

## Kankakee Outwash Plain

Between Indiana 2 and the area 2 miles south of the Kankakee River, I-65 crosses 8 miles of the Kankakee outwash plain. Torrents of meltwater flushed sand and gravel out of the ice from the north and east. The outwash fans and deltas grade gently southward. Most of this valley was swamps and wetland forests until the early settlers drained and cleared it. You can see the ditched Kankakee River from the interstate bridge.

## Fair Oaks Dune Plain

Interstate 65 passes through 14 miles of the Fair Oaks dune plain between the area 2 miles south of the Kankakee River and Indiana 14. It is a broad area of blanket sands and sand dunes. Strong winds blew the sand off barren outwash plains after the last ice age ended. Hundreds of small dunes, some rising as much as 25 feet, formed where the sand was deepest. Crops

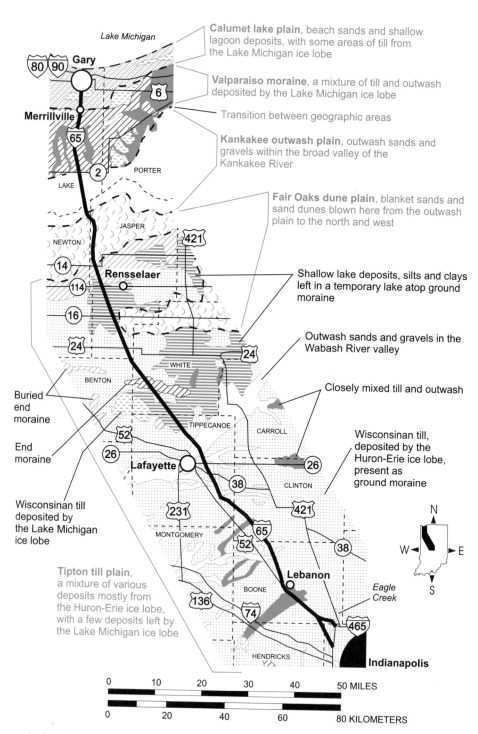

Lake Michigan

**Gary** 80 90

**Merrillville** 65 6

2

LAKE  PORTER

JASPER

NEWTON

14

114 **Rensselaer**

16

24

WHITE

BENTON

TIPPECANOE  CARROLL

52

26 **Lafayette** 38 26

CLINTON

Buried end moraine

End moraine

231  421

Wisconsinan till deposited by the Lake Michigan ice lobe

MONTGOMERY  65

52  38

421

**Tipton till plain,** a mixture of various deposits mostly from the Huron-Erie ice lobe, with a few deposits left by the Lake Michigan ice lobe

**Lebanon**

BOONE

136

74

*Eagle Creek*

465

HENDRICKS  **Indianapolis**

**Calumet lake plain**, beach sands and shallow lagoon deposits, with some areas of till from the Lake Michigan ice lobe

**Valparaiso moraine**, a mixture of till and outwash deposited by the Lake Michigan ice lobe

Transition between geographic areas

**Kankakee outwash plain**, outwash sands and gravels within the broad valley of the Kankakee River

**Fair Oaks dune plain**, blanket sands and sand dunes blown here from the outwash plain to the north and west

Shallow lake deposits, silts and clays left in a temporary lake atop ground moraine

Outwash sands and gravels in the Wabash River valley

Closely mixed till and outwash

Wisconsinan till, deposited by the Huron-Erie ice lobe, present as ground moraine

N
W — E
S

0   10   20   30   40   50 MILES

0   20   40   60   80 KILOMETERS

*Geology along I-65 between Gary and Indianapolis. Legend on page 208 further describes map patterns.*

and trees now stabilize the sand, but the wind still makes blowouts by removing sand where the cover is broken. The thickness of the glacial cover is between 50 and 100 feet. In this area the interstate crosses the divide between the Kankakee and Iroquois Rivers, which flow west into Illinois.

### Tipton Till Plain

Between Indiana 14 and I-465, I-65 crosses 97 miles of mostly ground moraine within the Tipton till plain. Several other types of glacial deposits interrupt the monotony. The till is the Trafalgar formation from the Huron-Erie ice lobe.

Four miles of buried end moraine extend between the junction with Indiana 14 and the area 1 mile north of Indiana 114. It is a band that runs about 34 miles in a general southeast to northwest direction. The Lake Michigan ice lobe deposited the hilly end moraine, then the later Huron-Erie ice smeared a thin layer of Trafalgar formation till over it.

The highway crosses 9 miles of lake sands and silts between Indiana 114 and the area 2 miles south of Indiana 16. They accumulated in a shallow lake dammed between the high end moraine to the north and the melting Huron-Erie ice lobe. At its greatest extent, this lake probably covered more than 550 square miles in parts of six counties. Blanket sands and sand dunes cover these lake deposits east of the highway. South of Indiana 16, I-65 crosses the subtle divide between the Iroquois and Wabash Rivers.

Where I-65 intersects U.S. 231, the highway crosses 3 miles of Wedron formation till, hilly end moraine deposited from the Lake Michigan ice lobe. From that area to about 1.5 miles northwest of the Wabash River, I-65 passes over another 9-mile stretch of shallow lake sands and silts, a continuation of the same deposits to the north.

Near Lafayette, I-65 offers three views of deep valleys eroded in the Trafalgar formation till. The first is a wide view of the Wabash Valley and the outwash materials within it. A fairly large tract of sand dunes is hidden in woods along the west bank of the river, north of the bridge. The second is 2 miles south of the Wabash River, where the interstate crosses Wildcat Creek. The third is 7 miles farther south where I-65 crosses hilltops west of one of the three major tributaries to Wildcat Creek. For additional discussion of the Lafayette area, see the roadlogs for U.S. 52 and Indiana 26.

Three miles south of Indiana 38, I-65 crosses 1 mile of outwash about 60 feet lower than the surrounding ground moraine. This channel fed material into the large outwash plain that U.S. 52 and U.S. 231 cross south and west of Lafayette. Between this outwash channel and I-465, the highway crosses 44 miles of flat ground moraine, almost all of it farmed. Near Lebanon, I-65 passes over the divide between small tributaries to the Wabash River and the West Fork White River.

### Fossilized Reefs around Rensselaer

Rensselaer sits near where limestone rich in chert forms rapids in the Iroquois River. Locals have quarried fossiliferous rocks of Devonian and Silurian age since the late 1800s. Some of it was used as building stone, some for road and railroad ballast, and some, particularly the older Silurian rock, was burned for lime.

The Silurian Wabash formation is more than 150 feet thick in a quarry southeast of Rensselaer. It records a time when a shallow sea dotted with patch and barrier reefs covered northern Indiana. Rocks of the Wabash formation yield brachiopods the size of golf balls and even larger clams, massive corals, bryozoans, nautiloid cephalopods with shells shaped like cones, and calcareous algae.

### Indianapolis

In 1820 the General Assembly appointed a commission to select a central site for a new state capital. The commission met near the mouth of Fall Creek, and all but one member agreed on the site. By the fall of 1824 Indianapolis was ready to receive the state records and the state treasury.

Indianapolis is near the southern edge of the Tipton till plain. About 80 percent of it stands on ground moraine at an elevation between 700 and 880 feet. The till is the Trafalgar formation. Approximately 20 percent of the city is in the valleys of the West Fork White River and two of its tributaries, Fall Creek and Eagle Creek, all filled with glacial outwash. The elevations of their floodplains range from 725 feet at the north side of the county to 650 feet at the south side. A small area of closely mixed till and outwash exists between Indiana 37 and U.S. 31, mostly south of I-465. It includes four prominent kames—hills made of outwash.

The glacial cover varies from less than 50 feet to more than 300 feet deep. It is less than 100 feet thick in the valleys, thicker in the Tipton till plain. A small segment of a completely filled bedrock valley just southeast of Geist Reservoir contains more than 300 feet of fill.

The oldest bedrock layers beneath the glacial deposits are late Silurian and early Devonian limestones and dolomites, across the eastern half of the

*Generalized surface and bedrock profiles along I-65.*

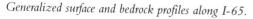
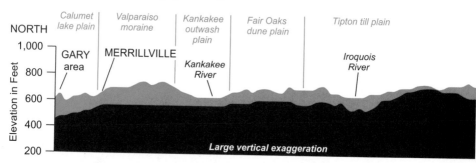

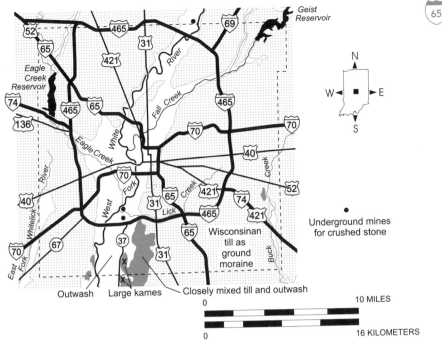

*Surface geology of Indianapolis and Marion County.*

city. The next youngest are black shales of middle Devonian to early Mississippian age. The youngest are middle Mississippian siltstones and shales in the southwestern corner of the city.

After the growth of the city curtailed sand and gravel mining in many places, a few companies turned to underground bedrock for crushed stone to meet the continued demand for aggregate. The Kentucky Avenue Mine opened in 1981 and the Harding Street Mine opened in the late 1980s; both are on the south side of the city. A third underground mine opened in 1987 on the north side of Indianapolis.

Indianapolis originally got its water from surface streams and wells in the outwash fill, but those sources eventually became inadequate. Geist and Morse

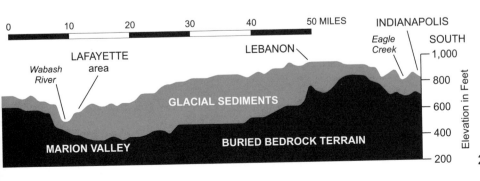

Reservoirs add to the water supply and also provide flood control and recreation. The newest impoundment, Eagle Creek Reservoir, is primarily for flood control and recreation, but it may provide water in an emergency.

The 9 mile stretch of Central Canal between the West Fork White River at Broad Ripple to the area west of the capitol survives because it carries water to the treatment plants. The legislature authorized it in 1836 as one of eight statewide canal, railroad, road, and survey projects. The first boat went through in about 1839. Water was leased to mills that processed cotton, paper, wool, grain, and lumber. The rest of the canal was never built.

In 1847 a flood on Fall Creek tore out the aqueduct that carried the canal over the creek. The empty ditch was sold in 1850 for $2,245, an anemic return on the $882,088 spent to build it. The Water Works Company provided chaotic management for the next thirty years. In 1881 the canal was sold to the Indianapolis Water Company and became an integral and orderly part of the water system. The Fall Creek aqueduct was replaced and destroyed by floods three times before the present massive concrete structure was built in 1904.

# Interstate 69
## Michigan Line—Indianapolis
**155 MILES**

Interstate 69 angles across the northeastern quarter of the state, mainly over farmland developed on ground moraine, end moraine, and valleys filled with outwash.

### Steuben Morainal Lake Area

Interstate 69 crosses 37 miles of the eastern end of the Steuben morainal lake area. The Huron-Erie ice lobe dumped the surface glacial debris as it melted. This area contains some of the thickest glacial cover in the state, between 250 and 400 feet deep.

Between the Michigan line and the area 2 miles south of U.S. 6, I-69 winds through 25 miles of low hills formed in closely mixed till and outwash, end moraine, and buried end moraine. In this stretch, the highway intersects two major outwash channels that ultimately connect with the Kankakee outwash plain farther west. One is between the areas 2 and 3.5 miles south of Indiana 727. It forks 1 mile to the west to hold Crooked Lake and Lake James, two of the state's largest natural lakes. The second channel is a 1-mile-wide depression, about 5 miles north of the line between Steuben and Dekalb Counties.

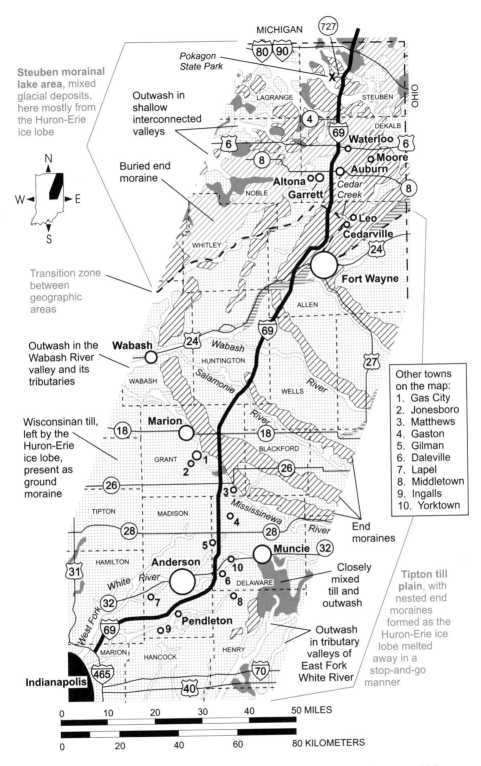

Geology along I-69 between the Michigan line and Indianapolis. Legend on page 208 further describes map patterns.

One mile south of Indiana 4, the highway ascends the divide that separates waters flowing northwest toward the Pigeon River from those flowing south and southwest to the Wabash River.

Interstate 69 crosses 6 miles of ground moraine between the area about 1 mile south of U.S. 6 and Cedar Creek about 2 miles south of Indiana 8. The highway crosses 6 miles of end moraine between the nearly invisible Cedar Creek near Auburn and its more prominent valley 2 miles south of the line between Allen and Dekalb Counties. This is one of the five nested end moraines in northeastern Indiana.

### Tipton Till Plain

The Tipton till plain underlies I-69 for 118 miles, from the Cedar Creek valley a few miles north of Fort Wayne to I-465. The glacial sediments vary from less than 50 feet to as much as 150 feet thick. Buried bedrock valleys exist just north of Anderson and just northeast of Marion.

Interstate 69 angles across two parts of one hilly end moraine and some intervening ground moraine in the 29 miles between Cedar Creek north of Fort Wayne and the line between Allen and Wells Counties. Within this end moraine, between U.S. 24 and the area 2 miles north of the line between Allen and Wells Counties, I-69 crosses a 2-mile-wide meltwater valley and 3 miles of ground moraine. A minor stream now flows through part of that valley, but torrents of meltwater once rumbled through when the ice melted at the end of the last ice age. The water left outwash later covered by shallow lake deposits.

Between the northern edge of Wells County and the exit for Indiana 18, I-69 traverses 31 miles of ground moraine. The valleys of the Wabash and Salamonie Rivers, with bedrock exposures and outwash deposits, interrupt the general flatness. The land near the two river valleys is more rolling than usual because buried bedrock hills are just below the surface. The highway crosses 3 miles of another end moraine just northeast of the Salamonie River, but it is not very obvious.

Interstate 69 crosses 6 miles of end moraine between the exit for Indiana 18 and the area 1 mile north of the Mississinewa River. Hills are more

*Generalized surface and bedrock profiles along I-69.*

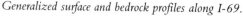
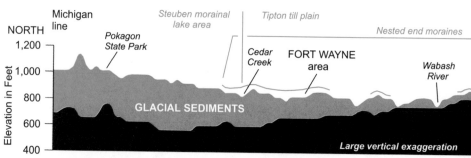

236

common than in the ground moraine to the north. This is the farthest southwest of Indiana's five major nested end moraines.

Between the area 1 mile north of the Mississinewa River and I-465, I-69 crosses 44 miles of ground moraine. Near Indiana 28, the highway crosses the divide between waters flowing west in the Wabash River basin and those flowing southwest in the basin of the West Fork White River. The highway crosses the West Fork White River valley, filled with outwash, near the exit for Indiana 32, just east of Anderson.

### Pokagon State Park

A visit to Pokagon State Park on the eastern side of Lake James in northern Steuben County provides a glimpse into the late Pleistocene history of northeastern Indiana. The entire park is mapped as closely mixed till and outwash. They were deposited at the edge of either the Saginaw or the Huron-Erie ice lobe, or both.

Lake James, the largest in the park, fills a series of at least three depressions left as large blocks of ice in the glacial sediments melted. Smaller kettle lakes and depressions dot the nearby landscape. The fate of kettle lakes is to fill with sediments and vegetation and thus become swamps or bogs. Watch for this progression in the low areas east of the Potawatomi Inn and north of the main campground.

Glacial erratics, including cobbles and boulders, provide examples of bedrock from faraway places and illustrate the power of the ice to move large rocks long distances. Hells Point is a hilly kame complex on the north border of the park. Part of the main campground is in another group of kames.

### Mastodons of Dekalb County

A nearly complete skeleton of a Pleistocene mammoth was unearthed in 1888 in a farm field near Waterloo; it now resides in the Carnegie Institute in Pittsburgh. In 1933 much of another skeleton was discovered south of Garrett, but the bones were scattered and the skull and tusks were in poor condition. These bones are now in the Denver Museum of Natural History. Scattered bones have also been found in the Butler and Auburn areas.

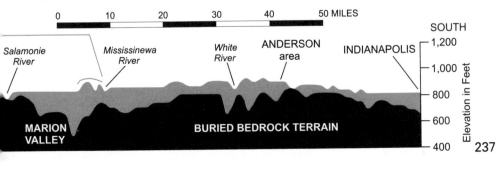

237

### Allen and Dekalb County Mineral Industries

The Trenton gas and oil boom hit Dekalb County in 1887. Three companies quickly formed and began drilling in the countryside, soon finding gas but no oil. At least six companies used clay from glacial tills near Auburn, Butler, Garrett, Grabill, and Spencerville to make ordinary brick for use in many early local buildings. Drain tile plants proliferated at Altona, Auburn, and Moore to make the pipes to help farmers drain the soggy soils on the impervious till. Outwash deposits yielded sand and gravel at a number of sites, especially southwest of Auburn. The Greenhurst Country Club is within an area once mined for sand and gravel.

### Stream Piracy near Cedarville

A great stream piracy happened west of Cedarville and Leo in northern Allen County while the Huron-Erie ice lobe melted. Cedar Creek began as a meltwater stream flowing from the northwest edge of the ice lobe as it laid down end moraine. Cedar Creek flowed west to the Eel River. As the ice melted to the east, a cross valley in the end moraine eroded deeply enough to capture the waters flowing on the other side of the moraine. Thus Cedar Creek came to reverse course and flow southeast to the St. Joseph River, and the Eel River lost part of its headwaters. Such drainage changes were commonplace while the ice sheets melted.

### Silurian Reefs in Northeastern Indiana

The Silurian Wabash formation and the underlying Pleasant Mills formation contain fossilized dolomitic reefs. Beginning about the 1870s, the need for construction material led to the establishment of limestone quarries near many towns in northeastern Indiana. Quarries operated near Albany, Bluffton, Eaton, Huntington, Marion, Markle, Montpelier, Point Isabel, Rockford, Sweetser, Wabash, and Wheeling. Active quarries still exist near some of these towns. Stone was removed first for construction and later for lime production. Competition and general economic conditions by the 1920s led to the consolidation and closing of many of the operations. Crushed stone predominates today.

Two nonquarry reef exposures exist at Wabash. One is the Wabash Reef at the east end of East Market Street near the edge of the Wabash Valley. A 750-foot-long railroad cut exposes the dolomite core of the reef. Look at the ends of the cut to see the flank rocks slope away from the core of the reef. Glacial ice scraped off its top. The second site is the South Wabash Reef farther south on Indiana 13 where it ascends the south bank of the Wabash Valley.

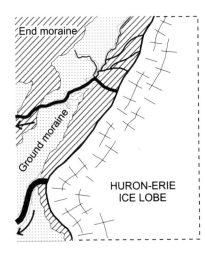

**Development of major westward valleys:**
The edge of the Huron-Erie ice lobe melted slowly enough to form a large end moraine. Westward-flowing meltwater poured forth and carved the Eel and Wabash River valleys. Meltwater also carved the precursor of the Cedar Creek valley across the end moraine. The modern valleys of the St. Joseph and St. Mary's Rivers did not exist. Ice blocked the eastward flow of water.

**Development of two new edge rivers:**
The south edge of the Huron-Erie ice lobe melted rapidly enough to form a wide area of ground moraine before pausing to deposit another end moraine. The north edge melted just enough to form a narrow valley before leaving more end moraine. Two new streams formed along the edge of the latest end moraine and contributed to the meltwaters still cutting the valleys of the Eel and Wabash Rivers. These two streams would later become the St. Joseph and St. Mary's Rivers. Where meltwater cut across the end moraine to the north, it deepened the valley for Cedar Creek.

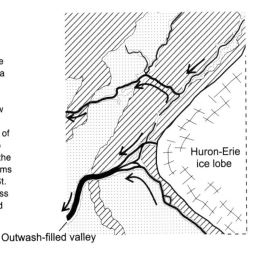

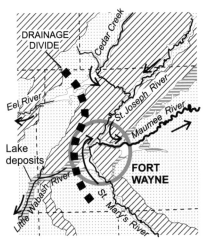

**The Fort Wayne area today:** After the ice melted, Cedar Creek followed the newly established regional slope to the east. It flowed south and east into the St. Joseph River, which joins the St. Mary's River to form the Maumee River, which flows eastward to Lake Erie. Thus the headwaters of the present-day Eel River were reduced. The area just west of Fort Wayne has a subtle east-west drainage divide that did not exist when the ice was present. Narrow areas east and west of Fort Wayne once held temporary lakes against the edge of the melting ice lobe. These short-lived lakes left behind unique deposits of sands, silts, and clays.

*Stages in the development of Cedar Creek, St. Joseph River, St. Mary's River, and Maumee River in the Fort Wayne area.*

*Abandoned quarry in Silurian reef rock near Markle.*

### Glass Factories and the Trenton Gas and Oil Boom

A manufacturing boom followed natural gas discoveries in the Trenton field in the 1880s and 1890s. Around 1900 at least one glass factory worked in each of the following towns: Albany, Alexandria, Anderson, Converse, Daleville, Dunkirk, Elwood, Fairmount, Fowlerton, Frankton, Gas City, Gaston, Gilman, Hartford City, Ingalls, Jonesboro, Lapel, Marion, Matthews, Middletown, Millgrove, Pendleton, Redkey, Summittville, Sweetser, Upland, and Yorktown. Many other towns had glass plants as well. The plants used the inexpensive natural gas to power the furnaces that melted the glass. The glass companies petered out with the gas about 1910. Companies survive at Dunkirk and Hartford City.

Indiana's first commercial gas well, the start of the Trenton gas and oil boom, was developed near Eaton in northern Delaware County. In 1870 a local railroad company drilled a 600-foot-deep hole looking for coal. They found no coal, but the abandoned hole produced a peculiar odor. Eaton residents visiting the Findlay, Ohio, area in 1886 smelled the same odor there and learned that the smell indicated natural gas. The well was deepened to 922 feet, breaking through a shale layer into the Trenton limestone, and the test flame burned as high as 10 feet.

Oil was discovered in the Trenton limestone some 1,000 feet below northern Blackford County in 1887. The population of Montpelier exploded and oil derricks and wooden storage tanks dotted the countryside. Production peaked in 1904, and the boom was over by 1912.

### Rock Wool

Small quarries east of Yorktown were once sources of dolomite and clay from the Mississinewa shale. The rock was hauled to the Union Fiber Company in Yorktown, dumped in piles, and left to harden by exposure over

*Steeply inclined strata of the Wabash formation form the walls of this quarry near Bluffton in Wells County.*

winter. The next summer, the weathered rock was heated to 3,800 degrees Fahrenheit and the melt steamblown into fluffy strands of rock wool, a type of insulation. Production at Yorktown ended in the 1920s, when the company opened a larger factory in Wabash. The clay-rich carbonates of the Mississinewa shale were quarried for rock wool production at Sweetser and Alexandria about the same time.

### The Muncie Area

A large quarry on the northeast side of Muncie exposes two Silurian units: 90 feet of the Pleasant Mills formation and more than 90 feet of the Salamonie dolomite. Quarrying began in the late 1800s when rock was produced along the West Fork White River for use in building construction. The city eventually spread over other areas that could have produced more rock.

A number of brick and tile plants dotted the Muncie area around 1900. A tile plant was located at Shideler. The raw material was clay in the glacial till, which averaged about 60 feet thick.

### Pendleton Sandstone

The waterfall in Falls Park at Pendleton tumbles over a ledge of middle Devonian Pendleton sandstone, part of the Jeffersonville limestone. The white to variably colored sandstone bed is about 7 feet thick. It lies on an old erosion surface on the Silurian Wabash formation. The Pendleton sandstone was used to make glass and was quarried for local buildings. The original waterfall, 10 to 15 feet high when first described in 1869, is long gone, and the quarry is filled with water.

### Mineral Industry in Hamilton, Madison, and Hancock Counties

Three counties near Indianapolis also had quarrying activities in the late 1800s that resembled, but did not match, those farther northeast. Several quarries operated in the Fishersburg-Lapel area, taking advantage of the Liston Creek limestone and Mississinewa shale members of the Silurian Wabash formation. The Wabash formation also supplied building stone from sites near Anderson, Frankton, Huntsville, and Rigdon. Two lime operations once worked near Ingalls. Quarrying was also important near Fortville in the late 1890s but was abandoned by the 1920s, and all traces are gone today.

# Interstate 80/90, Indiana Toll Road
## Ohio Line—Illinois Line
**157 MILES**

Interstate 80/90, the Indiana Toll Road, curves across the northernmost part of the state, crossing many glacial deposits left by the Huron-Erie, Saginaw, and Lake Michigan ice lobes.

### Steuben Morainal Lake Area

The toll road crosses 50 miles of the Steuben morainal lake area between the Ohio border and the boundary between Elkhart and Lagrange Counties. The 18 miles of low hills from the Ohio line to the area 3 miles west of the Angola interchange are closely mixed till and outwash at each end, with buried end moraine in between. These are from the Huron-Erie ice lobe. Near Ohio, the highway is within the basin of the Maumee River, which flows into Ohio.

From the area west of the Angola interchange to the line between Lagrange and Elkhart Counties, the highway crosses 30 miles of sands and gravels washed from the melting Huron-Erie and Saginaw ice lobes. These ice lobes deposited glacial sediments between 200 and 300 feet deep. This part of the highway passes through the basin of the Pigeon River, which flows into Michigan.

West of the Pigeon River, the toll road crosses a few miles of hilly sand dunes that merge westward into flat outwash, which probably supplied the sand for the dunes.

### Kankakee Outwash Plain

The toll road passes through 44 miles of the Kankakee outwash plain. The glacial deposits are generally 150 to 200 feet deep. Between the boundary of Elkhart and Lagrange Counties and the area 1 mile west of the St. Joseph

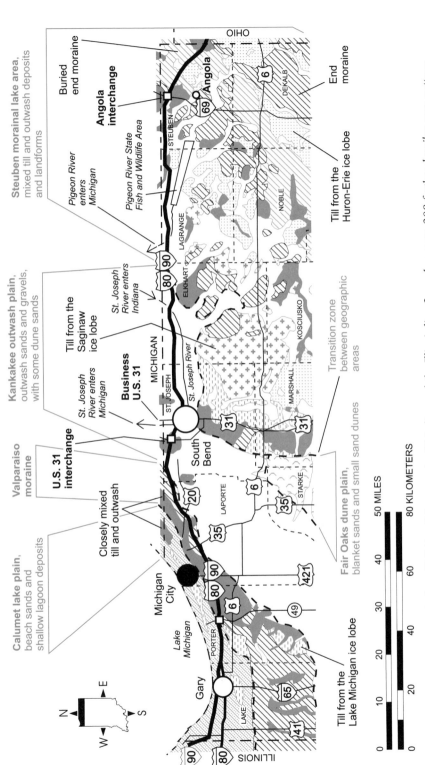

**Calumet lake plain,** beach sands and shallow lagoon deposits

**Valparaiso moraine**

Closely mixed till and outwash

**U.S. 31 interchange**

**Kankakee outwash plain,** outwash sands and gravels, with some dune sands

Till from the Saginaw ice lobe

St. Joseph River enters Michigan

St. Joseph River enters Indiana

**Business U.S. 31**

**Steuben morainal lake area,** mixed till and outwash deposits and landforms

Pigeon River enters Michigan

Pigeon River State Fish and Wildlife Area

Buried end moraine

**Angola interchange**

End moraine

Till from the Huron-Erie ice lobe

Transition zone between geographic areas

**Fair Oaks dune plain,** blanket sands and small sand dunes

Till from the Lake Michigan ice lobe

OIHO

Angola

DEKALB

STEUBEN

NOBLE

LAGRANGE

ELKHART

KOSCIUSKO

MICHIGAN

ST JOSEPH

MARSHALL

St. Joseph River

South Bend

LAPORTE

STARKE

Michigan City

Lake Michigan

Gary

PORTER

LAKE

ILLINOIS

N
W — E
S

0   10   20   30   40   50 MILES

0   20   40   60   80 KILOMETERS

*Geology along I-80/90 (Indiana Toll Road) between the Ohio line and the Illinois line. Legend on page 208 further describes map patterns.*

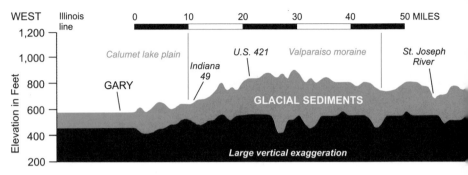

*Generalized surface and bedrock profiles along I-80/90.*

River, the road crosses 10 miles of dune sands. The narrow valley of the St. Joseph River, filled with glacial outwash, interrupts the sand. Between the dune sands and the hillside 3 miles west of Business U.S. 31, the road follows 25 miles of the St. Joseph River, which flows north to Michigan.

Three miles west of Business U.S. 31, the toll road crosses a hilly island of closely mixed till and outwash 6 miles wide. It is part of the divide between the St. Joseph and the Kankakee Rivers. The Kankakee River flows west into Illinois. West of that hilly area, the toll road crosses 3 miles of a valley filled with outwash. Watch for the change in the slope between the valley floor and the hillsides north and south of the road.

### Valparaiso Moraine

The Toll Road crosses 36 miles of the Valparaiso moraine between the area 6 miles west of the U.S. 31 interchange and Indiana 49. This is a hilly ridge of end moraine left by the Lake Michigan ice lobe. The glacial sediments thin from about 200 feet at the eastern end of the moraine to about 150 feet near Indiana 49. Two areas more than 300 feet deep, near U.S. 20 and U.S. 35, are parts of a buried valley.

Two areas of closely mixed till and outwash then top the end moraine: a 3-mile stretch just west of U.S. 20 and a longer stretch from the area 4 miles east of U.S. 421 to Indiana 49. Just west of U.S. 35, the road dips down to the edge of the outwash plain that slopes away southward from the moraine.

East of U.S. 421, the toll road crosses the divide that separates waters flowing south toward the Kankakee River from those seeping north toward Lake Michigan.

### Calumet Lake Plain

Between the Indiana 49 interchange and the Illinois border, the toll road cuts across 27 miles of the Calumet lake plain. The highway crosses former

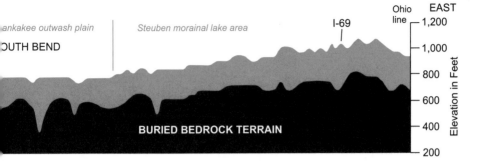

ankakee outwash plain    Steuben morainal lake area    I-69    Ohio  EAST
                                                                line
SOUTH BEND

**BURIED BEDROCK TERRAIN**

*Elevation in Feet*

1,200
1,000
800
600
400
200

beach and dune sands between interchanges 23 and 21, and just east of the I-65 interchange. The rest of the areas are sands, silts, and clays deposited in shallow lakes and lagoons behind the beaches. The glacial deposits thin westward, from about 200 feet near Indiana 49 to about 100 feet near the Illinois line. All these deposits, between 600 and 660 feet elevation, were left high and dry as the water level in Lake Michigan receded to its modern level of 580 feet. In this region, the highway winds through the watersheds of the Calumet River and other streams that flow into Lake Michigan between the Porter and LaPorte county line and Illinois.

### Pigeon River State Fish and Wildlife Area

Pigeon River State Fish and Wildlife Area, in eastern Lagrange County, protects part of the Pigeon River, which meanders wildly as it flows on an extremely flat landscape. More than fifty kettle lakes of varying size drain into it. Tannin seeping from peat bogs colors the river water a clear brown, like strong tea. The unusually cool water makes good trout habitat, something rare in Indiana.

# U.S. 6
# Ohio Line—Illinois Line
### 148 MILES

U.S. 6 steps across Indiana in a series of straight segments offset along survey lines. Across the eastern half the state, U.S. 6 is on deposits and landforms associated with the Huron-Erie ice lobe. Across the western half of Indiana, U.S. 6 passes over deposits and landforms left by the Lake Michigan ice lobe.

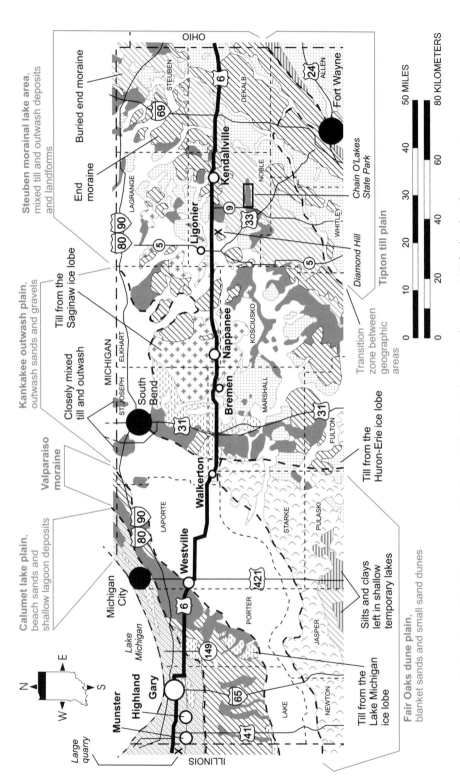

**Calumet lake plain,** beach sands and shallow lagoon deposits

**Valparaiso moraine**

**Kankakee outwash plain,** outwash sands and gravels

Till from the Saginaw ice lobe

Closely mixed till and outwash

**Steuben morainal lake area,** mixed till and outwash deposits and landforms

Buried end moraine

End moraine

Chain O'Lakes State Park

Diamond Hill

**Tipton till plain**

Transition zone between geographic areas

Till from the Huron-Erie ice lobe

Silts and clays left in shallow temporary lakes

Till from the Lake Michigan ice lobe

**Fair Oaks dune plain,** blanket sands and small sand dunes

Large quarry

OIHO

ILLINOIS

MICHIGAN

Lake Michigan

Fort Wayne

Kendallville

Ligonier

Nappanee

Bremen

South Bend

Walkerton

Westville

Michigan City

Munster

Highland

Gary

STEUBEN
DEKALB
ALLEN
LAGRANGE
NOBLE
WHITLEY
ST. JOSEPH
ELKHART
KOSCIUSKO
MARSHALL
FULTON
LAPORTE
STARKE
PULASKI
PORTER
JASPER
LAKE
NEWTON

24
6
69
80 90
5
9
33
5
31
31
421
149
65
41

0    10    20    30    40    50 MILES

0    20    40    60    80 KILOMETERS

N    E    S    W

*Geology along U.S. 6 between the Ohio line and the Illinois line. Legend on page 208 further describes map patterns.*

### Steuben Morainal Lake Area

U.S. 6 crosses 86 miles of mixed glacial deposits within the central part of the Steuben morainal lake area between the Ohio line and the area east of Walkerton. Here, the Huron-Erie, Saginaw, and Lake Michigan ice lobes all touched. The glacial deposits are about 300 feet deep at the Ohio line and more than 450 feet deep in the Kendallville area. They thin to about 150 feet west of Kendallville.

Between the Ohio line and its intersection with U.S. 33 south of Ligonier, U.S. 6 crosses 43 miles of deposits laid down along the northern edge of the Huron-Erie ice lobe. The landscape features low hills of mixed ground moraine and end moraine. These morainal surfaces were probably never continuous because of the volumes of meltwaters that cut numerous small valleys and filled them with outwash sands and gravels. All these minor valleys merge toward the Kankakee outwash plain.

A few miles east of Kendallville, U.S. 6 climbs the drainage divide that separates waters flowing southwest to Cedar Creek and the Maumee River from those flowing northwest toward the Elkhart River and on into Michigan.

Watch for Diamond Hill, a kame, 3.5 miles east of Ligonier near where U.S. 6 crosses the South Branch of the Elkhart River. It is 1 mile south of the highway. The road to Diamond Lake crosses it.

Between Indiana 5 and the valley west of Bremen, U.S. 6 passes through 28 miles of more low hills also formed in mixed ground and end moraine, this time deposited by the Saginaw ice lobe. Several more meltwater valleys filled with glacial outwash cut through this area. West of Nappanee, U.S. 6 ascends the indistinct divide that separates waters flowing north to the Elkhart River from those flowing west to the Yellow River, a tributary to the Kankakee River.

From west of Bremen to the area about 2.5 miles east of Walkerton, U.S. 6 crosses 15 miles of glacial deposits from the Lake Michigan ice lobe. Just west of Bremen, U.S. 6 enters a shallow, outwash-filled valley. Most of the rest of this stretch is over ground moraine, but there is some closely mixed till and outwash 1 mile or so east and west of U.S. 31.

### Kankakee Outwash Plain

U.S. 6 cuts diagonally across 28 miles of outwash, part of the great expanse of the Kankakee outwash plain, between the area 2.5 miles east of Walkerton and that just west of Westville. The topography near Walkerton is not as flat as the rest of the plain because small streams have dissected it. The glacial sediments here are 150 to 200 feet thick.

### Valparaiso Moraine

Between the area west of Westville and Indiana 149, U.S. 6 crosses 11 miles of the Valparaiso moraine, deposited when the Lake Michigan ice lobe temporarily stalled during the great melt at the end of the last ice age. The large end moraine divides the broad outwash plains to the south from the lakeshore deposits to the north, separating the respective rivers as well.

Most of the terrain here is closely mixed till and outwash. The outwash was deposited by meltwaters that poured over and through the end moraine along a 30-mile front that extends into Michigan. The area 3 or so miles east of Indiana 149 is end moraine but looks much the same.

### Calumet Lake Plain

U.S. 6 covers 23 miles of nearly flat country in the Calumet lake plain between Indiana 149 and the Illinois border. The glacial sediments thin westward from about 150 feet to less than 100 feet.

Shallow lake sediments that accumulated behind a barrier beach dominate most of this part of the route. There is a low, narrow ridge of beach sands just south of the intersection with I-80 and I-94 north of Deep River. Deep River eroded into the old lakebed and meanders northward to the Calumet River complex, emptying into Lake Michigan.

The bedrock that underlies this area is beautifully exposed in an enormous quarry a few miles west of the Illinois line where U.S. 6 is collocated with I-80/94. It is more than 200 feet deep, working in a Silurian reef that produces huge quantities of aggregate for the Chicago area.

Old U.S. 6, no longer marked, passes through Dyer along a low ridge of beach and dune sands. Early settlers built on this low ridge to avoid swampy areas.

### Wabash Portland Cement Company

In 1899–1900 the factory of the Wabash Portland Cement Company was constructed between Big and Little Turkey Lakes in Lagrange County to take advantage of the marl deposits in the lakes. This was the first such plant

Generalized surface and bedrock profiles along U.S. 6.

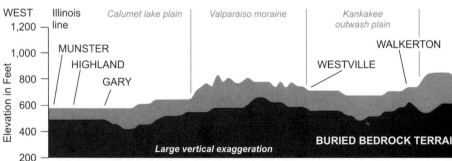

*View of the Wabash Portland Cement Company plant at Stroh, circa 1904.*
—Mark J. Camp Collection

built in Indiana. The towns of Elmira and Stroh were also built to support the operation.

Marl thickness ranged from a few feet to as much as 45 feet around the perimeters of the two lakes. Marl was mixed with clay while still wet, heated in a kiln, and then ground in mills to make portland cement. Peak production occurred in the 1920s, but the cement industry was changing and the plant closed by the 1940s. The old marl pits are now a public fishing area.

### Chain O'Lakes State Park

Chain O'Lakes State Park, just east of Indiana 9, has eleven kettle lakes in closely mixed till and outwash. The sands and gravels were left by meltwater flowing through fractures and tunnels in the melting Huron-Erie ice lobe. The lakes fill irregular depressions left where blocks of ice incorporated in the outwash finally melted. The surface elevations of the lakes decrease westward, only 5 feet from highest to lowest. The natural succession of aquatic

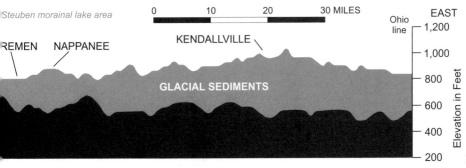

vegetation spreading from the banks has begun to fill the lakes. Mud and Weber Lakes are the ends of a much larger lake now almost filled with muck and peat. More than forty similar small lakes exist on private land north and west of this state park.

### Marl in Kosciusko and Elkhart Counties

Marl was also mined from the Lake Wawasee area to make portland cement between 1900 and 1919. Large deposits of gray marl, a fine-grained carbonate-rich lake sediment, were discovered in Lakes Wawasee and Syracuse. The Syracuse Portland Cement Company mixed in nearby clay and heated the mixture to make cement. They later went out of business when the industry began using limestone instead of marl. The Syracuse company was the only major attempt to mine marl in this area, although many marl pits were dug for local use.

Dewart, Tippecanoe, and Wabee Lakes, south of Syracuse, also contain extensive marl beds. Marl deposits between Big Barbee Lake and the six smaller lakes adjacent to it suggest they were once part of a large single lake.

# U.S. 24
## Ohio Line—Illinois Line
**155 MILES**

U.S. 24 traverses the state through two contrasting areas, both within the Tipton till plain. Between the Ohio border and Logansport, the highway follows the major meltwater channels of the Maumee and Wabash Valleys. Between Logansport and the Illinois border, the highway crosses ground moraine and related deposits from the Huron-Erie ice lobe.

East of Fort Wayne, the highway is within the Maumee River basin; between Fort Wayne and the west side of White County, the highway is within the Wabash River basin; and farther west it is in the basin of the Iroquois River.

U.S. 24 crosses 11 miles of ground moraine between the Ohio border and the area 1.5 miles east of Fort Wayne. The Maumee River, just north of the highway, now flows east, but it flowed west while the glacial ice melted. The glacial deposits are 50 to 100 feet deep. Gravel pits produce construction aggregate from the sands and gravels near the river.

For 19 miles the highway runs through a meltwater valley filled with outwash. Hilly tracts of end moraine, located between the area 1.5 miles east of Fort Wayne and that 4 miles west of its intersection with I-69, bracket the valley.

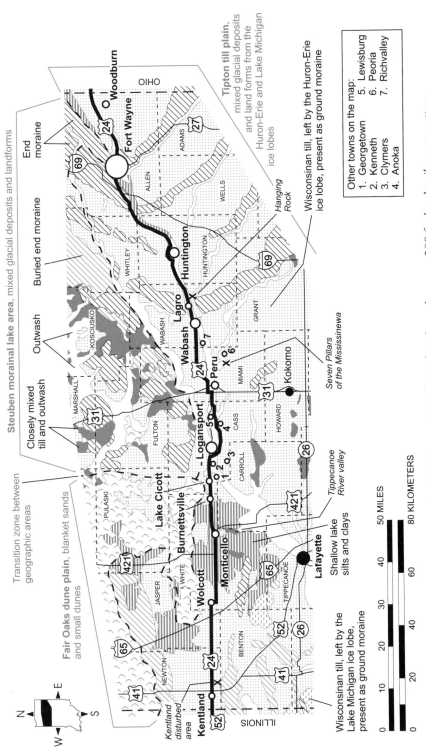

**Steuben morainal lake area,** mixed glacial deposits and landforms

End moraine

Buried end moraine

Outwash

Closely mixed till and outwash

Transition zone between geographic areas

**Fair Oaks dune plain,** blanket sands and small dunes

Kentland disturbed area

Wisconsinan till, left by the Lake Michigan ice lobe, present as ground moraine

**Tipton till plain,** mixed glacial deposits and land forms from the Huron-Erie and Lake Michigan ice lobes

Wisconsinan till, left by the Huron-Erie ice lobe, present as ground moraine

Shallow lake silts and clays

Tippecanoe River valley

Seven Pillars of the Mississinewa

Hanging Rock

Other towns on the map:
1. Georgetown    5. Lewisburg
2. Kenneth       6. Peoria
3. Clymers       7. Richvalley
4. Anoka

OIHO

ILLINOIS

*Geology along U.S. 24 between the Ohio line and the Illinois line. Legend on page 208 further describes map patterns.*

Between the area 4 miles west of I-69 and that 5 miles west of Logansport, U.S. 24 winds in and along the north side of the Wabash River valley for 69 miles. Meltwaters eroded the valley in Silurian and Devonian limestones and dolomites; the waning waters deposited some outwash sands and gravels, generally less than 50 feet thick. Bedrock and outwash terraces, relicts of the glacial flooding, create the apparent hilliness in the valley.

The Wabash River enters this valley just west of Huntington. To the northeast, the Little Wabash River is the diminutive occupant of the relatively large valley.

U.S. 24 leaves the Wabash Valley and crosses part of the ground moraine uplands in five places. One is the bypass north of Huntington. The second is the upland stretch between Wabash and Peru. These two areas appear somewhat rolling because of the small stream valleys eroded into the edge of the uplands. The glacial cover between Wabash and Peru thickens to more than 250 feet because the highway follows a buried bedrock valley.

The third and fourth departures from the river valley are in eastern Cass County, where old U.S. 24 crosses a small island of ground moraine within the outwash valley and passes next to a narrow ridge of ground moraine approaching Logansport. This ridge separates the converging Wabash and Eel Rivers. The fifth departure is where the new route of U.S. 24 crosses the Wabash River valley in eastern Cass County and climbs onto the ground moraine highlands south of the river. The new highway segment returns to the valley west of Logansport.

U.S. 24 crosses 56 miles of ground moraine and related shallow lake deposits between the area 5 miles west of Logansport and the Illinois line. The ground moraine in western Cass County also has a broad cover of windblown sands and dunes. The tree-covered dunes, about 20 feet high, are numerous near Lake Cicott where they help form the lake basin. The glacial cover is more than 250 feet deep because the highway crosses a downstream segment of a buried bedrock valley east of Peru.

A shallow glacial lake once existed in the 21 miles between the area 1 mile west of Burnettsville and that 1.5 miles east of Wolcott. The transitions

*Generalized surface and bedrock profiles along U.S. 24.*

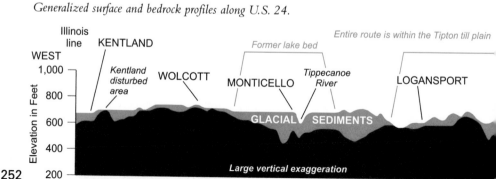

into and out of the area of the former lake are too subtle for easy notice. The glacial sediments are between 100 and 200 feet deep but thin westward to less than 50 feet.

The ground moraine near Illinois is part of the westernmost deposits of the Huron-Erie ice lobe within Indiana. The hilly areas are buried end moraine, left by the Lake Michigan ice lobe and later lightly covered by the Huron-Erie ice lobe. The glacial deposits are generally less than 50 feet deep but are 50 to 100 feet deep near the Illinois line. Near Kentland, U.S. 24 crosses the Kentland structure.

Just west of Wolcott, U.S. 24 crosses a subtle drainage divide that separates waters flowing east to the Tippecanoe River from those flowing west and north to the Iroquois River.

### Woodburn Quarry

Spoil heaps rise high above the flat terrain east of Fort Wayne, near the turnoff to Woodburn. They mark a deep quarry in the Silurian and Devonian formations of northeastern Indiana. The quarry floor is far below the level of the Maumee River, in Pleasant Mills dolomite. The quarry exposes nearly 100 feet of reef rock of the Wabash formation that overlie the Pleasant Mills dolomite. Above that are 35 feet of the Detroit River formation and 10 feet of the Traverse formation.

### Huntington—The Lime City

The Wabash formation is exposed along the Little Wabash River through Huntington. Quarries west of town produced flag and building stone around 1900. Twelve companies operated at least thirty-one lime kilns around Huntington in the 1870s. The kilns are gone now and little remains of the huge lime plants, but crushed stone is still big business in the Huntington area. A side trip along Meridian Road on the east edge of town will take you past a quarry that exposes some 150 feet of the Wabash and Pleasant Mills formations as well as more than 60 feet of Salamonie dolomite.

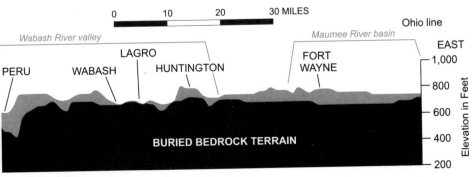

253

*A reef facies of the Silurian Wabash formation forms the walls of this quarry along U.S. 24 at Huntington.*

### Hanging Rock and Other Fossilized Reefs

The Wabash River eroded its valley between Huntington and Wabash through Silurian reefs. The central parts of the fossilized reefs, composed of dolomites in the Wabash formation, now stand as ridges, mounds, and knobs above the glaciated landscape.

Hanging Rock, 1.5 miles southeast of Lagro, shows the flat layers of the central reef and the sloping layers around its edges as well as flank deposits of reef blocks derived from wave erosion of the living reef. Fossils in this and other Silurian reefs are hard to recognize because the change from limestone to dolomite distorts them. Hanging Rock towers some 80 feet above the river. The view from the trail leading to the top is worth the short hike. Three more reefs jut from the floodplain 1 mile east of Hanging Rock.

Within Wabash, just east of a park at the former site of the passenger depot of the Big Four Railroad, a cut in the Wabash formation has attracted geologists for at least one hundred years. Dolomite, the core of a reef, extends about 750 feet along the tracks and rises nearly 40 feet above them. At the ends of the cut, the flank rocks slope away from the core of the reef. Glacial ice scraped off its top.

Another equally impressive dolomite reef core is exposed in a 50-foot-deep roadcut south of Wabash along Indiana 13, where it climbs the south bank of the Wabash River valley.

A fossilized reef is nicely exposed at Shanty Falls, south of the river, 1 mile southwest of Wabash. The vertical drop from the top of the cliffs to the valley floor is as much as 80 feet in some places. Along the base of the cliff,

*Hanging Rock, just upstream from Lagro, is a classic example of an eroded Silurian reef exposure.*

*The deep railroad cut through the Wabash reef in downtown Wabash.*

the rock layers tilt down to the east on the east side of the reef, lie flat on its top, and tilt down to the west on the west side of the reef.

### Wabash Valley Flagstone

Many quarries operating before 1900 in the Wabash Valley between Lagro and Richvalley now escape notice. They are relics of flagstone production, an important early industry. Flagstone is any rock that splits into slabs or flags suitable for foundation, pier, or wall construction. Some layers in the Wabash formation make good flags. Look for them in the foundations of older buildings and in old sidewalks and curbing throughout Wabash County.

### Seven Pillars of the Mississinewa

Before it joins the Wabash River just east of Peru, the Mississinewa River flows through a valley with some impressive features, including the Seven Pillars of the Mississinewa. The pillars are 2 miles northwest of Peoria and were eroded out of the dolomite of the Wabash formation. Water dissolved the bedrock along fractures in the cliff to isolate the pillars. Small caves pock the cliff.

The Mississinewa River eroded most of its valley during the latter part of the Wisconsinan ice age, when it was a meltwater channel. The Frances Slocum State Recreation Area, southeast of Peru, includes waterfalls, cliffs, and springs, as well as several historical sites.

### Quarries from Peoria to Peru

Slabby Wabash dolomites were quarried around Peoria in the late 1800s for use as flagstone and building stone. Other quarries worked along the Wabash River at Peru, making lime until about 1900. The Mississinewa shale is still quarried on the northwest edge of Peru.

### Logansport

Logansport was settled in the 1820s at the juncture of the Eel and Wabash Rivers. Nearby quarries supplied stone for locks, walls, and bridges on the Wabash and Erie Canal. Logansport became a center for lime production by the late 1850s. Look for crumbling abandoned vertical kilns east of Logansport.

Georgetown, a few miles down the Wabash valley, was the site of a quarry established in the 1830s during the era of canal building. The Georgetown stone was used in canal stonework and many early buildings, including Logansport's first courthouse.

Other quarries were once active near Kenneth, Clymers, Anoka, and Lewisburg. Lime production began in the 1870s and ended in the 1940s. Other products included crushed stone, flux stone for steel mills, and dimension stone for construction.

Quarries are still important near Logansport. The Wabash formation provides crushed stone from operations along U.S. 35 south of Logansport and along U.S. 24 at Kenneth. A cement plant began operating near Clymers, off Indiana 25, just southwest of town in 1962. It also uses glacial till as raw material.

*The Seven Pillars of the Mississinewa, southeast of Peru.*

*Slabs of Silurian limestones from the banks and riverbed of the Wabash River were the basis of the flagstone industry around Peru in the late 1800s. A few pools of oil were located in the Wabash River valley near Peru outside the more prosperous Trenton field. Note the oil rig in the distance. Photo circa 1905.* —Mark J. Camp Collection

An iron forge briefly operated along the Wabash and Erie Canal east of Logansport in the mid-1850s. Bog iron ore was shipped in from White County to the west. The forge was abandoned by 1860 because it was not close to a source of ore.

### *A Lake on the Ground Moraine*

At its greatest extent, the temporary glacial lake on the ground moraine along the western part of U.S. 24 stretched across part of northwestern Carroll County and most of White County. Its irregular shoreline extended as much as 27 miles north, 15 miles south, and 18 miles west of the U.S. 24 area. Its water was impounded when the edge of the Huron-Erie ice lobe blocked the natural drainage a few miles to the east. After the ice melted and the lake drained, blanket sands and dunes blew out of the Kankakee River outwash plains to the northwest and covered much of the old lakebed.

The valley of the Tippecanoe River at Monticello cuts the flat lake plain and the underlying till. The river eroded the 100-foot-deep valley after the blanket sands to the north blocked its original path west to the Kankakee River valley.

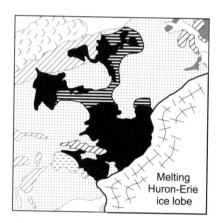

The ice melted eastward but still blocked any full drainage, so a progressively larger lake was dammed at its edge. Solid black areas represent visible lake deposits and black-striped areas represent possible lake areas buried by later sediments.

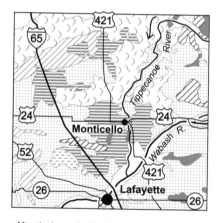

After the ice melted farther east, the lake drained into the Wabash River Valley. Blanket sands and small dunes later covered part of the lakebed. The sands diverted the Tippecanoe River southward to carve a new valley through the middle of the old lakebed.

*Development of a shallow, ice-dammed lake atop ground moraine in western Indiana.*

# U.S. 27
## Fort Wayne—Ohio Line
### 111 MILES

U.S. 27 begins in Fort Wayne in thick glacial deposits that thin farther south as they cap hills eroded in bedrock of Ordovician age.

## *Tipton Till Plain*

Between Fort Wayne and Richmond, U.S. 27 crosses the eastern side of the Tipton till plain. The section features nested end moraines (also called recessional moraines) that record five stages in the melting, or recession, of the Huron-Erie ice lobe.

U.S. 27 parallels the west edge of an end moraine for 19 miles between U.S. 24 in Fort Wayne and the St. Mary's River north of Decatur. The topography is flatter than that of most end moraines. Small streams have eroded the edge of the moraine, making it hilly. The thickness of the glacial material is between 50 and 100 feet.

The outwash sands and gravels are only about a half-mile wide where U.S. 27 crosses the St. Mary's River. The river flows where it does because meltwater was trapped between the ice to the north and the rise of the land to the south.

Between Decatur and Berne, U.S. 27 crosses 12 miles of ground moraine. Between Berne and the Wabash River, U.S. 27 crosses 3 miles of another end moraine. The glacial cover is 50 to 100 feet thick. The drainage divide that separates waters flowing north to the St. Mary's River from those flowing west to the Wabash River is south of Berne.

The highway crosses less than a half-mile of outwash sands and gravels in the valley of the Wabash River. A buried bedrock valley that contains more than 300 feet of glacial materials trends northeast, at a right angle to the modern drainage.

The highway traverses 9 miles of ground moraine between Ceylon at the Wabash River and the area 3 miles north of Portland. It then crosses end moraine—though it is hard to see—between the areas 4 and 2 miles north of Portland. The glacial sediments are 50 to 100 feet thick.

U.S. 27 crosses 8 miles of ground moraine between the areas 2 miles north and 6 miles south of Portland. The highway passes over the Salamonie River a dozen miles from its source. Very little, if any, outwash was deposited this far upstream. A buried bedrock valley that contains more than 250 feet of fill trends more or less parallel to the modern drainage.

Between the area 4.5 miles south of Portland and the Mississinewa River north of Deerfield, U.S. 27 runs through 4 miles of end moraine in two sections. A 1-mile-wide area of ground moraine separates the two end

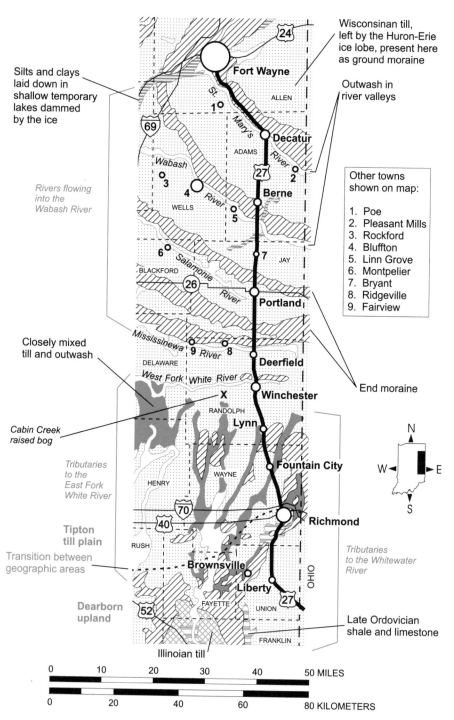

Wisconsinan till, left by the Huron-Erie ice lobe, present here as ground moraine

Silts and clays laid down in shallow temporary lakes dammed by the ice

Outwash in river valleys

Rivers flowing into the Wabash River

Other towns shown on map:

1. Poe
2. Pleasant Mills
3. Rockford
4. Bluffton
5. Linn Grove
6. Montpelier
7. Bryant
8. Ridgeville
9. Fairview

End moraine

Closely mixed till and outwash

Cabin Creek raised bog

Tributaries to the East Fork White River

N
W ◄—►E
S

Tipton till plain

Transition between geographic areas

Tributaries to the Whitewater River

Dearborn upland

Late Ordovician shale and limestone

Illinoian till

**Towns and roads along route (top to bottom):**
24 — Fort Wayne — ALLEN — Poe (1) — St. Mary's River — Decatur — ADAMS — 27 — Pleasant Mills (2) — Berne — Rockford (3) — Wabash River — Bluffton (4) — WELLS — Linn Grove (5) — 69 — Montpelier (6) — Salamonie River — BLACKFORD — 26 — Bryant (7) — JAY — Portland — Mississinewa River — Fairview (9) — Ridgeville (8) — Deerfield — DELAWARE — West Fork White River — Winchester — X — RANDOLPH — Lynn — Fountain City — WAYNE — HENRY — 70 — 40 — Richmond — RUSH — Brownsville — Liberty — FAYETTE — UNION — 52 — 27 — FRANKLIN — OHIO

0    10    20    30    40    50 MILES

0       20       40       60    80 KILOMETERS

*Geology along U.S. 27 between Fort Wayne and the Ohio line. Legend on page 208 further describes map patterns.*

moraines just north of the line between Jay and Randolph Counties but is difficult to distinguish.

Between Deerfield and the area 1 mile south of Lynn, U.S. 27 crosses 18 miles of ground moraine. The glacial cover is 150 to 200 feet thick. The clay-rich till of the Lagro formation grades into the less clayey till of the Trafalgar formation at the White River, but you cannot see this change in the landscape.

A drainage divide about 1 mile north of Winchester separates waters flowing north to the Mississinewa River from those flowing west and southwest through the West Fork White River. A divide about 2 miles north of Lynn separates the West Fork White River from that of the Whitewater River.

Northeastern Wayne County has the highest area in Indiana at 1,257 feet. Part of the elevation is due to the underlying bedrock topography and part to the layers of surface glacial deposits. This area of Indiana is along the crest of the Cincinnati Arch, a broad fold in the bedrock layers.

U.S. 27 crosses 15 miles of hills and valleys between U.S. 36 at Lynn and U.S. 40 at Richmond. Both end and ground moraine deposits cap the hills, and closely mixed till and outwash fill the valleys. The streams near Lynn and Fountain City feed the West Fork Whitewater River. The East Fork flows through Richmond. Numerous small streams have dissected the uplands and made them look a bit hillier. The glacial cover is 150 to 200 feet thick but slightly thinner in the valleys.

### Dearborn Upland

Between U.S. 40 in Richmond and the Ohio line, U.S. 27 winds 22 miles across the northeastern corner of the Dearborn upland. Thin glacial deposits cover the buried bedrock.

Between U.S. 40 in Richmond and Elkhorn Creek, 4 miles south of Richmond, U.S. 27 runs over 6 miles of hilly terrain capped by end moraine, generally less than 50 feet thick. Late Ordovician shales and limestones of the Whitewater formation are exposed in the south-flowing river valleys.

Between Elkhorn Creek and the Ohio border, U.S. 27 crosses 16 miles of ground moraine atop the same bedrock exposed in the valleys near Richmond. North of Liberty, streams have almost exposed the buried bedrock by eroding the shallow glacial cover, less than 50 feet thick.

Southeast of Liberty, up to 150 feet of glacial deposits fill a buried bedrock valley that trends northeast toward Ohio. The Pleistocene glaciers drastically changed some of the regional drainage patterns.

### Fort Wayne Area

Fort Wayne stands on three upland areas, parts of the last two end moraines laid down at the edge of the melting Huron-Erie ice lobe. The older end moraine is north and west of the St. Joseph and St. Mary's Rivers and has the least urban development. The younger is east of the St. Joseph and St. Mary's Rivers, and the Maumee River cuts through it. The rivers have eroded some 60 feet through the moraines. The edges of the moraines are rugged because streams have eroded small valleys into the hillsides. The thickness of the glacial sediments is between 50 and 100 feet.

The two end moraines are adjacent north of the city and about 10 miles apart south of the city because the Huron-Erie ice lobe melted unevenly. Ice covered the Fort Wayne area while the western moraine accumulated, and its meltwater poured down the valleys of the Wabash and the Little Wabash Rivers. Then the northern edge of the ice melted back about 4 miles, while the southern edge melted back 10 to 12 miles.

As the Huron-Erie ice lobe held its eastern position and deposited the second end moraine, its meltwaters eroded two new valleys. The St. Joseph River flowed south between the two end moraines and the St. Mary's River flowed at the edge of the forming end moraine. The two rivers met and poured their waters and outwash sediments down the large valley cut through the western moraine. After the eastern moraine formed and the ice melted back farther, the continued flow of meltwater cut the eastern moraine as easily as it had the western one. Meltwater continued to flow west and deposit outwash through this gap, even after the ice front melted back into northwestern Ohio (see map on page 239).

As the Huron-Erie ice lobe melted completely, the newly exposed land sloped down to the east. Then the St. Joseph and St. Mary's Rivers combined to make the Maumee River, which drains east to Lake Erie.

Meanwhile, the large meltwater valley west of the moraines became a shallow lake that accumulated silts and clays in its floor until it finally drained. Indians, fur traders, and explorers who came by canoe along the Maumee and Wabash Rivers used the valley for a portage. The frontier Fort Wayne was built to control this portage. The northeastern part of Fort Wayne stands on an end moraine, an extension of the Steuben morainal lake area. The land on all other sides of the city is part of the Tipton till plain.

The best view of the bedrock beneath Fort Wayne is at the Ardmore Avenue quarry on the southwest side of the city. The owners maintain a

*Generalized surface and bedrock profiles along U.S. 27.*

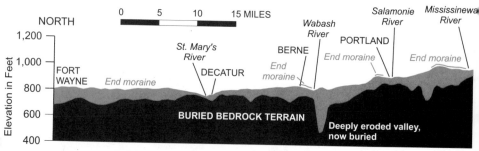

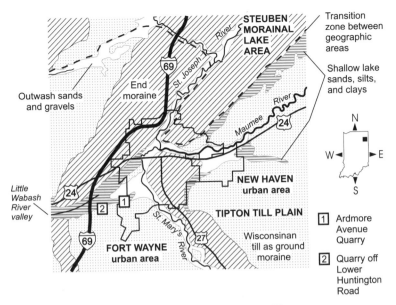

Transition zone between geographic areas

Shallow lake sands, silts, and clays

Outwash sands and gravels

End moraine

STEUBEN MORAINAL LAKE AREA

Little Wabash River valley

NEW HAVEN urban area

TIPTON TILL PLAIN

Wisconsinan till as ground moraine

FORT WAYNE urban area

1 Ardmore Avenue Quarry

2 Quarry off Lower Huntington Road

*Geology and geography in the greater Fort Wayne area.*

public viewing stand on the north wall along Sand Point Road. Sand and gravel were mined at this site before the pit was extended into bedrock around 1950. The quarry is nearly 300 feet deep, exposing the Wabash formation and the overlying Detroit River and Traverse formations, with a thin cap of Wisconsinan tills and outwash. Its floor is in the Silurian Pleasant Mills formation.

Blocks of gray dolomite of the Wabash formation lie around the viewing stand. These rocks are part of the Fort Wayne Bank, the great area of Silurian reefs that stretches across northern Indiana. The upper 10 feet of the formation are riddled with irregular openings called vugs that contain colorful crystals of fluorite, the mineral form of calcium fluoride. Larger vugs, opened by solution of the rock, and fractures filled with greenish sandstone exist at the top of the formation. These probably formed right after Silurian time, when the region was above sea level and eroding.

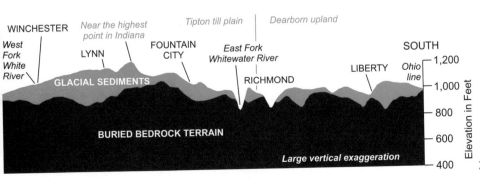

WINCHESTER

Near the highest point in Indiana

Tipton till plain

Dearborn upland

West Fork White River

LYNN

FOUNTAIN CITY

East Fork Whitewater River

SOUTH

GLACIAL SEDIMENTS

RICHMOND

LIBERTY

Ohio line

1,200

1,000

800

BURIED BEDROCK TERRAIN

*Large vertical exaggeration*

600

400

Elevation in Feet

From this viewing platform, visitors may watch the operation of a typical limestone quarry. This quarry is located off Ardmore Avenue in southwestern Fort Wayne.

Another quarry is north of Lower Huntington Road, about 2 miles southwest of the Ardmore Avenue operation. It exposes a similar column of Silurian to Devonian strata, although the Wabash formation here is less than half as thick as it is at the Ardmore Avenue quarry, a typical fluctuation.

Fort Wayne was the site of the highest section of the Wabash and Erie Canal. The first shovels of dirt were turned in 1832. The canal reached downstream to Huntington by 1836. The sections to the east were completed by 1843, as were the sections west to Lafayette.

During the canal's brief heyday, Fort Wayne was home to several thousand people. Boat builders, ship chandlers, foundries, smithies, breweries, brickyards, wagon manufacturers, joineries, sawmills, and flour mills all operated in Fort Wayne. Three blocks of canal warehouses shipped and received products.

The Wabash and Erie Canal was too little, too late. Costs far exceeded revenue, and the railroads eliminated dependence on rivers. The canal sections west of Fort Wayne were abandoned by 1870, those to the east by 1888. Only overgrown ditches and historical records remain.

### Quarries South of Fort Wayne

Silurian bedrock is close to the surface at many sites south of Fort Wayne. Quarries there produce crushed stone and aggregate. The oldest exposed rock is the Salamonie dolomite at quarries near Bryant, Fairview, Linn Grove,

*Silurian-Devonian strata along Lower Huntington Road on the southwest side of Fort Wayne.*

Pleasant Mills, Portland, and Ridgeville. The overlying Pleasant Mills formation is exposed at Bluffton, Bryant, Linn Grove, Montpelier, and Pleasant Mills. The youngest rock is the Wabash formation, exposed in quarries near Bluffton and Rockford. About 100 feet of the Wabash formation are exposed in a quarry along the St. Mary's River near Poe. Like other exposures of Silurian rocks across northern Indiana, these quarries feature reefs and their associated fossils.

### Decatur Mineral Industries

A quarry on North Second Street in Decatur, now full of water, opened in 1880. The company sold Silurian limestone for building stone and crushed stone, and burned it for lime. Another quarry on Piqua Road marketed a dimension stone called Decatur Stone. A brick plant operating in Decatur as early as 1882 used surface clays. The plant was enlarged in 1892 and drain tile was added to the product line. The plant functioned until the early 1970s.

### Cabin Creek Raised Bog

From U.S. 27 at Winchester, follow Indiana 32 west for 8 miles and then turn south for 2 miles on Indiana 1. You will find a mound of organic sediments that stands as much as 10 feet above the floodplain of Cabin Creek. This is a raised bog, the only one known in Indiana. The Cabin Creek raised bog originally developed as marl and organic matter accumulated in a small lake surrounded by ice. The marl and vegetation accumulated to a considerable depth, then the surrounding land dropped as the ice melted.

Test borings in the bog show between 20 and 23 feet of marl and organic debris. The marl formed as groundwater seeped out of the surrounding glacial sediments and precipitated calcite in the lake. Plants filled the basin, forming peat with moss and sedge fragments.

Such a raised bog would normally drain because it is higher than the surrounding terrain, but an artesian flow of groundwater keeps the Cabin Creek bog wet. The groundwater maintains an alkaline environment that favors mosses and sedges, prairie grasses, sumac, hazelnut, and lady's slipper orchids.

## A Giant Beaver and a Mastodon

The Joseph Moore Museum, on the Earlham College campus in Richmond, provides a good introduction to the geology and natural history of eastern Indiana. Joseph E. Moore served Earlham College from the 1850s until his death in 1905 as professor of geology, curator of the museum, and president. He assembled a collection of thousands of fossils, minerals, shells, artifacts, and preserved and stuffed animals from around the world.

Moore acquired the museum's first Pleistocene mastodon skeleton from New Paris, Ohio, in 1874. The skeleton was nearly complete, and the museum used parts of two other mastodons from Randolph County, north of Richmond, to fill in the missing sections. The completed skeleton was early Richmond's biggest attraction.

In 1889 ditch diggers in Randolph County uncovered the bones of an unknown animal. They were displayed in a Winchester bank until Moore identified them as the extinct giant beaver of Pleistocene time. This giant beaver skeleton is the most complete ever found.

Beginning in 1888 the collections were placed in the newly constructed Lindley Hall. In 1924 fire destroyed Lindley Hall along with part of the collection, but the mastodon and giant beaver skeletons survived. The present museum, completed in 1952, includes a dinosaur and a dire wolf.

## Whitewater Formation

Fossiliferous shales and limestones of the late Ordovician Whitewater formation abound in the stream valleys around Richmond. The layers are so thin that the shale and limestone beds are hard to differentiate. Watch for roadcuts 1 mile south of Richmond. They provide a nice view of the formation and its fossil brachiopods, clams, and bryozoans.

## German Stone Arches

A German stone mason, George Heim, came to Union County in the 1850s to help construct a rail line from Hamilton, Ohio, to Rushville. The

266

Heim family masons were regarded as the best builders of stone arches in Germany. Heim's arches of hand-hewn limestone still carry the tracks across the deeper valleys between Liberty and Brownsville.

# U.S. 31
## Michigan Line—Indianapolis
### 141 MILES

### Kankakee Outwash Plain
Between the Michigan line and the southern edge of South Bend, U.S. 31 crosses 8 miles of the Kankakee outwash plain—sands and gravels deposited from the Lake Michigan, Saginaw, and Huron-Erie ice lobes. The glacial cover is 100 to 150 feet thick. The business route crosses outwash in the St. Joseph River valley. The bypass arcs west of the city across flat outwash and two hilly areas of closely mixed till and outwash, one northwest and the other south of the city. The hilly area to the northwest was isolated by meltwater floods that left it as an island in a sea of outwash. The hilly area south of the city is part of an end moraine left by the Lake Michigan ice lobe, near but not part of the Valparaiso moraine.

### Steuben Morainal Lake Area
U.S. 31 cuts through the western edge of the Steuben morainal lake area. The glacial sediments are generally 150 to 200 feet thick, but reach more than 400 feet in a filled bedrock valley 5 miles north of the Eel River.

The highway runs through 26 miles of low hills deposited by the Lake Michigan ice lobe between South Bend and the area 3 miles south of Plymouth. The hills are ground moraine, end moraine, and mixed till and outwash. The glacial till is the Wedron formation. The low areas and small valleys are filled with outwash.

About 2 miles south of Argos, U.S. 31 crosses the drainage divide that separates waters flowing north and west toward the Yellow and Kankakee Rivers from those flowing south and west to the Tippecanoe, Eel, and Wabash Rivers.

Between the area 3 miles south of Plymouth and the Eel River, U.S. 31 traverses 38 miles of similar low hills deposited by the Huron-Erie ice lobe. Near Rochester, the highway crosses 5 miles of outwash sands and gravels in the Tippecanoe River valley.

### Tipton Till Plain
U.S. 31 crosses 69 miles of the Tipton till plain between the Eel River and I-465. The land is mostly flat ground moraine, deposited by the

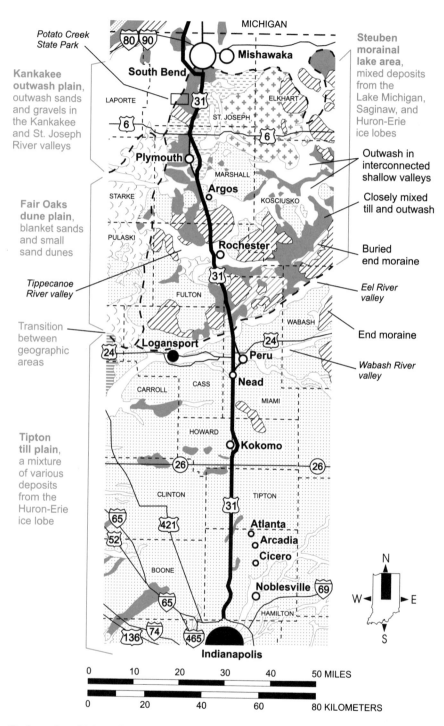

Geology along U.S. 31 between the Michigan line and Indianapolis. Legend on page 208 further describes map patterns.

Huron-Erie ice lobe. The thickness of the glacial cover varies from less than 50 feet to more than 150 feet. This part of U.S. 31 travels over two buried bedrock valleys more than 300 feet deep, one north of the Wabash River and the other a forked valley in southern Tipton County and northern Hamilton County.

U.S. 31 crosses 14 miles of uplands capped with Lagro till between the area just north of the Eel River valley and that 1 mile south of Nead. The Lagro till contains more clay than the Trafalgar till. The valleys of the Eel and Wabash Rivers cut this small area of Lagro till into thirds.

U.S. 31 crosses the level surface of ground moraine for 55 miles between Nead and Indianapolis. This flatness is precisely what geologists expect of a till plain. Only a few small creeks cut the surface. In southern Tipton County, the highway crosses the subtle divide between waters flowing north and west to the Wabash River from those flowing south to the West Fork White River.

### Cement Production from Marl

In 1877 South Bend was the site of the first successful manufacture in this country of portland cement from a mixture of marl and clay. The marl was dredged on the campus of Notre Dame University from St. Joseph's and St. Mary's Lakes. Glacial clay was shipped in from Bertrand, Michigan. The cement was known for its high quality and great strength, but the plant closed before 1900.

### Iron Forges

An ironworks in Mishawaka operated from 1834 to 1856, smelting bog iron ore dug along the nearby St. Joseph River. Bog iron forms in shallow water where vegetation is lush and dissolved iron content is high. Iron precipitates on lake or marsh bottoms in irregular masses called nodules. More abundant ores from the Missouri and Lake Superior districts replaced the limited amounts of bog ore. Marl was used for flux, an aid to the smelting process.

The Catalan forge at Mishawaka was a type of blast furnace, the first of its kind in the state. Catalan forges were set up where the market was limited and capital was scarce. They heated the iron to a paste but did not melt it. They consumed more fuel and produced less iron than ordinary blast furnaces, but they were cheap to operate.

A Catalan forge was also built near Plymouth in 1840. It made wrought iron products until around 1850. Another forge, possibly near Rochester, operated from 1840 to 1850. No traces of any of the Catalan forges exist today.

### Potato Creek State Park

Potato Creek State Park includes some of the best examples of the hilly terrain in this part of northern Indiana. The west half of the park is end

*One of the tusks of the Rochester mastodon before extraction and preservation.*
—Ansel Gooding photo

moraine and the east half is closely mixed glacial till and outwash, but the greatly variable appearance of the many small hills shows how indistinct the transition between them is. The marshy valley of Potato Creek was dammed to make a recreational lake.

### Mastodon near Rochester

A nearly complete skeleton of a mastodon was dug from a drainage ditch 5 miles west of Rochester in 1959 and 1960. The ground is mostly glacial outwash and dune sands, with low spots floored in muck and peat deposited in former ponds and bogs. The mastodon likely got stuck in the soft muck and marl of one of the ponds, drowned, and was buried in the accumulating

*Generalized surface and bedrock profiles along U.S. 31.*

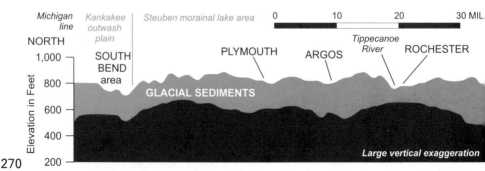

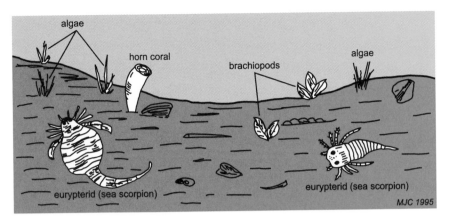

*Silurian seascape of northern Indiana, showing eurypterids, or sea scorpions. Fossils of these arthropods came from Kokomo area quarries.*

marl. A log buried below the bones yielded a radiocarbon age of 12,000 years. Analysis of pollen and snail shells indicate the beast died sometime around 11,000 years ago. The bones are on display in the Joseph Moore Museum at Earlham College in Richmond.

### Kokomo Sea Scorpions

Kokomo's Markland Avenue quarry, now filled with slag, once exposed the Kokomo limestone member of the Wabash formation. The site was well known for its fossils of large brachiopods, ostracods, and particularly its eurypterids, or sea scorpions. Eurypterids are best known from rocks of similar age in New York state and are scarce elsewhere.

Eurypterids were first noted in dolomites in Kokomo quarries in the late 1880s. Most eurypterid fossils are fragmental and incomplete, but the Kokomo locality yielded a few excellent impressions of nearly complete animals. Good examples are in the Smithsonian Museum.

The old Yeoman quarry, 1.5 miles west of the quarry at Markland Avenue, exposes 26 feet of Kokomo limestone underlain by 40 feet of the Liston Creek member of the Wabash formation. This site also yielded eu-

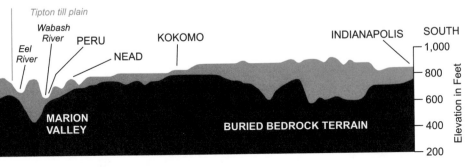

rypterids. Fine laminations in the dolomite, an abundance of large ostracod and algae fossils, and the eurypterids all suggest a sea with slightly higher than normal salinity.

### Glass Factories of North-Central Indiana

U.S. 31 lies just west of several old glass factories. At least four plants started business in Kokomo between 1888 and 1909. Glass factories also flourished in Atlanta, Arcadia, Cicero, and Noblesville. All these companies used the readily available natural gas and oil in the underlying Trenton rocks. The glass industry faded when the fuel ran out.

# U.S. 41
# Whiting—Attica
**102 MILES**

U.S. 41 crosses a wide variety of glacial deposits of the Wisconsinan ice age. The Lake Michigan ice lobe dumped some of them, the Huron-Erie ice lobe the rest.

### Calumet Lake Plain

U.S. 41 crosses 15 miles of the Calumet lake plain between the Illinois line and U.S. 30. The plain was deposited along the southern edge of Lake Michigan when its water levels were slightly higher than now. Two beach ridges are visible at the north edge of Hammond and in downtown Dyer, along old U.S. 6. Shallow lake deposits accumulated in low areas behind the beach ridges. The low areas once held perennial wetlands, most of which were drained to accommodate the expanding urban area. The glacial deposits range from 100 to 150 feet thick.

### Valparaiso Moraine

U.S. 41 crosses 17 miles of the Valparaiso moraine between U.S. 30 and the area 3 miles north of Schneider. It is a hilly end moraine deposited where an edge of the Lake Michigan ice lobe temporarily stalled as it melted back toward Lake Michigan. The till deposited from this ice lobe is the Wedron formation. The glacial deposits are 100 to 150 feet thick. In the northern part of this end moraine, the highway climbs an indistinct drainage divide that separates waters flowing north to Lake Michigan from those flowing south to the Kankakee River.

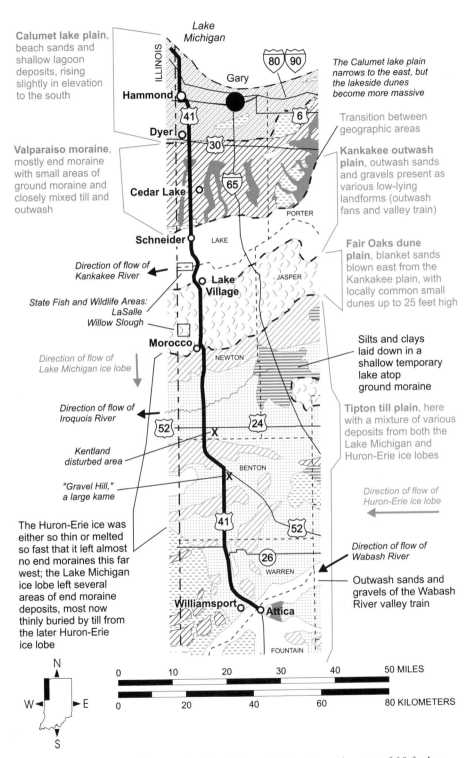

**Calumet lake plain**, beach sands and shallow lagoon deposits, rising slightly in elevation to the south

*Lake Michigan*

ILLINOIS

80 90

Gary

Hammond

41

Dyer

30

65

Cedar Lake

PORTER

Schneider LAKE

*Direction of flow of Kankakee River*

Lake Village JASPER

*State Fish and Wildlife Areas: LaSalle Willow Slough*

Morocco NEWTON

*Direction of flow of Lake Michigan ice lobe*

*Direction of flow of Iroquois River*

52

24

*Kentland disturbed area*

X

BENTON

*"Gravel Hill," a large kame*

X

41

52

The Huron-Erie ice was either so thin or melted so fast that it left almost no end moraines this far west; the Lake Michigan ice lobe left several areas of end moraine deposits, most now thinly buried by till from the later Huron-Erie ice lobe

26

WARREN

Williamsport

Attica

FOUNTAIN

*The Calumet lake plain narrows to the east, but the lakeside dunes become more massive*

Transition between geographic areas

**Kankakee outwash plain**, outwash sands and gravels present as various low-lying landforms (outwash fans and valley train)

**Fair Oaks dune plain**, blanket sands blown east from the Kankakee plain, with locally common small dunes up to 25 feet high

Silts and clays laid down in a shallow temporary lake atop ground moraine

**Tipton till plain**, here with a mixture of various deposits from both the Lake Michigan and Huron-Erie ice lobes

*Direction of flow of Huron-Erie ice lobe*

*Direction of flow of Wabash River*

Outwash sands and gravels of the Wabash River valley train

**Valparaiso moraine**, mostly end moraine with small areas of ground moraine and closely mixed till and outwash

N

W E

S

| 0 | 10 | 20 | 30 | 40 | 50 MILES |
| 0 | 20 | 40 | 60 | 80 KILOMETERS |

*Geology along U.S. 41 between the Illinois line and Attica. Legend on page 208 further describes map patterns.*

### Kankakee Outwash Plain

U.S. 41 crosses 8 miles of sands and gravels of the Kankakee outwash plain between the area 3 miles north of Schneider and that near Lake Village. This is part of a broad area of glacial outwash that meltwaters dumped in the valley of the Kankakee River. The deposits here are 50 to 100 feet deep.

### Fair Oaks Dune Plain

U.S. 41 passes through 15 miles of blanket sands and sand dunes, part of the Fair Oaks dune plain, between Lake Village and Morocco. Strong winds blew this thin cap of sand, 40 to 60 feet thick, from the wide outwash plains to the north and west at the end of the last ice age. The wind also created hundreds of sand dunes, 20 to 40 feet high. They are especially prominent in Conrad, but watch for low, forested mounds across the plain.

Windblown sands lap onto the edge of the Tipton till plain to the south. The deep drainage ditches lowered the water table to allow farming.

### Tipton Till Plain

U.S. 41 covers 47 miles of ground moraine within the Tipton till plain between the area just north of Morocco and Attica. As it melted, the Huron-Erie ice lobe left the Trafalgar till atop the landscape, perhaps 12,000 years ago.

Between central Newton County and southern Benton County, the highway crosses mostly flat ground, except for three hilly areas of buried end moraine. The Lake Michigan ice lobe stalled and deposited them, and later the Huron-Erie ice lobe laid thin deposits over them. The northernmost area extends from just north of Morocco to 4 miles south, where it grades into ground moraine. The middle area extends from the line between Benton and Newton Counties to just west of Earl Park, about 5 miles. The third area of buried end moraine is 3 miles across, centered 4 miles north of Boswell. In this area you also cross the drainage divide between the Iroquois River and the Wabash River.

*Generalized surface and bedrock profiles along U.S. 41.*

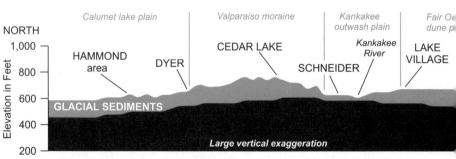

*A county road cuts through a sand dune in the Fair Oaks dune plain, near Enos.*
—Graham T. Richardson photo

The Iroquois River flows west to Illinois atop gently sloping ground moraine. The till here is 50 to 100 feet thick but thins to almost nothing at Rensselaer, 15 miles to the east. U.S. 41 passes through Kentland, just west of the world-famous Kentland structure.

Southeast of Earl Park, U.S. 41 passes near several kames—low elongated hills of outwash that accumulated in cracks in the melting ice or along its edge. Kames are excellent sources of sand and gravel ready for use as either construction aggregate or gravel roads.

The ground moraine between the area 2.5 miles north of Boswell and Attica is rather hilly, due in part to the valleys of small tributaries that flow east to Mud Pine and Big Pine Creeks. The glacial debris near Boswell is more than 350 feet deep because it fills an old valley that trends east-west

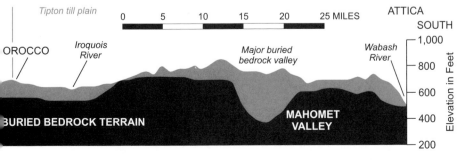

along the line between Warren and Benton Counties. Hills near Attica reflect the preglacial bedrock terrain buried beneath less than 50 feet of glacial debris.

U.S. 41 crosses the Wabash River at Attica in a valley about 175 feet deep and 1.5 miles across. Exposures of sandstone, siltstone, shale, and limestone of the Mississippian Borden group crop out along the valley walls, but the dense plant cover makes them hard to see. The outwash sands and gravels in the valley are less than 50 feet thick.

### Lake Michigan Wetlands

Many wetlands in the western Calumet lake plain were filled during the late 1800s to produce dry land for industrial, commercial, and residential development. Wolf Lake, west of U.S. 41, is one of the last large remnants of the marshes and lakes that formerly flooded the low areas between the old beaches and tracts of sand dunes that parallel the shore of Lake Michigan.

### Kettle Lakes and Mixed Glacial Drift

The small kettle lakes that dot the Valparaiso moraine fill depressions left where blocks of ice incorporated in the till melted. Cedar Lake is larger than most in northwestern Indiana, but larger kettle lakes exist in northeastern Indiana.

Two valleys filled with closely mixed till and outwash parallel U.S. 41 where it crosses the Valparaiso moraine. Kettle lakes and deposits of organic material such as muck, peat, or marl are typical of these valleys. They are about 1 mile wide and 12 to 13 miles long. Seven other such valleys cross the moraine farther east.

### Kankakee River

Swamps once covered the Kankakee outwash plain, but the modern Kankakee River is little more than a drainage ditch. Before settlers entered the region in the late 1800s, the Kankakee River did not really flow west into Illinois. It oozed through swamps and undergrowth that harbored abundant game and fish along with malarial mosquitoes. A rock ledge in eastern Illinois served as a natural dam. In the 1890s Hoosiers paid to remove that rock ledge and channelize the upper Kankakee River, reducing its length from 250 to 85 miles.

By 1925 the swamps were drained and the trees cleared to produce agricultural land. The history of that process is a tale of controversy and intrigue. The Kankakee State Fish and Wildlife Area was reflooded to restore a small part of the old wetlands.

### *Willow Slough State Fish and Wildlife Area*

Willow Slough State Fish and Wildlife Area is at the extreme southern edge of the Fair Oaks dune plain, just northwest of Morocco. It includes a few sand dunes. The second-growth plant cover and the lakes provide some idea of what the Kankakee region looked like before farmers drained and cleared it for agriculture.

### *Williamsport Falls*

Williamsport Falls are a quarter mile south of Indiana 28 in Williamsport. Fall Branch cascades 80 feet over a cliff of Pennsylvanian sandstone into a rocky gorge on its way to the Wabash River. An abandoned sandstone quarry at the foot of the falls provided building stone for many local homes and businesses.

*Williamsport Falls, circa 1900.* —Mark J. Camp Collection

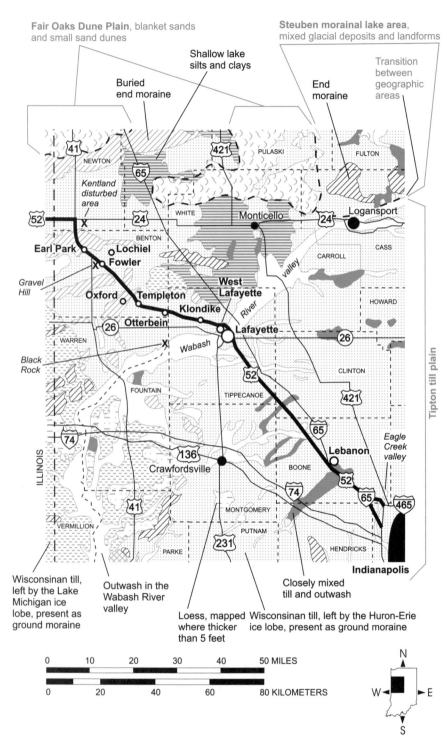

**Fair Oaks Dune Plain**, blanket sands and small sand dunes

Shallow lake silts and clays

Buried end moraine

**Steuben morainal lake area**, mixed glacial deposits and landforms

End moraine

Transition between geographic areas

NEWTON

*Kentland disturbed area*

PULASKI

FULTON

WHITE

Monticello

Logansport

BENTON

Earl Park

Lochiel

Fowler

CARROLL

CASS

*Gravel Hill*

Oxford

Templeton

West Lafayette

HOWARD

Klondike

Otterbein

Lafayette

WARREN

Wabash

*Black Rock*

River valley

CLINTON

FOUNTAIN

TIPPECANOE

Eagle Creek valley

Tipton till plain

Lebanon

BOONE

ILLINOIS

Crawfordsville

MONTGOMERY

Indianapolis

PUTNAM

VERMILLION

PARKE

HENDRICKS

Wisconsinan till, left by the Lake Michigan ice lobe, present as ground moraine

Outwash in the Wabash River valley

Loess, mapped where thicker than 5 feet

Closely mixed till and outwash

Wisconsinan till, left by the Huron-Erie ice lobe, present as ground moraine

| 0 | 10 | 20 | 30 | 40 | 50 MILES |

| 0 | 20 | 40 | 60 | 80 KILOMETERS |

N
W — E
S

*Geology along U.S. 52 between Indianapolis and the Illinois line. Legend on page 208 further describes map patterns.*

# U.S. 52
## Indianapolis—Illinois Line
**100 MILES**

U.S. 52 crosses a wide expanse of glacial deposits in the southwestern part of the Tipton till plain between I-465 and the Illinois line. Most of the route traverses nearly level ground moraine formed from glacial till of the Trafalgar formation deposited by the Huron-Erie ice lobe, which advanced southwest across Indiana.

Between I-465 and the area east of the Wabash River, U.S. 52 crosses 53 miles of mostly ground moraine. The highway parallels a buried bedrock slope. Northeast of U.S. 52, the glacial cover is generally between 200 and 300 feet thick; southwest of the highway, the cover generally thins to less than 100 feet.

About 7 miles south of Lebanon, U.S. 52 passes over the drainage divide between waters flowing west to the Wabash River from those flowing south and southeast to the West Fork White River.

Just south of Lafayette, glacial meltwater pouring across the countryside deposited a wide outwash plain. The water broke through two low areas southeast of Lafayette and spread a thin plain of sand and gravel 4 miles wide that connects with a larger outwash terrace to the west. The northern edge of this outwash plain is a few miles south of Lafayette, but it is hard to identify because it merges gradually into the ground moraine near the city. The southern edge of this outwash plain is much more visible 8 miles south of Lafayette, where U.S. 52 climbs 50 feet in a short distance.

The Wabash River valley at West Lafayette and Lafayette is narrow by Wabash Valley standards, about 1.5 miles wide, and deep by Indiana standards, about 200 feet. As grand as the modern Wabash River looks, it is a small remnant of the mighty torrent that once passed through here. The highway crosses a relatively narrow portion of the Wabash River valley's massive deposits of outwash sands and gravels that extend upstream and downstream for many miles. Their thickness is 100 to 200 feet. At the west bank of the Wabash River, U.S. 52 ascends 180 feet through a large and impressive roadcut in ground moraine.

Between the Wabash River and Earl Park, U.S. 52 covers 34 miles of mostly flat ground moraine. This area contains some of the most productive and intensively farmed land in the United States.

Between Templeton and Earl Park, U.S. 52 crosses ground moraine and buried end moraine deposits that do not show the usual contrast between flat and hilly appearances. A few miles west of Templeton, U.S. 52 enters a narrow hilly area of buried end moraine that quickly grades down to the lower ground moraine to the east. Some of the land immediately south of

Fowler is part of the drainage divide that separates waters flowing north and west into Illinois from those flowing south to the Wabash River. The thickness of the glacial cover varies from less than 50 feet to more than 300 feet. The gentle landscape hides two buried bedrock valleys that connect with a major buried valley farther south along the line between Warren and Benton Counties.

Two miles west of Fowler, near a crossroads named Gravel Hill, an elongated kame appears as a low hill about 90 feet high, southwest of the highway. Kames formed as sand and gravel filled cracks in the ice or accumulated as alluvial fans along its edge. They are excellent sources of road gravel and construction aggregate.

Between Earl Park and the line between Benton and Newton Counties, the highway crosses 5 miles of buried end moraine of Wedron till. This till was laid down along a temporarily stable edge of the Lake Michigan ice lobe, then buried under thin till of the Trafalgar formation deposited by the Huron-Erie ice lobe. The glacial cover is 50 to 100 feet thick.

Between the Benton and Newton County boundary and the Illinois line, U.S. 52 crosses 6 miles of fairly flat ground moraine that ranges from 50 to 100 feet thick. This land slopes toward Illinois and is within the drainage basin of the Iroquois River.

### The Wabash and Erie Canal at Lafayette

The commercial success of the Erie Canal across New York state in the 1820s inspired early Hoosiers to build one for themselves. They chose the Wabash River valley for one of a series of canals. In January 1832 the legislature finally authorized the borrowing of $200,000 to survey and construct a canal to connect towns along the Wabash River to the western end of Lake Erie in Ohio.

Construction of a channel 40 feet wide and 4 feet deep proceeded slowly westward from the Ohio line. It was 1843 before the Wabash and Erie

*Generalized surface and bedrock profiles along U.S. 52.*

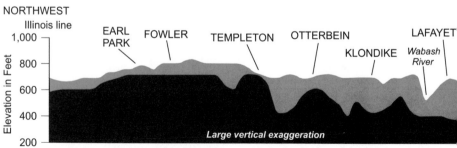

Canal reached Lafayette, 1849 before it reached Terre Haute, and 1851 before it extended to Evansville.

When the canal was completed, the speed, capacity, and connections of the railroads were already making it obsolete. Gross receipts never exceeded construction costs, and regular maintenance and flood damage only drove costs higher. The canal's commercial value fell in the 1850s, but the sections around Lafayette maintained some utility until 1874. While in operation, the canal and its support works helped build Lafayette.

Some difficulties in construction were due to the physical geology of the Wabash Valley. The porous outwash sands and gravels of the valley did not help the canal retain water and made poor foundations for lock gates. The planners also largely ignored the Wabash River's floods and made poor use of tributaries to supply water.

### Bedrock near West Lafayette

Bedrock outcrops exist in several areas west of West Lafayette, but none are visible from U.S. 52. Some years ago, a small housing development near Klondike was built without basements because the planners did not recognize numerous small sandstone boulders in the lots as the tops of bedrock hills not completely buried under glacial sediments. A bedrock bluff, Black Rock, overlooks the Wabash River valley 8 miles south of Otterbein. These and other small exposures of bedrock testify to the hilly preglacial landscape.

### Mineral Industries of Benton County

Drainage tile manufacture was big business in Benton County in the 1880s, when the land was being cleared and swamps drained for farmers. Tile factories at Fowler, Lochiel, Oxford, and Templeton all used yellow clay that was available just below the rich topsoil. This clay is a product of normal soil weathering since the glaciers melted.

Small quarries in Pine and Sugar Creeks, north of Earl Park, worked Mississippian Harrodsburg limestone in the 1880s. The stone went into the foundations of many early local buildings.

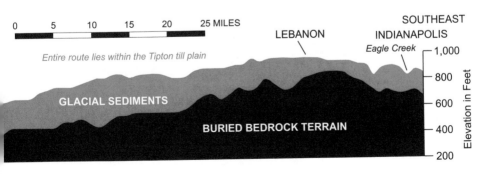

SOUTHEAST
LEBANON   INDIANAPOLIS
Eagle Creek

Entire route lies within the Tipton till plain

GLACIAL SEDIMENTS

BURIED BEDROCK TERRAIN

Elevation in Feet — 1,000 — 800 — 600 — 400 — 200

0   5   10   15   20   25 MILES

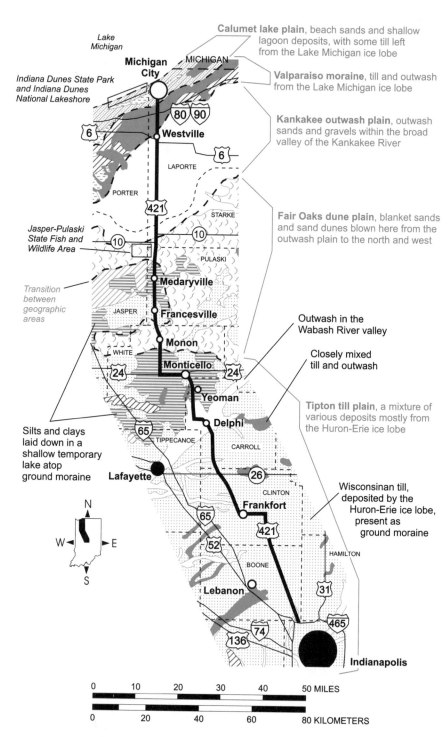

Calumet lake plain, beach sands and shallow lagoon deposits, with some till left from the Lake Michigan ice lobe

Valparaiso moraine, till and outwash from the Lake Michigan ice lobe

Kankakee outwash plain, outwash sands and gravels within the broad valley of the Kankakee River

Fair Oaks dune plain, blanket sands and sand dunes blown here from the outwash plain to the north and west

Outwash in the Wabash River valley

Closely mixed till and outwash

Tipton till plain, a mixture of various deposits mostly from the Huron-Erie ice lobe

Wisconsinan till, deposited by the Huron-Erie ice lobe, present as ground moraine

Silts and clays laid down in a shallow temporary lake atop ground moraine

Transition between geographic areas

Lake Michigan

Indiana Dunes State Park and Indiana Dunes National Lakeshore

Jasper-Pulaski State Fish and Wildlife Area

Michigan City

MICHIGAN

Westville

80 90

6

6

LAPORTE

PORTER

421

STARKE

10

10

PULASKI

Medaryville

Francesville

JASPER

Monon

WHITE

Monticello

24

24

Yeoman

Delphi

65

TIPPECANOE

CARROLL

Lafayette

26

CLINTON

Frankfort

65

421

52

HAMILTON

BOONE

Lebanon

31

74

465

136

Indianapolis

N
W ◄ ► E
S

0    10    20    30    40    50 MILES

0    20    40    60    80 KILOMETERS

*Geology along U.S. 421 between Michigan City and Indianapolis. Legend on page 208 further describes map patterns.*

# U.S. 421
## Michigan City—Indianapolis
**143 MILES**

## Calumet Lake Plain

U.S. 421 passes through 6 miles of the Calumet lake plain between Lake Michigan and the area 3 miles south of Michigan City. It features beach and dune sands, shallow backwater deposits, and a patch of glacial till. The till belongs to the Wedron formation deposited from the Lake Michigan ice lobe. It extends 2 miles south of U.S. 20. The glacial sediments are 100 to 200 feet thick.

## Valparaiso Moraine

U.S. 421 crosses 5 miles of the Valparaiso moraine between the area 3 miles south of Michigan City and that just north of Westville. This part of the moraine is mainly till chaotically mixed with sands and gravels deposited in small meltwater channels. The glacial cover is between 150 and 250 feet thick. Between the toll road and Westville, U.S. 421 crosses the drainage divide between waters flowing north to Lake Michigan and those flowing south to the Kankakee River.

## Kankakee Outwash Plain

U.S. 421 crosses 24 miles of the Kankakee outwash plain between the area just north of Westville and the northern intersection with Indiana 10. The surface elevation only drops 30 feet from north to south across those miles, making this about the flattest area in the state. The glacial cover varies from 50 to nearly 100 feet deep across this plain, thickening rapidly to the east and thinning to the west.

## Fair Oaks Dune Plain

Between the northern intersection with Indiana 10 and the area 1.5 miles south of Monon, U.S. 421 runs for 26 miles within, and along the edge of, the Fair Oaks dune plain. This is an eastern extension of the blanket sands and dunes blown out of the enormous outwash plains along the Kankakee River to the north and west. Some of the best dunes are in and near the Jasper-Pulaski State Fish and Wildlife Area, where the dunes rise as high as 50 feet.

In the area north of Medaryville, U.S. 421 traverses a subtle drainage divide between the basin of the Kankakee River and that of the Tippecanoe River, a tributary of the Wabash River. This area also contains the easternmost drainage divide of the Iroquois River.

The areas around Medaryville and Francesville are actually within an edge of the Tipton till plain. Shallow lake sediments and till grade imperceptibly into the blanket sands of the surrounding dune plain.

Six miles of blanket sands and small dunes cover part of southern Pulaski County and northern White County, obscuring a small area of Silurian and Devonian limestone and dolomite that exists around Francesville and Monon. This was part of the highest local preglacial bedrock topography.

### Tipton Till Plain

U.S. 421 crosses about 82 miles of the Tipton till plain between the area 1.5 miles south of Monon and I-465. The glacial cover ranges from zero to more than 350 feet in two buried valleys, one parallel to the Tippecanoe River south of Monticello, the other in a broad lowland in Clinton and Boone Counties.

The glacial cover north of Delphi includes lake sediments and blanket sands. Sands, silts, and clays deposited in a large, shallow lake cover the glacial till in a 17-mile-wide area in central White County. This large lake existed along the edge of the melting Huron-Erie ice lobe.

U.S. 421 crosses 8 miles of glacial outwash between the area 1 mile south of Yeoman and that 1.5 miles southeast of Delphi, in the valley of the Wabash River. Where U.S. 421 crosses the Wabash River, watch for bedrock outcrops north of the bridge. U.S. 421 passes over these same rock formations farther north. A nearby quarry works a large Silurian reef structure for crushed aggregate.

Fifty-five miles of virtually uninterrupted Trafalgar till deposited as flat ground moraine underlie the highway between Delphi and I-465. East of Lebanon, the highway crosses another subtle drainage divide between waters that flow west and south to the Wabash River and those that flow south and west to the West Fork White River.

*Generalized surface and bedrock profiles along U.S. 421.*

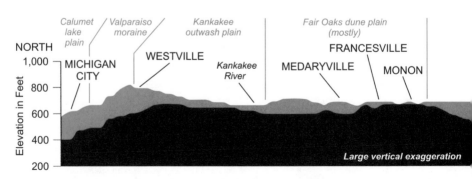

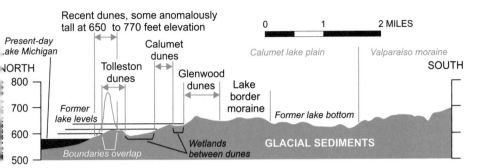

*Generalized surface profile across dunes and moraines in the area of the Indiana Dunes State Park, just west of Michigan City.*

## Indiana Dunes State Park and Indiana Dunes National Lakeshore

These two areas include more than 6,000 acres of nearly untouched land, with some dunes more than 120 feet high. The beach and dune sands of the Calumet lake plain record more than one hundred former shorelines along the southern margin of Lake Michigan as it dropped some 80 feet to its present level of about 580 feet.

The beach and dune sequences in the park and lakeshore record the three major lake levels before the present one. The uppermost is the Glenwood level, which developed when Glacial Lake Chicago, the precursor of Lake Michigan, stood at about 640 feet. The Calumet level developed at elevation 620 feet. The Tolleston level, the youngest, developed when the lake stood at 605 feet. The Tolleston level lasted from about 8,000 to about 2,000 years ago, when the lake began to drain east through the other Great Lakes instead of south through Illinois.

The dunes display a succession of plant covers related to the time available for their development. The foredunes, the youngest and closest to the modern lakeshore, support pioneer species—cottonwood trees and dune

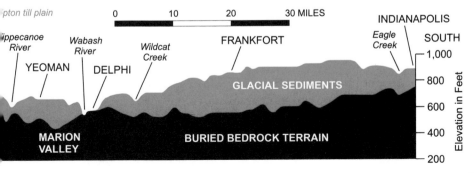

*Dunes along Lake Michigan in Indiana Dunes State Park.*

grasses. The second line of dunes supports pine and juniper trees. The oak dunes are next, featuring oak, basswood, and elm trees. The dunes farthest inland support a cover of beech and maple trees. Bog vegetation grows in the wetlands between dunes.

### Tippecanoe River State Park

East of U.S. 421 and south of Bass Lake, U.S. 35 passes a subtle sand barrier that diverted the Tippecanoe River south toward the Wabash River. Tippecanoe River State Park between Bass Lake and Winamac is a good place to see these sand dunes. The first mile of the entrance road winds through dunes 20 to 45 feet high, long stabilized by trees. These are but a few of the thousands of dunes that strong winds blew eastward across the blanket sands.

In its floodplain the Tippecanoe River meanders its way south to the Wabash River. Watch for abandoned stream channels and meanders. If the blanket sands and dunes had not accumulated as they did, the Tippecanoe River might still flow west to the Kankakee River.

## Francesville Gas Field

In 1867 a well struck natural gas at about 600 feet in Silurian limestone 1 or 2 miles southwest of Francesville. The owner used the fuel in the operation of his farm, and for many years a large lamp burned bright on the Indiana prairie. The gas ran out in the 1880s.

## Delphi Reefs and Lime

Lime was produced from Silurian rocks near Delphi, an early business center on the Wabash and Erie Canal, as early as the 1830s. By the 1890s, lime from this area had a reputation for its high quality. Delphi was a leading lime producer until the 1920s. Crushed stone production continued after that.

Three quarries on the east bank of the Wabash River at Delphi expose more than 160 feet of the Wabash formation. The south quarry is in the central part of the reef complex, estimated to be at least 400 feet thick. The North Vernon limestone of Devonian age laps onto the reef at the north quarry.

Tilted layers of Devonian shale overlap the Silurian rocks, which continue to considerable depth. Early geologists tried to visualize upheavals that somehow brought knobs of Silurian rock to within a few feet of the Earth's surface. Later studies showed that the knobs were old reefs that resisted compaction and that the Devonian rocks were draped over them. It is easy to see how these unusual structures puzzled the old-timers.

*The Silurian Wabash formation forms the highwalls of this quarry at Delphi.*

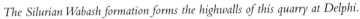

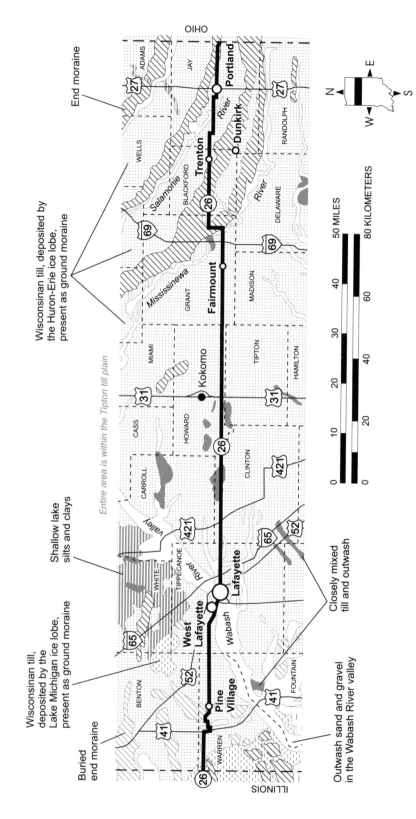

ADAMS

JAY

Portland

End moraine

27          27

WELLS          Dunkirk

Trenton          River

26          RANDOLPH

Salamonie          DELAWARE

Wisconsinan till, deposited by          BLACKFORD          River
the Huron-Erie ice lobe,
present as ground moraine          69

Mississinewa          69

Fairmount

GRANT          MADISON

*Entire area is within the Tipton till plain*

MIAMI          Kokomo          TIPTON

31          31          HAMILTON

Shallow lake          CASS          HOWARD
silts and clays

26

Wisconsinan till,          CARROLL          CLINTON          421
deposited by the
Lake Michigan ice lobe,          421          65          52
present as ground moraine
WHITE          Valley          65          52

TIPPECANOE          River          Lafayette          Closely mixed
till and outwash

65          West          Wabash
Lafayette
Buried          52
end moraine
BENTON          Pine          41
41          Village          FOUNTAIN

WARREN          Outwash sand and gravel
26          in the Wabash River valley

N  E
W  S

0   10   20   30   40   50 MILES

0   20   40   60   80 KILOMETERS

*Geology along Indiana 26 between the Ohio line and the Illinois line. Legend on page 208 further describes map patterns.*

# Indiana 26
## Ohio Line—Illinois Line
### 153 MILES

Indiana 26 cuts a straight line across Indiana, near the center of the Tipton till plain, and is on ground moraine most of the way. It also crosses three end moraines, four minor stream valleys, and one major stream valley. The entire route is within the basin of the greater Wabash River system. Almost all the glacial deposits and landforms were left by the Huron-Erie ice lobe; the Lake Michigan ice lobe left some deposits on the far western side of the state.

Between the Ohio state line and the area 4.5 miles west, Indiana 26 parallels the edge of one of the four nested end moraines that curve across northeastern Indiana. This end moraine is not as hilly and irregular as most. Its thickness is less than 50 feet.

Between the area 4.5 miles east of Portland and that 1 mile west of Trenton, Indiana 26 covers 23 miles of flat ground moraine. The thickness of the glacial sediments is less than 50 feet near Portland; it is more than 150 feet near Trenton. The highway passes over a buried bedrock valley more than 300 feet deep near the line between Blackford and Jay Counties.

Between the area 1 mile west of Trenton and the Mississinewa River, Indiana 26 crosses 6 miles of one end moraine, 4 miles of ground moraine, and 4 miles of another end moraine. The two end moraines join farther east and north. The landscape provides little clue to the changes between types of moraines.

Indiana 26 follows a straight line across 73 miles of ground moraine between the Mississinewa River and Lafayette. A few miles east of Lafayette, Indiana 26 crosses two forks of Wildcat Creek. Their valleys, now full of outwash, once carried meltwaters that flowed west.

The glacial cover thins from 150 feet at the Mississinewa River to less than 50 feet in central and western Grant County. It thickens to more than 250 feet at Lafayette. Between downtown Lafayette and the area a half-mile west of Purdue University, Indiana 26 crosses 2 miles of outwash terraces in the valley of the Wabash River, some 150 feet below the ground moraine highlands. The valley sediments are 100 to 150 feet thick.

Thirty-five miles of flat ground moraine lie between the area a half-mile west of Purdue University and that 1 mile east of the Illinois line. The highway parallels the south edge of a buried bedrock valley filled with more than 330 feet of glacial deposits.

West of the Wabash River valley, Indiana 26 crosses three small areas of a locally hilly landscape. These areas include the valleys of Indian Creek, 7 miles west of West Lafayette, and Little Pine Creek at Pine Village. Hills east

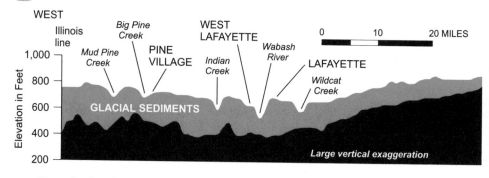

*Generalized surface and bedrock profiles along Indiana 26.*

and west of the intersection with U.S. 41 are mostly buried end moraine, till from the Lake Michigan ice lobe thinly covered by younger till from the Huron–Erie ice lobe.

In its last mile in western Indiana, Indiana 26 crosses ground moraine deposited by the Lake Michigan ice lobe. The later Huron–Erie ice lobe left its own ground moraine deposits atop the Lake Michigan material.

*Outwash terraces in the Lafayette-West Lafayette area.* —Modified from Richardson and West, 1977

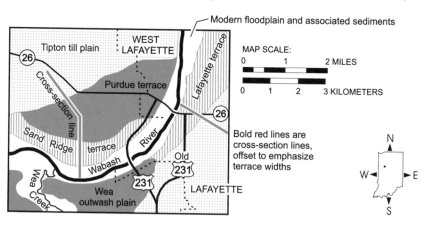

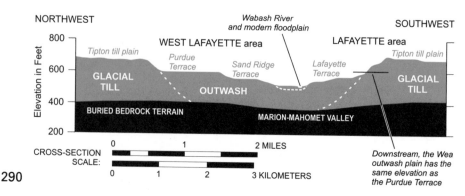

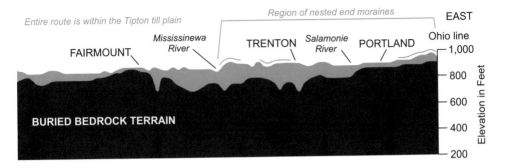

## Indiana Glass Company at Dunkirk

Dunkirk sank its first natural gas well in 1887. Nine years later, the Beaty-Brady Glass Company opened, using the readily available fuel for its ovens. In 1908 the company was renamed the Indiana Glass Company. When the gas supply dwindled, most of the local glass companies went out of business. The Indiana Glass Company, however, survived.

## Outwash Terraces at Lafayette and West Lafayette

The earliest visitors camped in the river bottomlands, but later settlers preferred the slightly higher riverside outwash terraces, where Lafayette was first surveyed in 1825. The villages that preceded West Lafayette were laid out in 1845. Since that time, the two cities have outgrown the original terraces and expanded onto the ground moraine uplands.

Downtown Lafayette is on the Lafayette terrace, 50 to 100 feet above the Wabash River floodplain. Note the steep climbs to ground moraine highlands east and south of the downtown area. Purdue University and the southern part of West Lafayette were built across the Purdue terrace, about 100 to 125 feet above the river. The Sand Ridge terrace, south of the Purdue terrace, corresponds to the elevation of the Lafayette terrace.

# GLOSSARY

**aggregate.** Sand, gravel, and crushed stone added as filler material in mortar or concrete, or used alone as a construction medium.

**anhydrite.** A mineral form of calcium sulfate, but without the water that gypsum contains. Typically forms by evaporation of water.

**aragonite.** A mineral form of calcium carbonate, common in some caves.

**arch.** An upward bend or fold of rock layers, also called an anticline.

**artesian.** Refers to a spring or well that produces water because the aquifer that feeds it is at a higher elevation.

**arthropod.** Animal with jointed legs, an external skeleton, and a segmented body. Insects, spiders, crabs, and lobsters are common members of this diverse group.

**barite.** A mineral form of barium sulfate, found in some sedimentary rocks as fracture or pore fillings.

**basin, sedimentary.** A more-or-less circular concavity in sedimentary strata.

**bed.** A layer of sedimentary rock.

**bedrock.** Solid rock in place, not transported.

**bituminous coal.** A sedimentary rock formed from compression and gentle heating of peat. The most common kind of coal.

**blastoid.** A stalked echinoderm of Paleozoic time that possessed a body enclosed within an armor of thirteen plates. Related to crinoids, starfish, and sea urchins.

**blowout.** A depression in a sandy area caused by the mass removal of sand by wind.

**bog iron ore.** A spongy hydrated iron oxide found below some swamps and bogs.

**brachiopod.** An animal that looks superficially like a clam, but is not one. Brachiopod shells are symmetrical about a surface that bisects the shells. Common during Paleozoic time, less so since.

**bryozoan.** A tiny colonial animal that builds a variety of calcareous structures. Common during Paleozoic time, less so since.

**calcite.** The mineral form of calcium carbonate, common in limestone and the main cementing material in many other kinds of sedimentary rocks.

**cannel coal.** A waxy coal composed mostly of fossil plant spores and pollen.

**cephalopod.** A group of animals that includes nautiloids, squids, and the extinct ammonoids. Tentacles surround their heads.

**channeler.** A quarry machine used to score building stone so that it can be removed in large blocks.

**chert.** A microscopically fine form of quartz. Typically occurs as nodules or thin layers in sedimentary rocks. The main raw material for Indian arrowheads.

**clay.** A sedimentary material composed of different types of weathered silicate minerals with grain sizes less than $\frac{1}{256}$ millimeter in diameter.

**concretion.** A mass of mineral matter formed around a nucleus. Concretions differ in composition from the rocks that enclose them.

**conglomerate.** A sedimentary rock composed of rounded pebbles or cobbles cemented together in a mass.

**conodont.** Barely visible fossils that look like minuscule jaws. Common in Paleozoic sedimentary rocks.

**crinoid.** A stalked echinoderm with many arms and a body enclosed in solid plates of calcite. Common in Paleozoic time, less so since.

**crossbedding.** Layers of sediment within larger layers, typically in more or less intricate patterns showing deposition by running water.

**cyclothem.** A repetitive series of sedimentary layers including sandstone, siltstone, shale, and limestone associated with coal seams of late Paleozoic time. Caused by changes in the depositional environment.

**cystoid.** A stalked echinoderm common in early Paleozoic time but since extinct. Body enclosed within an armor of calcite plates.

**delta.** An accumulation of sediment deposited where a river enters an ocean or lake.

**dimension stone.** A rock free enough of cracks and zones of weakness that it can be cut into blocks or slabs for use in building and bridge construction.

**dolomite.** The mineral form of calcium and magnesium carbonate. A common constituent of some sedimentary rocks. The name also refers to sedimentary rocks made of dolomite.

**dome.** A more-or-less circular upfold in sedimentary strata.

**dragline.** A huge power shovel used in strip mines.

**echinoderm.** A group of animals that typically have five part symmetry and a stony or spiny outer skeleton. Starfish and sea urchins are common echinoderms, as were crinoids, blastoids, and cystoids.

**end moraine.** A ridge of till that builds up along the edge of an ice sheet when the glacier is not advancing or receding.

**entrenched meander.** A deeply cut, curving channel of a stream with steep banks. Former floodplain is elevated above the stream level as a terrace.

**esker.** A winding ridge of sand and gravel once deposited in a meltwater tunnel or channel carved into an ice sheet.

**eurypterid.** Extinct aquatic arthropods that looked much like a modern scorpion. Found only in Paleozoic rocks.

**facies.** Different types of rocks deposited in different, yet connected, areas at the same time.

**fault.** A fracture in rocks along which one side slides past the other.

**flagstone.** A sedimentary rock that readily splits into slabs or plates.

**floodplain.** The part of a valley floor that is underwater during floods.

**flowstone.** A smooth deposit of calcium carbonate precipitated from groundwater trickling down the walls of caves.

**fluorite.** The mineral form of calcium fluoride. It generally forms cubic crystals in a variety of transparent colors, most commonly purple or yellow.

**flux.** Material used to lower the melting temperature of ore.

**foraminifera.** A group of single-cell animals with tiny shells common in oceans.

**formation.** A body of rock distinctive enough to be recognizable from one place to another. A formation may vary in age or appearance.

**galena.** The mineral form of lead sulfide. Typically occurs as dense gray cubes. Weathered surfaces are dull gray, but fresh surfaces display a silvery metallic sheen.

**geode.** A hollow nodule lined with crystals, most commonly of quartz. Geodes may weather out of their host rock and accumulate in streambeds.

**glacial erratic.** A glacially transported rock that generally differs in type from local bedrock. Erratics are often rounded and found in till.

**glacier.** A mass of slowly moving ice.

**ground moraine.** Till plastered on the landscape by melting glaciers. Areas of ground moraine vary from flat to gently rolling terrain.

**group.** Two or more formations that form a mappable unit.

**gypsum.** The mineral form of hydrous calcium sulfate. Used in manufacture of plaster and wallboard.

**gulf.** An elongate depression formed by collapse or sinking in an area of soluble limestone, often exposing an underground stream.

**helictite.** A branching wall and ceiling growth of aragonite present in some caverns.

**ice lobe.** A tongue of glacial ice along the advancing or receding edge of an ice sheet, typically controlled by the underlying topography.

**kame.** A hill of outwash originally deposited on or at the edge of a glacier, then let down onto the landscape as the ice melted.

**karst.** A hilly landscape of caves and sinkholes that develops on some dissolving limestone formations.

**kettle.** A depression left where a block of ice, left behind in glacial sediments, finally melted.

**lime.** Calcium oxide, often made from limestone.

**limestone.** A sedimentary rock composed mainly of calcite. Typically forms in shallow warm seas or lakes.

**lithographic limestone.** A very fine-grained limestone.

**loess.** A deposit of windblown silt.

**mammoth.** An extinct species of elephant that favored grasslands and lived in North America until about 10,000 years ago.

**marcasite.** A mineral form of iron sulfide.

**marl.** A calcareous mud precipitated in lakes and streams.

**mastodon.** An extinct species of elephant that favored forests and lived in North America until about 10,000 years ago.

**meltwater.** Water derived from the melting of an ice sheet. Meltwater erodes valleys and distributes outwash.

**member.** A subdivision of a formation based on distinctive rock characteristics.

**mineral wool.** Mineral product composed of intertwining fine filaments made from exposing certain melted rocks or slag to a blast of air. Used as insulation.

**mudstone.** Sedimentary rock of clay-size (less than $\frac{1}{256}$ millimeter in diameter) particles with no evident layering.

**nodule.** A rounded mass of mineral matter differing in composition and resistance from the enclosing rock. Essentially the same as a concretion.

**oolite.** A small spherical to ellipsoidal mass of calcite found in some sedimentary rocks, most commonly limestone or dolomite.

**ostracod.** A minute arthropod related to shrimps with a shell that looks like a miniature clam shell. Ostracods are common in many sedimentary rocks, where they typically look like sesame seeds.

**outcrop.** A surface exposure of bedrock.

**outwash.** Sand and gravel washed from glacial deposits by meltwater.

**overburden.** Geologic material that overlies a rock of economic value.

**oxbow lake.** An abandoned stream meander filled with water.

**paver.** A hardened thick brick used for street paving.

**pig iron.** Crude iron directly from a blast furnace.

**pothole.** A circular depression or hole eroded in rock from swirling sediments in a stream.

**proglacial.** A term applied to any temporary landscape feature, such as a lake, associated with the edge of an ice sheet.

**pyrite.** The mineral form of iron sulfide. Typically crystallizes into cubes with a metallic appearance and the color of pale brass. Many people call it fool's gold.

**quartz.** The mineral form of silica, silicon dioxide. Quartz is probably the most common of all minerals, the main constituent of sand and silt. It is very hard.

**rise.** A spring where groundwater rises from fractures in limestone.

**sand.** Weathered mineral grains, most commonly quartz, greater than $\frac{1}{16}$ millimeter in diameter.

**sedimentary rocks.** Sediments of whatever kind hardened into solid rocks. Typically occur in layers.

**shale.** A common sedimentary rock composed mainly of clay.

**shattercone.** A rock showing fractures that appear like stacked cones resulting from high-pressure impact.

**siderite.** The mineral form of iron carbonate. Sometimes found in concretions.

**silt.** Weathered mineral grains larger than clay but smaller than sand (between $\frac{1}{256}$ and $\frac{1}{16}$ millimeter in diameter).

**siltstone.** A sedimentary rock composed of particles of silt.

**sinkhole.** A surface hole formed through collapse of a cave.

**sphalerite.** The mineral form of zinc sulfide.

**strata.** Layers or beds of sedimentary rock.

**strip mine.** A mine worked from an open pit, named so because overburden is stripped to expose the material of value.

**swallow hole.** A sinkhole where a stream goes underground.

**terminal moraine.** A ridge of till marking the farthest advance of an ice sheet. A type of end moraine.

**terrace.** A flat shelf or plain above the floodplain of a stream. Terraces are remnants of old floodplains formed when the channel was at a higher elevation.

**terra rossa soil.** A reddish soil common in cave and sinkhole landscapes.

**tile.** Drain pipe, in a variety of sizes and designs, made from locally available clay. Placed into excavated channels in farm fields to drain water.

**till.** A chaotic deposit of all sizes of sediments dumped from glacial ice.

**trilobite.** A common arthropod of Paleozoic seas, now extinct. Trilobites had hard-shelled skeletons divided into three lobes across the body.

**unconformity.** An old erosion surface buried under younger sedimentary rocks.

**underclay.** A layer of clay beneath a Pennsylvanian coal seam. Almost every such seam has its underclay.

**underfit stream.** A stream that appears too small for the size of its valley. The stream has experienced a great decrease in flow over geologic time.

**valley train.** Outwash filling a valley beyond the reach of the glacial ice sheet. Deposited by meltwater torrents.

**whetstone.** A sandstone or siltstone used for sharpening tools.

# ADDITIONAL READING

We urge the interested reader to consult the many publications of the Indiana Geological Survey and its predecessors. More recent publications are available by mail or in person at the publication sales office on the Indiana University campus in Bloomington. Many Indiana libraries, and especially those on university and college campuses, have new as well as out-of-print studies. The geological survey offers two annotated bibliographies of Indiana geology. Pamphlets on the geology of many Indiana state parks are available through the survey.

The *Proceedings of the Indiana Academy of Science,* available at many libraries, contain many excellent articles on the geology of Indiana. Also look in issues of *Outdoor Indiana* and *Traces.* County historical books often contain references to scenic geologic sites and mineral resources. Below are a few selected publications of interest.

Davis, R. A. 1992. *Cincinnati Fossils.* Cincinnati: Cincinnati Museum of Natural History.

Fatout, P. 1972. *Indiana Canals.* West Lafayette, Ind.: Purdue University Press.

Flint, R. F. 1971. *Glacial and Quaternary Geology.* New York: John Wiley and Sons.

Graham, R. W., J. Holman, and P. Parmalee. 1983. *Taphonomy and Paleoecology of the Crhistensen Bog Mastodon Bone Bed, Hancock County, Indiana,* Illinois State Museum, Reports of Investigations No. 38.

Gray, H. H. 1982. *Map of Indiana Showing Topography of the Bedrock Surface.* Miscellaneous Map 36, Indiana Geological Survey, Department of Natural Resources.

Gray, H. H. 1983. *Map of Indiana Showing Thickness of Unconsolidated Deposits.* Miscellaneous Map 37, Indiana Geological Survey, Department of Natural Resources.

Gray, H. H. 1989. *Quaternary Geologic Map of Indiana.* Miscellaneous Map 49, Indiana Geological Survey, Department of Natural Resources.

Gutshick, R. C. 1983. Geology of the Kentland Dome structurally complex anomaly, northwestern Indiana. In *Field Trips in Midwestern Geology*, vol 1, edited by R. H. Shaver and J. A. Sunderman, p. 105–38. Bloomington, Ind.: Geological Society of America, Indiana Geological Survey, and Indiana University of Geology.

Hall, R. D. 1989. *Geology of Indiana*. Dubuque, Iowa: Kendall/Hunt Publishing Company.

Hasenmueller, N. R., and J. R. Tankersley. 1987. *Annotated Bibliography of Indiana Geology 1956 through 1975*. Bulletin 60, Indiana Department of Natural Resources, Geological Survey.

*The Indiana Atlas and Gazetteer.* 1998. Freeport, Maine: Delorme Mapping.

Indiana Geological Survey. 1970. *Map of Indiana Showing Bedrock Geology.* Miscellaneous Map 16. Department of Natural Resources.

Jackson, M., ed. 1997. *The Natural Heritage of Indiana*. Bloomington: Indiana University Press.

Lindsey, A. A., ed. 1966. *Natural Features of Indiana*. Indiana Sesquicentennial Volume. Indianapolis: Indiana Academy of Science.

Logan, W. N., E. R. Cummings, C. A. Malott, S. S. Visher, W. M. Tucker, and J. R. Reeves. 1922. *Handbook of Indiana Geology*. Publication No. 21, Indiana Department of Conservation.

Malott, C. A. 1922. The physiography of Indiana. In *Handbook of Indiana Geology*, p. 59–256. Publication No. 21, Indiana Department of Conservation.

Malott, C. A. 1932. Lost River at Wesley Chapel Gulf, Orange County, Indiana. *Indiana Academy Science Proceedings for 1931*, vol. 41, p. 285–316. Indianapolis: Indiana Academy of Science.

McPherson, A. 1991. *Nature Walks in Southern Indiana*. Indianapolis: Hoosier Chapter/Sierra Club.

Melhorn, W. and J. Kempton, eds. 1991. *Geology and Hydrogeology of the Teays-Mahomet Bedrock Valley System*. Geological Society of America Special Paper 258. Boulder, Colo.: Geological Society of America.

Nevers, G. M., and R. D. Walker. 1962. *Annotated Bibliography of Indiana Geology through 1955*. Bulletin 24, Indiana Department of Conservation, Geological Survey.

Powell, R. L. 1961. *Caves of Indiana*. Circular 8, Indiana Geological Survey.

Richardson, G. and T. West. 1977. Post-glacial deltas in the region of the Great Bend of the Wabash River. In *Proceedings of the Indiana Academy of Science for 1976*, p. 317–25. Indianapolis: Indiana Academy of Science.

Shaver, R. H., et al. 1986. *Compendium of Paleozoic Rock-Unit Stratigraphy in Indiana—A Revision.* Bulletin 59, Indiana Geological Survey, Department of Natural Resources.

Taylor, R. M., Jr., E. W. Stevens, M. A. Ponder, and P. Brockman. 1992. *Indiana: A New Historical Guide.* Indianapolis: Indiana Historical Society.

Wayne, W. J., 1956. *Thickness of Drift and Bedrock Physiography of Indiana North of the Wisconsin Glacial Boundary.* Report of Progress 7, Indiana Geological Survey, Department of Conservation.

# INDEX

Mecca, 160, 180, 189–92
Medaryville, 282–84
Medora, 107–10
Memphis, 32, 34, 38
Merom, 155, 182, 193
Merrillville, 229–30, 232
Metamora, 56–57, 59–60
meteorite, 96, 216
Miami County, 225, 251, 268
Michigan, Lake, 221, 285–86
Michigan Basin, 5–7, 209
Michigan City, 4, 9, 208, 225–26, 243, 246, 282–84
Middlefork Creek, 66
Middletown, 235, 240
Milan, 50, 52
Mill Creek, 130, 201–3
Milltown, 37, 76, 92, 104–5
mineral springs, 32, 34–35, 37, 49, 51–52, 96, 105–6, 112, 114, 116–18, 125, 134, 137, 141, 172, 186, 207
Minnehaha State Fish and Wildlife Area, 193
Minshall, 189–90
Mishawaka, 268–69
Mississinewa River, 13, 211, 219, 235–37, 255–56, 259–62, 288–89, 291
Mississinewa shale, 21, 33, 36, 240, 242, 256
Mississippian time, 1, 73–74, 76, 91, 110, 116, 122, 141
Mitchell, 80, 83, 109, 121, 123, 126, 130
Mitchell plain, 81, 83–84, 88–89, 91–92, 95, 100, 104, 107–8, 115, 117, 122–23, 132, 140–41, 169–70, 173, 198–200
mollusks, 18, 21, 46, 178, 211
Monon, 282–84
Monroe City, 195, 197
Monroe County, 79–81, 86, 112, 121–23, 125–27, 140–41, 158
Monroe Reservoir, 80, 123, 126
Monte Cassino, 165–66
Montezuma, 160, 190–91
Montgomery County, 158, 176–77, 179, 198, 225
Monticello, 251–52, 258, 278, 282, 284
Montpelier, 238, 240, 260, 265
Moore, 235, 238
Moore's Hill, 50, 54

Morgan County, 79, 81, 88–89, 121–22, 126, 170, 201
Morocco, 273–75, 277
Mounds State Recreational Area, 60
Mt. Carmel fault, 6, 79–80, 125–26
Mud Pine Creek, 275, 290
Mumford Hills, 155–56
Muncie, 222, 226, 235, 241
Munster, 246, 248
Muscatatuck regional slope, 27–28, 30, 44, 46–47, 50–53, 56, 58–59, 63–65, 67, 69
Muscatatuck River, 28, 31, 52, 54–55, 64, 67, 109

Napoleon, 50, 54, 63–64
Nappanee, 246–47, 249
Nashville, 80, 126, 141
natural bridge, 148, 190
nautiloid, 18, 211, 232
Nead, 268–69, 271
New Albany, 4, 9, 14, 16, 27, 30, 34, 37, 72, 81, 88, 91–93, 95–96, 101, 115
New Albany shale, 2, 4, 22–23, 32–33, 37, 54–55, 71, 73–74, 213, 215–16
New Amsterdam, 14, 92, 104
New Goshen, 170, 175
New Harmony, 60, 145, 162–63, 167–68
New Harmony fault, 166
New Madrid faults, 167
New Providence shale, 2, 75, 94, 109
New Salem, 56, 59
New Salisbury, 96
Newberry, 198, 205
Newburgh, 155–56, 165
Newton County, 215, 225, 230, 251, 273–74, 278, 280
Noble County, 225, 246
Noblesville, 268, 272
nodules, 22, 35, 154, 188
Norman Station, 80, 126
Norman upland, 30, 32, 50, 74–75, 88, 91–92, 95–96, 104, 107, 109, 115, 117, 120, 122, 140–41, 143, 169
North Vernon, 37, 50, 52, 54, 57, 222
North Vernon limestone, 2, 4, 22, 25, 33, 35–36, 54, 57, 71, 213, 287
Nyesville, 189–90

Odon, 198, 205
Ohio County, 67
Ohio River, 12–16, 29
oil, 160, 164, 166–67, 183, 193–94, 204, 213, 220–24
Oolitic, 80, 86–87, 121, 123–24, 126, 128–29
Orange County, 80–81, 83, 89, 115, 119, 121, 125, 158
Orangeville, 119, 131–33, 134
Orangeville Rise, 132–34
Ordovician time, 2, 17, 45, 51, 52–53, 59, 64, 70
Orleans, 80, 121, 123, 126, 131–33
Osgood, 50, 54, 63
Osgood member, 20, 65, 209
ostracods, 19, 271–72
Otterbein, 278, 280–81
Owen County, 77, 81, 112, 140, 158, 198
Owen, David Dale, 84, 145, 167–68
Owensville, 166–67
Owensville fault, 166
Oxford, 278, 281

Palmyra, 115–17
Paoli, 81, 115–16, 119, 121–24, 134–35
Paoli limestone, 2, 76, 83, 91, 97, 104, 119, 131–32, 171
Parke County, 155–56, 158, 162, 182, 185, 188–91
Parkersburg, 198–99
Patoka, 167, 194
Patoka formation, 2, 154
Patoka River, 13, 115, 156, 163, 182–83, 185, 195, 201, 205–6
Patriot, 66–68
Paxton, 182–83
peat, 62, 224–25, 227, 266, 270, 276
Pedestal Rock, 186
Peerless, 121, 128
Pendleton, 235, 240, 241
Pennsylvanian time, 1, 2, 91, 116, 119, 151
Peoria, 251, 255–56
Perry County, 78, 81, 90, 92, 112, 121, 156, 158, 163
Peru, 251–53, 255–57, 268, 271
Petersburg formation, 2, 154, 165, 204
petroleum. See oil

Pigeon River, 13, 242–43
Pigeon River State Fish and Wildlife Area, 243, 245
Pike County, 158, 160, 163, 165–66
Pilot Knob, 92
Pine Hills Nature Preserve, 186
Pine Village, 288, 290
placoderm, 21, 71
Pleasant Mills, 260, 265
Pleasant Mills formation, 2, 210, 238, 241, 253, 263, 265
Pleasantville, 192–93
Pleistocene time. See ice age; glaciation
Plummer, 160, 198, 204–5
Pluto Water, 117–18
Plymouth, 267–70
Poe, 260, 265
Pokagon State Park, 235–37
Pompey's Pillar, 64
Porter County, 225, 243, 246
Portersville, 200, 205
Portland, 259–60, 262, 265, 288–89, 291
Portland Arch State Nature Preserve, 151, 184–86
Posey County, 154–55, 163
Potato Creek State Park, 268–70
potholes, 120, 188, 200, 203
pottery, 25, 68, 114, 191, 159, 175
Precambrian rocks, 1, 2, 7, 39
Princeton, 167, 182–83, 185, 193
Prospect, 115–16
Pulaski County, 225, 282, 284
Purdue terrace, 290–91
Putnam County, 76, 81, 158, 169–72, 197–98
Putnamville, 170–71

Raccoon Creek, 13, 147, 156, 181–82, 184–85, 190
Raccoon Creek group, 2, 4, 78, 124, 151, 179, 191, 199, 201–2
Ragsdale, 192–93
Ramp Creek formation, 2, 75, 95
Randolph County, 260–61, 266
Raven Rock, 200
reclamation, coal, 158–59
reefs, Silurian, 125, 205, 210–12, 232, 238, 248, 254–55, 263, 265, 284, 287

snails, 18, 21, 24, 48, 52, 62, 73, 117, 142, 201, 211, 271
South Bend, 4, 9, 208, 225–26, 243, 245, 267–70
South Wabash Reef, 238
Speed, 31–32, 34, 36, 105
Spencer, 140–42, 146, 198–200
Spencer County, 90, 153, 158, 163, 197–98, 205
Spergen Hill, 115–16
Spiceland, 40, 42
Spiceland kame complex, 40, 42–43
Spickert Knob formation, 2, 75, 79, 95, 142–43
sponges, 18, 60
Spring Mill State Park, 83, 121, 130–31
Squire Boone Caverns, 98
stalactites, 84, 98, 103
stalagmites, 84, 98, 102–3
Stanford, 121, 127
starfish, 21
Starke County, 225
Staunton formation, 2, 154, 189, 204–5
Stephensport group, 2, 4, 77, 137
Steuben County, 225, 234–35, 237, 243
Steuben morainal lake area, 226–28, 234–36, 242–49, 251, 263, 267–68, 270–71, 278
Stilesville, 170, 172–73
Stinesville, 84–85, 121, 140, 146
Stobo crinoid mound, 140, 144
stone, building, 25, 84, 128, 150, 204, 232, 238, 241, 253, 265, 281
Stoney Lonesome, 140, 142–43
stream piracy, 238
strip mines, 157–58, 165, 173, 176, 192–93, 205
stromatoporoids, 18, 20, 39
Sugar Creek, 13, 32, 42, 46, 58, 64, 156, 177–79, 182, 184, 186–89, 198–200, 281
Sullivan, 182–84, 192–93
Sullivan County, 154–55, 158, 160, 182, 192–93, 204
Sulphur, 92, 94, 105, 136
Sulphur Springs, 92, 105
Sunbury shale, 2, 4, 213

swallow hole, 83, 132–33. *See also* sinkhole
Sweetser, 238, 240–41
Switzerland County, 67

Tar Springs formation, 2, 78, 111, 124
Taswell, 121, 137
Teays River, 218, 220–21
Tell City, 15, 72, 81, 88, 120–21, 123–24, 137–38, 152, 161, 163
Templeton, 278–81
terra rossa, 34, 37, 83–84, 97, 123
terraces, 57, 156, 183, 203, 252, 289–91
Terre Haute, 4, 9, 152, 158, 160–61, 169–72, 175, 182–85, 192, 226, 281
Terre Haute Bank, 210, 212
Tertiary time, 81
tile, drainage, 25, 35, 57, 62, 64, 68, 109, 160, 191, 238, 241, 265, 281
Tioga bentonite bed, 213
Tippecanoe County, 197–98, 230, 278, 288
Tippecanoe River, 13, 219, 251–53, 258, 267–68, 270, 283–86
Tippecanoe River State Park, 286
Tipton County, 268–69
Tipton till plain, 27, 88, 161, 226–27, 231, 236, 259, 267–69, 274, 278–79, 282, 284, 288–90
Tobinsport formation, 2, 78
Trafalgar till, 9, 58, 155, 176, 181, 197, 217, 231, 261, 269, 274, 279–80, 284
Traverse formation, 2, 4, 213, 253, 263
Trenton, 57, 288–89, 291
Trenton gas and oil field, 160, 175, 220, 222–23, 240, 257
Trenton limestone, 2, 126, 220
trilobites, 17–18, 21, 48–49, 60, 211
Troy, 138, 155, 59
Tunnelton, 107–8
Turkey Run State Park, 182, 187, 189
Twin Bridge, 148–49

Union County, 60, 260, 266
Unionville, 80, 126
Unionville dome and gas field, 125–26
Utica, 34, 37

# ABOUT THE AUTHORS

**Mark J. Camp** began his teaching career at Earlham College in Richmond, Indiana, before joining the faculty at the University of Toledo where he teaches introductory geology, historical geology, and paleontology. His recent studies of the use of building stones in historical buildings, quarry and mine development, and the architecture of railroad depots reflect his long-standing interest in turn-of-the-century history. He holds a Ph.D. in geology from Ohio State University.

**Graham T. Richardson** became interested in geology during undergraduate studies at Purdue University where, as a biology major, he was introduced to glacial geology. Following a tour of duty in the U.S. Navy, he returned to Purdue and earned a M.S. in geology and remote sensing with an emphasis on geomorphology.

We encourage you to patronize your local bookstore. Most stores will be happy to order any title that they do not stock. You may also order directly from Mountain Press by mail, using the order form provided below, or by calling our toll-free number and using your Visa or MasterCard. We will gladly send you a catalog upon request.

## Some geology titles of interest:

| | |
|---|---|
| _____ROADSIDE GEOLOGY OF ALASKA | 16.00 |
| _____ROADSIDE GEOLOGY OF ARIZONA | 18.00 |
| _____ROADSIDE GEOLOGY OF COLORADO | 16.00 |
| _____ROADSIDE GEOLOGY OF HAWAII | 20.00 |
| _____ROADSIDE GEOLOGY OF IDAHO | 18.00 |
| _____ROADSIDE GEOLOGY OF INDIANA | 18.00 |
| _____ROADSIDE GEOLOGY OF LOUISIANA | 15.00 |
| _____ROADSIDE GEOLOGY OF MAINE | 18.00 |
| _____ROADSIDE GEOLOGY OF MONTANA | 20.00 |
| _____ROADSIDE GEOLOGY OF NEW MEXICO | 16.00 |
| _____ROADSIDE GEOLOGY OF NEW YORK | 20.00 |
| _____ROADSIDE GEOLOGY OF NORTHERN CALIFORNIA | 15.00 |
| _____ROADSIDE GEOLOGY OF OREGON | 15.00 |
| _____ROADSIDE GEOLOGY OF SOUTH DAKOTA | 20.00 |
| _____ROADSIDE GEOLOGY OF TEXAS | 20.00 |
| _____ROADSIDE GEOLOGY OF UTAH | 16.00 |
| _____ROADSIDE GEOLOGY OF VERMONT & NEW HAMPSHIRE | 12.00 |
| _____ROADSIDE GEOLOGY OF VIRGINIA | 12.00 |
| _____ROADSIDE GEOLOGY OF WASHINGTON | 18.00 |
| _____ROADSIDE GEOLOGY OF WYOMING | 18.00 |
| _____ROADSIDE GEOLOGY OF THE YELLOWSTONE COUNTRY | 12.00 |
| _____AGENTS OF CHAOS | 14.00 |
| _____COLORADO ROCKHOUNDING | 20.00 |
| _____NEW MEXICO ROCKHOUNDING | 20.00 |
| _____FIRE MOUNTAINS OF THE WEST | 18.00 |
| _____GEOLOGY UNDERFOOT IN DEATH VALLEY AND OWENS VALLEY | 16.00 |
| _____GEOLOGY UNDERFOOT IN ILLINOIS | 15.00 |
| _____GEOLOGY UNDERFOOT IN SOUTHERN CALIFORNIA | 14.00 |
| _____NORTHWEST EXPOSURES | 24.00 |

**Please include $3.00 per order to cover postage and handling.**

Send the books marked above. I enclose $_____

Name_____

Address_____

City_____State_____Zip_____

☐ Payment enclosed (check or money order in U.S. funds)

Bill my:☐VISA ☐MC  Expiration Date:_____ Daytime Phone_____

Card No._____

Signature_____

**MOUNTAIN PRESS PUBLISHING COMPANY**
**P.O. Box 2399 • Missoula, MT 59806 • Order Toll-Free 1-800-234-5308**
**E-mail: mtnpress@montana.com • Website: www.mtnpress.com**